M000170348

Catastrophic Risk

Business Strategy for Managing Turbulence in a World at Risk

Richard L. Alfred

Routledge
Taylor & Francis Group

A PRODUCTIVITY PRESS BOOK

First published 2022
by Routledge
600 Broken Sound Parkway #300, Boca Raton FL, 33487

and by Routledge
2 Park Square, Milton Park, Abingdon, Oxon, OX14 4RN

Routledge is an imprint of the Taylor & Francis Group, an informa business

ISBN: 978-0-367-42532-6 (hbk)
ISBN: 978-0-367-42386-5 (pbk)
ISBN: 978-0-367-85330-3 (ebk)

Typeset in Garamond
by Apex CoVantage, LLC

Contents

Contents

Foreword

Dick Alfred and I got to know one another as we shared faculty appointments in the School of Education at the University of Michigan. My appointment was joint with the Ross School of Business, and Dick's was an appointment in the Center for the Study of Higher and Postsecondary Education. Dick's scholarly work in the areas of strategy, organizational effectiveness and performance, and leadership had a significant national impact on colleges and universities, particularly on community colleges which form the backbone of higher education in America. His leadership had an extraordinary influence on the development of this unique sector of higher education and the important role it plays in the lives of millions of students and their families.

In several forums and conferences, Dick and I shared the podium, sat on discussion panels together, and listened to one another's presentations regarding our individual areas of interest. It is no surprise that Dick's interest in the broader societal context of higher education and the impact of organizations on society have led him toward developing this book.

The book addresses several of the most critical and pressing issues of our time, namely, the global pandemic, climate change, economic strain, social inequality, polarization, and changing cultural norms. Dick's insights highlight a number of important, memorable, and noteworthy points regarding these issues and the potentially catastrophic risk they present individually and in combination. You will, no doubt, make important discoveries as you read Dick's analysis of these sources of risk, and each chapter deserves careful attention. Some examples of insights that I found to be especially worthy of consideration, contemplation, and action include:

- A variety of sociological and psychological inhibitors have impeded awareness regarding the gravity of the challenges currently being faced. Behavioral mechanisms to minimize and ignore threats are widely used, and awareness helps us confront them.
- Inaction on the part of individuals, and especially leaders and business organizations, can escalate current challenges and turn them into existential threats. Business strategy has a critical role to play in mobilizing action.
- Viewing disruptive challenges as single problems rather than in systemic terms contributes to escalating potential of existential risks.
- Three kinds of risk exist—*operational* (daily issues), *strategic* (the competitive world), and *existential* (survival of humankind). Business must broaden its purview to attend to risks beyond mere operational risk.
- The impact of the global pandemic extends well beyond the loss of life and disrupted lifestyles. It includes a serious impact on social institutions that will have long-term societal consequences.
- The role of organizations and leaders—aside from government action—will be crucial in responding to and limiting the impact of climate change. Business has a central role to play.

- Societal inequality—especially in the form of conflict-induced displacement, economic displacement, climate change displacement, disaster-induced displacement, and opportunity displacement—can, and should be, addressed by enlightened organizations and leaders. Inequality is the prerogative of business strategy.

- Political polarization can be characterized on two dimensions—*form* (liberal–conservative) and *intensity* (strong–weak). Leaders and organizations have an important role in managing and leading change, especially if no *center* exists in the political arena.

- The widespread dissemination—mainly through media outlets—of mistruths, falsehoods, accusations, offensive language, canceling opponents' speech, and escalating scandals are examples of changing cultural norms. Understanding truth is crucial and movement from reaction to reflection is an imperative for organizations and leaders.

- A widening gap between early adopters of change and laggards or refugees from change being left behind is a challenge for leaders and organizations, especially when difficult trade-offs must be made between advantaging one group by disadvantaging another.

- New forms of leadership, new strategic options, and a new focus on communities rather than mere organizations are among the prescriptions offered to address the potentially catastrophic risks that are a growing threat in our environment.

- Leaders in business organizations of the future will be faced with unprecedented challenges that can escalate to existential risk if not addressed; consequently, intelligently addressing major challenges that have not yet become existential is a critical imperative.

Dick offers key insights and informed advice regarding the strategic directions that leaders and organizations must consider. His guidance is timely and cogent. This book highlights and clarifies not only the key challenges we face in our current environment, but also the practical and insightful prescriptions for addressing potentially catastrophic risks are a special strength of the book. You will find the wisdom of Dick to be astute, helpful, and prescient.

Kim Cameron
William Russell Kelly Professor of Management and Organizations
University of Michigan

Preface

The book you are holding was conceptualized in 2019 and written over two years leading up to publication in 2021. It is not a product of advance planning nor is it part of a professional agenda. *Catastrophic Risk: Business Strategy for Managing Turbulence in a World at Risk* is the capstone of years of watching human inaction in response to risk. Risk beyond the boundaries of everyday life fueled by three forces: truth compromised by fallacy, partisan antipathy, and outrageous conduct at the highest levels of government. The intersection of these forces became a personal call to action. Media headlines played into the call as well as did scientific findings and critical analysis by pundits.

The spark that lit the fire came from author and journalist Mort Rosenblum, who, when asked at the conclusion of a speech what it would take to move people from passivity to action in the face of risk, responded "You have to scare the hell out of them." That stuck with me. A tipping point had been reached and I was off and running. A precis was developed, media resources were plumbed for literature and research on causative factors in risk, and hours each day were spent building the basis of business strategy in a world edging toward catastrophic risk. The result was a book integrating theory and research from business and the sciences, wide-ranging ideas from disparate disciplines, and media accounts of the relationship between people and risk. My goal was twofold: to bring catastrophic risk to the world of business and to further business engagement in service to the common good.

To the Reader

This book is not a pop press, quick-fix business book, and it is not for the casual reader. It is a carefully researched work that blends theory, literature and research, and practice to examine the relationship between risk, human behavior, and business strategy. Readers accustomed to receiving and processing information in sound bites will be challenged by ideas that are complex and wide-ranging in terms of their application to business. The chapters on behavioral dynamics and climate change, in particular, will test the patience of readers because of the volume and technical nature of the information presented. I contemplated reducing the narrative in these chapters to create an easier read, but climate change and human behavior are preeminent factors contributing to catastrophic risk and the time has arrived to act on them. Ultimately, this is a book about risk, social forces, and human behavior—a relationship that is critically important for business and best understood through the lens of the sciences. For the reader, this will mean careful attention to concepts and ideas and re-reading as necessary to get the full benefit of information.

Risk, Social Forces, and Behavior

Catastrophic risk is global in scope and calamitous in impact. When it becomes transgenerational (affecting future generations) and terminal (capable of extinguishing civilized life), it is classified as "existential risk." My interest in catastrophic risk had its genesis in our changing climate—climbing temperatures, more frequent and intense weather events, and warming oceans. One could swim in the ocean in southeastern Maine in June rather than having to wait until August. The reality of a warming climate seemed obvious to me, but legions of naysayers believe otherwise. Their refusal to accept scientific evidence thrust human behaviors such as denial, normalization, and intuitive thinking which shape perception and response to risk into a domain of risk. Behavior does not take shape in a vacuum—it is conditioned by social forces that influence what people think and do. Among the forces shaping behavior in American society today are polarization, social inequality normative transition, and the experience of pandemic. When these forces are played out in the context of risk, a cause-and-effect relationship is realized: *social forces shaping human behavior determine response to risk and power its effect and consequences.*

Many *forces* are at work in our society and one could reasonably ask, "Why these forces and not others?" The answer lies in their power over people's lives and their profound influence on thought and behavior. Polarization and social inequality are pervasive in American society. Singly and in combination, they have the power to color perception, obscure consequences, and impede response to risk. Social norms accentuate risk by sculpting perception and channeling it into arenas of acceptable group conduct. And then there is the experience of pandemic—a disaster that will forever influence the outlook on risk of those who have lived through it. In the domain of *behavior*, people meet risk in different ways depending on background, cognition, and societal conditions. Awareness of different behavioral modes is important if we are to effectively mobilize communities in response to risk. In the world of *business*, there are looming questions about the scope and depth of business commitment to social responsibility. Knowing what it will take to broaden business purpose in service to the common good is imperative in the evolving world of risk.

What's Inside

This book is divided into three parts that describe the relationship between risk, societal forces, and human behavior and their implications for business strategy: (1) *Setting the Context*, (2) *Challenges and Deterrents*, and (3) *Shaping the Future*.

Part I, *Setting the Context*, takes the reader into the world of risk and human behavior. The opening chapter ("A World at Risk") describes different forms of risk and differentiates catastrophic risk from conventional risk. Habitats of catastrophic risk are presented as part of a "new abnormal" with climate change and rogue technology singled out as imminent threats to humanity. A perfect storm is presented at the close of the chapter to illustrate the compounding effect of thought and behavior on risk. The focus in Chapter 2 ("Deterrents to Action") shifts to the human side of risk—thinking and behavior people employ in response to risk. Behavior is described as *societally induced, change-induced*, and *stasis-induced* with behaviors in each category having the potential to compound the effects of risk. Societally induced behavior is a function of societal conditions—polarization, anomie, and information overload—which deter response to risk by coloring perception. Change-induced behavior refers to the impact of cognition on risk—the inability of people to put risk in perspective due to flawed cognition. Stasis-induced behavior describes actions that deter response to risk by normalizing it and making it part of everyday life. Alternative interpretations of risk are sought until an acceptability threshold is reached, thereby avoiding the need to change personal outlook and behavior.

Part II, *Challenges and Deterrents*, examines societal forces that condition human behavior in response to risk. Six forces are presented: *the experience of pandemic, climate change, social inequality, polarization, changing norms*, and *social disparity*. Chapter 3 ("The Power and Peril of Pandemic") describes the pandemic's impact on people and organizations and implications for business in a post-COVID world. Chapter 4 ("Climate Change: Default, Mitigation, or Adaptation?") turns the focus to climate change and its impact as a graduated march toward catastrophe. The changing condition of atmosphere, oceans, and land is examined in detail to reveal the significance of global warming as a threat to civilized life. Response strategies ranging from adaptation to mitigation are discussed and new roles for organizations and leaders are stipulated. In Chapter 5 ("Social Inequality"), inequity and its effect on the capacity of people and communities to respond to risk are described. The extent of inequality is revealed through data, its harmful effects are described using economic and social arguments, and its importance for business is profiled through the human rights commitment in companies of principle. Chapter 6 ("Polarization: Factions, Filters, and Antipathy") and Chapter 7 ("Changing Social Norms") consider the impact of partisan antipathy and normative transition on perception of risk. The diminishing ideological "center" of American society and the phenomenon of normalization are examined in terms of their effect on perception and response to risk. Business is challenged to find the "center" in relationship to risk and embrace and invest in social responsibility or be left behind. In Chapter 8 ("Navigating and Falling Behind Change"), disruption caused by asymmetry among organizations and workers impacted differentially by change is profiled using industry data and reports. Business is called on to broaden the conception of work to include investment in societal well-being—specifically, service to communities in times of crisis.

Part III, *Shaping the Future*, moves to the domain of business strategy and what companies must do to bring value to communities. Chapter 9 ("Rethinking Business Purpose and Strategy") introduces relational strategy as a means of delivering value to communities during crisis. Relational strategy avoids the trap of "frontloading"—building strategy on the basis of anticipated conditions—by backloading strategy to human needs in crisis. It is the basis for delivery of optimal value to communities by moving from competition to collaboration to alliance and, ultimately, to the goal of business as social purpose. The closing chapter ("Mobilizing") takes the reader to tactics that business will need to employ to mobilize communities in response to risk. Leaders will need a greater understanding of behavioral dynamics and enhanced capacity to relate to people on an emotive basis to meaningfully help communities in times of crisis. This will require contextual understanding and an enduring commitment to societal well-being.

At the close of a 40-year career as an executive and university professor in academe, I thought my writing days were over. The fire still burns, however, and it burns brightly. Risk took on new meaning and urgency when coupled with growing evidence of climate change and the immediate impact of pandemic. Add to this, the behavior, of people—heroic and otherwise—and it became impossible to sit on the sidelines and watch words, behavior, and events turn our nation and world upside down. Much of what was happening was stunning in impact and consequence—a state of affairs that confirmed once again how easy it is to tear down institutions and how difficult it is to rebuild them. The ideas in this book will have a short or long life depending on what readers do with them. If there is one idea, however, that readers take from this book, hopefully, it will be that the business of business is not business; ultimately, it is service to the common good.

Richard L. Alfred
Ocean Park, Maine

Acknowledgments

The catalyst for this book was author and journalist, Mort Rosenblum. Years of watching mounting evidence of risk met by human inaction reached a point in 2019 where enough had become enough. The time was January 2019, the place was Tucson, Arizona, and the occasion was a seminar sponsored by The University of Arizona under Mort's direction, "Keeping Tabs on a Mad World: A Correspondent's Guide to Global News That Matters." Mort's approach was direct and his message was clear—we have more speed-of-light access to information than ever before, and yet we've never been so badly misinformed. His goal was to equip people who care with an idea of how to follow and act on news that matters. In that, he succeeded and I am grateful to him for the spark that mobilized me to action.

Good fortune comes in many forms, and for me it is my partner in life, Patricia Carter. Pat is a vital part of the thought process that went into this book—its early development, chapter narrative, and finished editing before submission to the publisher. She is a brilliant content editor and was in the right place at the right time with an idea, a sentence, a word—whatever it took to get the message across. The last set of eyes on the book before it was delivered to the publisher belonged to Pat. I owe a similar debt of gratitude to Kristine Mednansky, Senior Editor, Business Improvement-Health Care Management at Taylor & Francis Group. Kris is the consummate professional one would hope to work with in creating and bringing a book to completion. She was involved throughout the process—answering questions about protocol and procedure, providing advice about form and content, and helping me through a section of the book that stretched the limits of reality. I am also indebted to Noah Brown, President and CEO of the Association of Community College Trustees. Noah reviewed the idea for this book at an early stage and recognized its potential for contribution to the world of business. His experience with professionals across a wide variety of organizations and disciplines was especially important in framing ideas in key sections of the book.

I have benefitted greatly from the wisdom and creative scholarship of Kim Cameron, William Russell Kelly Professor of Management and Organizations at the University of Michigan. I have listened to presentations by Kim for two decades—in particular, frame-breaking research on organizational abundance and positive organizational scholarship which has dramatically expanded our understanding of organizations. Kim's creative ideas about emerging directions in organizational scholarship informed my work and opened up new fields of inquiry. My research and writing over the past two decades have been informed to a considerable extent by Kim's work. He was an obvious choice to craft the Foreword and I am honored that he agreed to do so.

Countless hours went into this book—hours that tested family and personal responsibilities. I recognize this and express my heartfelt thanks to Pat for her encouragement, for her support, and for being there. The privilege of sharing life with her is beyond words.

About the Author

Richard L. Alfred is an Emeritus Professor of Higher Education at the University of Michigan. Prior to joining the graduate faculty at Michigan in 1980, he served as an executive officer in the City University of New York and the Metropolitan Community Colleges in Kansas City, Missouri. He is the author of numerous books among them *Developing Tomorrow's Leaders: Context, Challenges and Capabilities* (2015), *Performance: The Dynamic of Results in Postsecondary Organizations* (2012), and an award-winning book on organizational strategy, *Managing the Big Picture in Colleges and Universities: From Tactics to Strategy* (2006). Over the course of a 50-year career in academe, he has consulted with hundreds of organizations in the areas of strategy, organizational effectiveness and performance, and management and leadership. Foresight into the future—a hallmark of his books and written works—has shaped management and leadership practice in colleges and universities throughout North America.

Dick holds a bachelor of arts degree from Allegheny College and master's and doctoral degrees from Penn State University. He and his wife Pat reside in Ocean Park, Maine.

SETTING THE CONTEXT 1

Chapter 1

A World at Risk

There is no beginning without an end, no day without night, no life without death. Our whole life consists of the difference, the space between beginning and ending.

Angela Merkel
Chancellor of Germany, 2019

Our world is a rapidly changing amalgam of convention and chaos. In 2019, when this book was conceptualized and writing began, the driving force in catastrophic risk was climate change. COVID-19 changed everything. The coronavirus took the world by storm, spread with lightning speed, and outran efforts toward containment. Almost overnight, it shut down business and commerce, put millions out of work, brought economies to the brink of collapse, and dramatically reshaped human life. Life after COVID-19 would not return to a pre-COVID "normal." A new normal would evolve and a retrospective look in its wake would reveal much about how we think and act. It would disclose that we are vulnerable to risk that can run the table on human life, we are interconnected as part of a world community, and we are capable of heroic deeds and episodes of stunning ignorance.

Lethal as it was, the pandemic was not risk at the level of climate change. It ran its course, exacted horrible suffering, and was eventually brought under control through human intervention. Climate change is different. It has evolved over time and much of its impact—both actual and potential—is already beyond human intervention. It is the very essence of catastrophic risk. When combined with societal forces and human behavior, its ultimate effect on civilized life is beyond our imagination. Scientists describe it as a "new abnormal—searing temperatures, rising sea levels, extreme weather events, flooding and drought that could lead to a collapse of civilization, and extinction of much of the natural world if met by reticence.[1]

The upshot of the "new abnormal" is a dangerous sense of paralysis in which complexity on a scale never before realized splinters the civilized world into disparate groups that hinder one another. Catastrophic risk is an almost insurmountable problem in and of itself. When compounded by human behavior which exacerbates its effect, it defies resolution. Business is an entity with an extraordinarily important role in a world edging toward crisis. Its impact will not be felt, however, in the absence of a comprehensive understanding of catastrophic risk and behavior that deters response to risk. In the pages that follow, the reader is introduced to hazards and behavioral dynamics that bring catastrophe to the domain of risk.

What Is Risk?

Risk is part of every human endeavor. It is ubiquitous, enduring, and subject to multiple interpretations, some of which are contradictory. Is it risk only if it is quantifiable? Is it a function of probability? Is it an outcome or consequence? Is it positive or negative? Is it associated with reward and opportunity? Does it involve danger or threat?

Conventional Risk

Early thinking on risk centered on a distinction between quantification and uncertainty. Pioneering thinkers such as Knight (1921) defined only quantifiable uncertainty to be risk.[2] Almost a century later, Holton (2004) argued that two dimensions must be present for risk to exist: uncertainty about the outcome of an event and importance—the outcome must be important.[3] Multiple conceptions of risk are at work in organizations today ranging from negative to positive, possibility to probability, and objective to subjective. Adding to its complexity are different forms of application in multiple disciplines from insurance to engineering to portfolio theory.

Risk has an attribute of *paradox*. There is a strong association between risk and negative occurrences and between risk and reward.[4] A primary focus of organizations is the elimination of risk, but it is almost impossible to achieve gains without some degree of risk. Risk also has *quantifiable and non-quantifiable* dimensions. In the objective domain, it can be quantified in terms of probability.[5] In the subjective domain, it is an amalgam of feelings and emotions that cannot readily be quantified.[6] Risk can be differentiated according to *scale and consequence*. Strategic risk is associated with high-level decisions focused on organizational purpose, objectives, and resources.[7] Operational risk is centered on day-to-day operations that get work done.[8] While seemingly less important than strategic risk, operational risk can impair performance if neglected because of an excessive focus on strategy.

Numerous forms of risk are at work in organizations—competitive risk, economic risk, legal risk, quality risk, reputational risk, pure risk, speculative risk, compliance risk, and resource risk. Most of the forms fall into the realm of *unsystematic* risk—risk related to a particular firm that can be reduced or eliminated through action taken by the firm.[9] When risk shifts to factors beyond a firm's control, *systematic risk* is introduced—risk embedded in events affecting aggregate outcomes such as the impact of extreme weather on a supply chain.[10] Risk beyond organizational and industry boundaries driven by randomly occurring factors introduces yet another realm of risk—*stochastic risk*.[11] Examples include naturally occurring phenomena, unresolved conditions caused by human activity, and calamitous events orchestrated by humanity. The distinction between unsystematic risk, systematic risk, and stochastic risk is a function of *scale*, *control*, and *impact*. Unsystematic risk is specific to, and controlled by, an individual firm. Systematic risk is part of total risk caused by factors beyond the control of a firm. Stochastic risk is rooted in random factors beyond industry and market control; its impact is large-scale and volatile.

Catastrophic Risk

On January 23, 2020, the Doomsday Clock was moved to 100 seconds to midnight—an index of humanity's proximity to destroying itself by twin threats of nuclear weapons and climate change.[12] Going into 2020, the hands stood at two minutes to midnight, the closest they had been in the 75 years the Bulletin of the Atomic Scientists has been issuing numerics on the Doomsday Clock. Multiple factors went into the 100-second setting: the U.S. decision to withdraw from the Intermediate Range Nuclear Forces treaty with Russia, Iran's departure from the nuclear-control agreement reached under the Obama Administration, and North Korea's announcement that it no longer felt bound by a self-imposed nuclear moratorium.[13] On par with the threat of nuclear war was the ascent of human-caused climate change from an academic curiosity to a global threat. A sixfold increase in greenhouse gas emissions and warming of 1°C over a half century brought climate change center stage to world leaders.[14]

> It's 2020, and we're closer than we have ever been to annihilation. It's worth noting, that if Doomsday does arrive, it will not be the result of a global plague we did not see coming and were helpless to stop, or of an asteroid strike like the one that wiped out the dinosaurs. Instead, we will be the authors of our own end, a species, in effect, committing global suicide.
>
> (Jeffrey Kluger, January 23, 2020)[15]

Catastrophic risk is global in scope and perceptible in intensity.[16] When it becomes transgenerational in scope (affecting future generations) and "terminal" in intensity, it is classified as *existential risk*.[17] Global catastrophic risk will extinguish the majority of life on Earth, but humanity could still potentially recover. Existential risk, on the other hand, will extinguish humanity entirely and prevent any chance of civilization recovering.

Bostrom has distinguished four classes of catastrophic risk as presented in Table 1.1.[18] Catastrophic and existential risks threaten the survival of intelligent life and have become a global priority. For the purpose of simplicity, these risk forms are merged under the heading **catastrophic risk** throughout the book. They are interchangeable and their impact is terminal—they are a threat to humanity and all forms of life.

Table 1.1   Classes of Catastrophic Risk

Human extinction	Humanity goes extinct prematurely before reaching technological maturity.
Permanent stagnation	Humanity survives but never reaches technological maturity.
Flawed realization	Humanity reaches technological maturity but in a way that is dismally and irremediably flawed.
Subsequent ruination	Humanity reaches technological maturity in a way that provides promising future prospects, yet subsequent developments cause the permanent ruination of those prospects.

Habitats of Catastrophic Risk

Global catastrophic risks take the form of risk caused by humans (*anthropogenic risks*) and risk caused by natural forces (*non-anthropogenic risks*).[19] Natural forces include disasters of epic proportion which threaten life such as an outbreak of disease, supervolcanic eruptions, and earthquakes. Domains of risk caused by human activity include the spread of disease, climate change, global conflict, social inequality, and rogue technology—the potential for innovations such as biotechnology and artificial intelligence to grow out of control and become an insurmountable problem. The effect and consequences of risk are compounded by human behavior that deters response to threats. Illustrations are abundant—for example, the paralyzing effect of polarization that divides society into subcultures with divergent views that constrain collective action in response to threats.

Humanity has survived risk posed by natural forces for hundreds of thousands of years. Scientific models suggest that the likelihood of extinction through naturally occurring events is extremely small.[20] In stark contrast is catastrophic risk driven by human activity. Technological development has radically expanded our ability to manipulate the external world and our own biology.[21] As demand for energy and technological power has grown so too has the scale of its potential consequences. In particular, there is deepening concern about catastrophe embedded in climate change, advanced forms of warfare, and artificial intelligence.

Climate Change

Extreme temperatures, rising sea levels, more frequent and intense weather events, flooding, weather patterns that threaten food production, wildfires, insect-borne disease—climate change is global in scope and unprecedented in scale. Scientific consensus maintains that climate change is due primarily to burning of fossil fuels such as oil and coal which release greenhouse gases into the air and trap heat in the atmosphere.[22] Agriculture and deforestation also contribute to the proliferation of greenhouse gases—farming and logging account for nearly a quarter of greenhouse gas emissions.[23] Forests and wetlands absorb significantly greater amounts of CO_2 than they have emitted, but deforestation, soil degradation, and destruction of land-based ecosystems reverse that trend by causing land to release more carbon dioxide than it absorbs.[24]

Climate is now changing faster than at any point in human history. The atmospheric concentration of CO_2 did not rise above 300 parts per million (ppm) until 1900. Today, it is 400 ppm and rising.[25] The Earth's average temperature has increased 1.4°F over the past century. Without human intervention, it is projected to rise by as much as 11.5°F over the century.[26] The effects of global warming are potentially catastrophic:

- rising sea levels and warming ocean temperatures fueling more frequent and powerful storms,
- rainfall associated with extreme weather events producing regularly occurring 100-year floods,
- increasing incidence and severity of wildfires threatening habitats, homes, and lives,
- heat waves contributing to drought and food shortages, insect-borne disease, and rising levels of human mortality.[27]

In October 2018, the Intergovernmental Panel on Climate Change (IPCC) issued a special report on the impact of global warming at 1.5°C. Limiting warming to 1.5°C rose to the top as a policy recommendation—an initiative that would require rapid and unprecedented transitions in land

and energy use, industry and buildings, and transportation and cities.[28] To curtail the effects of climate change, global net human-caused emissions of carbon dioxide would need to diminish by 45 percent from 2010 levels by 2030 and reach "net zero" by 2050.[29] Essentially, CO_2 emissions would need to be balanced by removal of an equivalent amount of CO_2 from the air.

Despite the objections of naysayers who believe that global warming attributed to human activity is part of natural variations in the Earth's climate, climate change is a reality that will change the way we live.[30] Our approach to using water and energy, moving from place to place, and consuming food will need to change.[31] To conserve water, we will need to adjust patterns of daily use. To reduce carbon emissions, our approach to transportation will need to change through new vehicular and employment policies—a shift to production of electric cars, regulated use of gasoline-driven cars, rationing of gasoline, and greater emphasis on public transportation.[32] The manner in which we produce, consume, and dispose of food will need to change to reduce methane from agricultural products and waste management.[33] Consuming less meat and adopting a plant-rich diet will lower methane associated with livestock and the fertilizer needed to sustain them.[34] The relationship between carbon emissions and human consumption is significant. Whether through transportation, energy and water usage, or waste management, altering this relationship is no longer an option—it is an imperative.

Warfare and Mass Destruction

The global security landscape has darkened in recent years as nations and leaders have fallen short in efforts to address humanity's most pressing challenges. Hyperbolic rhetoric and provocative actions of leaders have fueled strident nationalism—a circumstance that threatens a tenuous world order balanced on international agreements and nuclear deterrence.[35] Newspaper headlines bring the severity of circumstance into focus: "N. Korea Threatens to Restart Nuclear Testing" (*The Boston Globe*, July 17, 2019); "U.K. Warns Iran of 'Consequences' for Seizing Tanker" (*New York Times*, July 21, 2019); "Afghanistan Recoils at Trump's Talk of Wiping Out Country" (*New York Times*, July 24, 2019); "U.S. Ends Cold War Missile Treaty, to Counter Arms Buildup by China" (*New York Times*, August 2, 2019); "U.S. to Test New Missile as Arms Treaty with Russia Ends" (*Portland Press Herald*, August 3, 2019); "Erosion of Nuclear Deal Puts World on Brink of New Arms Race" (*New York Times*, August 9, 2019); "Further Enhancing Arsenal, North Korea Says It Tested New Type of Missile" (*New York Times*, August 12, 2019); and "Fatal Explosion in Russia Gives United States Pause" (*New York Times*, August 12, 2109). The last headline—an explosion involving a new class of Soviet missiles designed to evade American defenses—illustrates the intensity of the arms race with nations leapfrogging one another to gain advantage.

The existence of thousands of nuclear weapons continues to pose a serious global threat. Nine countries—China, India, Israel, France, North Korea, Pakistan, Russia, the United Kingdom, and the United States—hold nearly 16,000 nuclear weapons, enough to destroy the planet several times over.[36] The likelihood of a nuclear war between the United States and Russia has decreased, but the continued presence of large stockpiles makes nuclear weaponry a persistent threat. Among nations, there is growing concern that:[37]

■ weapons held by countries known to possess nuclear capability could be detonated accidentally
■ nuclear capability could proliferate through the diffusion of weapons technology to additional nations
■ nuclear weapons could reach the hands of terrorists.

The risk of nuclear weapon proliferation among countries has been limited in the past by the Nuclear Non-Proliferation Treaty (NPT) signed in 1968 by five countries and the 1987 Intermediate-Range Nuclear Forces Treaty (INF) between the United States and Russia. Both treaties call upon nations to adhere to a complex set of understandings easily subject to violation. The NPT, for example, is a complex agreement that discriminates between nuclear have and have-not countries.[38] Developing third world nations have agreed not to receive nuclear weapons or their components, while nuclear weapon states have agreed not to furnish these items. Nuclear states are further obligated to assist developing nations in the peaceful application of nuclear energy and, simultaneously, to work toward the elimination of nuclear weapons. Herein lie inherent weaknesses of non-proliferation agreements: non-nuclear states can readily convert nuclear material into weaponry and nuclear states adhering to a principle of deterrence have few, if any, incentives to reduce nuclear stockpiles.

Nuclear states vault over one another in a race for advantage. Russia tested a missile with an on-board nuclear reactor capable of reaching any point in the world in 2019.[39] In August 2019, the United States terminated its participation in the 1987 Intermediate-Range Nuclear Forces Treaty (INF) to pursue development of a new class of missiles to counter Soviet advantage. Nuclear weapons constitute perhaps the most threatening outcome of the interaction of science and technology in human history. If a nuclear weapon exploded in a major city, the blast epicenter would be hotter than the surface of the sun; tornado-strength winds would spread the flames; and a million or more people could die. Survivors would have no electricity, transportation, or phones, and hospitals would be overwhelmed—if they were still standing.

Social Inequality

Despite growth in income and wealth across economies, variability in economic means has widened and societies worldwide are enmeshed in a growing inequality gap. According to the International Monetary Fund (IMF), over the past three decades, more than half of the countries in the world have seen an increase in income inequality with the trend particularly pronounced in advanced economies.[40] Inequality exists in multiple forms, but the common thread is uneven access to goods, resources, and opportunity on the basis of race and ethnicity, geographical location, age and gender, income and occupation, and power and prestige.[41]

Social scientists have long posited a relationship between social inequality and conflict—a relationship that is the central premise of conflict theory. Social order is maintained by domination and power, rather than consensus and conformity.[42] Those with wealth and power maintain position by suppressing those without power while those without power seek to enhance position by challenging the status quo.[43] Conflict theory has been used to explain a wide range of social phenomena including war and revolution, wealth and poverty, and discrimination and domestic violence. It rests on four assumptions—structural inequality, competition, revolution, and war.[44]

- *Structural Inequality* is endemic to all human relationships and social structures. Some individuals and groups acquire more power and reward than others. Beneficiaries of a social structure will work to maintain that structure to retain or enhance their power.
- *Competition* exists as a result of resource scarcity. Resources are zero-sum in nature—whatever is gained by one side is lost by the other. Competition escalates into conflict when the distribution of resources shifts unevenly to advantage groups with power.

- *Revolution* is a potential outcome of conflict between those with and without power. Change in the power dynamic between groups does not happen as a result of adaptation; it evolves from conflict that is abrupt and large scale, rather than gradual and evolutionary.
- *War* is the result of cumulative conflict between individuals and groups and between whole societies. It can be a unifying or destructive force capable of uniting a society in competition with other societies or, if not channeled, destroying a society from within.

Social inequality has dramatic consequences which stunt the capacity of societies to grow and develop. Among the consequences are contraction of growth, rising incidence of crime, attenuation of health, and constriction of educational access and attainment.[45] Research has shown that wealth inequality correlates with a higher incidence of poverty, crime, and poor public health—conditions that place a burden on economic growth.[46] In an essay on the consequences of economic inequality, Birdsong (2015) pieced together relationships that illustrate the serial effects of social inequality.[46]

> In the face of rising prices for goods and lower incomes, wealthy citizens maintain disproportionate purchasing power compared to impoverished citizens. As the gap between rich and poor swells, the incentive to commit crimes grows as fewer methods of lawfully obtaining resources are available to indigent citizens. Further complicating the lives of these citizens is a lack of access to education and quality health care. Unequal societies tend to underinvest in programs that provide a financial path for impoverished citizens to access education and health care. Poor nutrition and diminished access to health care make impoverished citizens vulnerable to illness at a higher rate than the general population.

The consequences of social inequality are exceedingly diverse. A common belief is that inequality creates perpetually oppressed minorities, exploits disadvantaged populations, and leads to numerous social problems. A contrary belief is that inequality is a natural part of social progress. These contradictory perspectives anchor a belief spectrum that is wide-ranging but neglectful of one overarching aspect of inequality—the importance of individual needs and the role they play in motivation. Social inequality exacerbates the threat and consequences of risk when the unmet needs of a major segment of society mitigate response to crisis. In Maslow's hierarchy of needs, physiological and safety needs must be met before individuals become motivated to pursue higher-level needs.[47] If physiological needs are unmet, personal discomfort rises and incentives to reduce the discrepancy between need and satisfaction increase.[48] In the domain of risk, the price of inequality is reduced capacity to mobilize in response to risk as impoverished groups put basic needs ahead of societal needs.

Rogue Technology

Like other revolutions, artificial intelligence comes with promise and peril. It has been suggested that superintelligent learning computers could become capable of creating unintended results or that robots could eventually outperform humans.[49] It has also been suggested that the exceptional organizational capabilities and novel technologies of super computers could become matchless and unrivaled—capable of producing almost any outcome and able to foil any attempt to block their path.[50] Promise or peril, a humane AI-enabled future will require much more than technologists.

It will require the involvement of ethicists, social scientists, policy makers, and the people that will be affected by these systems.

In *Superintelligence: Paths, Dangers, Strategies*, Bostrom argues that if machines were to surpass humans in general intelligence, superintelligence could replace humans as the dominant life-form on Earth.[51] He reasons that technology will yield superintelligence in the next 30–80 years through computational models, full brain emulation, or collective enhancement.[52] Computational models are developing rapidly and becoming part of everyday life through computer vision, voice recognition, and predictive models. If these models are refined and their hardware capabilities scaled up, superintelligence would follow. Full brain emulation is the process of scanning the human brain and translating its properties into digital signals. This process in combination with higher frequency of calculation in digital machines will lead to faster-operating consciousness, which in turn could lead to superintelligence.[53]

Bostrom is among a growing number of voices registering concern about the evolution of superintelligence. Physicist Stephen Hawking, Microsoft founder Bill Gates, and Space X founder Elon Musk have voiced concerns about AI with Hawking theorizing that superintelligence could "spell the end of the human race."[54] AI would run a course from creation of a superintelligent unit to a superintelligence explosion through continuous iteration over its own code in a short period of time. The system would quickly find a way to outsmart humans and achieve its own goals through "infrastructure profusion"—a process wherein AI builds quickly to enhance its cognitive abilities and in so doing becomes an existential threat to humankind.[55]

Outbreak of Disease

The outbreak of disease creates unprecedented hardship through forced separation and communities crippled by economic downturn. The COVID-19 pandemic challenged the boundary between disaster and catastrophe by incorporating elements of each. Similar to a catastrophe, it created wide-ranging impacts at the global level. Unlike catastrophe, however, it did not cause widespread destruction of infrastructure nor did it unravel regional leadership which remained intact. Disease has a beginning and an end. Its impact and consequences can be remedied through human intervention. A catastrophe, on the other hand, is of such scale and magnitude that its effects may linger long after onset and remediation may not be possible. For this reason, the outbreak of disease is not classified as catastrophic risk.

Human Behavioral Dynamics

The tornado that devastated Lee County, Alabama, on March 3, 2019, came as a shock but not a surprise. Meteorologists had warned of severe weather days in advance and forecasters had monitored the area closely, issuing warnings as soon as individual tornadoes were detected. Despite those efforts, 23 people died.[56] How, one must ask, can we be so good at predicting dangerous weather and still lose so many lives in a single day? The answer lies in understanding not only extreme weather but also people and behavior. Demographics and human psychology stand in the way of mobilization in response to risk.

There is ample evidence to suggest that demographics play an important role in access and use of information including information about risk. Information about risk is widely available, but where one lives, one's income and social class, one's race and ethnicity, and one's age and background have a lot to do with how and when information is accessed and used.[57] People unable to access media because of resource limitations and lack of exposure are at a disadvantage in understanding and responding to risk—a deterrent of circumstance, not of choice.

There is another side to the relationship between information and risk. What if response to risk is driven more by personal choice than by circumstance? For example, what if people avoid risk by denying that it exists? This prompts questions: Why do some with full access to information respond proactively to risk while others waver or default? What types of behavior are part of risk avoidance? What are the sociological and psychological dynamics of default behavior?

If a small group of time-traveling scientists living on a parched Earth in 2050 were to travel back three decades and wanted to know why advanced economies like the U.S. did not respond more aggressively to increasingly severe conditions of climate change, what would you tell them?[58] You might mention that social inequality became more prevalent across much of the advanced world and large segments of the population had disengaged from society. You might indicate that people, barraged by waves of contradictory information, were no longer able to discern truth from falsehood and did not know what to believe about climate change. They followed gut feelings and disavowed the reality of climate change. When they were confronted with facts that contradicted personal beliefs, they reverted to behavior that made them feel more comfortable—denial, alternative explanations, and substitution of falsehoods for facts. They searched for alternatives that fit their outlook and glommed onto them as a way of interpreting climate change. Ultimately, with repeated exposure to extremes—heat waves, flooding, and food and water shortages—they "normalized" conditions that were once considered abnormal. Instead of asking "why" climate had changed, they acclimated by acquiring clothing that kept them warmer or cooler and devices that regulated temperature.

The time-traveling scientists would find this list rather depressing, but would also view each problem on the list as discrete, with its own cause and potential solutions. "How unfortunate," they might say, "when conditions changed so quickly, the need for action should have been obvious." But what if these behavioral dynamics are all part of the same phenomenon?[59] Maybe, for example, inequality is contributing to immobility because people lacking access to education, health care, and nutrition have little choice but to place basic needs ahead of everything else. Climate change is not among their priorities. Convincing impoverished civilians to shift their focus from basic needs to risk mitigation is not realistic. Maybe immobility is a consequence of lack of access to information about causes and effects of climate change or maybe it is a function of information overload. People exposed to volumes of information may rely on intuition to process the information—a process that may not be informed by scientific evidence. Trapped in a chasm between evidence and intuition, people may assuage their discomfort by avoiding risk altogether.

Collectively these behaviors constitute a dynamic that shapes response to risk. Conditions contributing to this dynamic—anomie, polarization, intuitive thinking, cognitive dissonance, satisfice, and normalization—are briefly described here to elucidate the relationship between behavior and immobility. They are described in greater depth in the following chapter.

Societal Conditions and Immobility

Anomie is a condition of social instability causing unrest and anxiety resulting from a breakdown of norms and values.[60] It is an outcome of rapid change in the social, economic, and political institutions of society—a transitional period when commonly accepted norms are no longer valid and new ones have yet to evolve and take their place. *Polarization* is a function of hostility and distrust between groups holding sharply contrasting opinions and beliefs in a society divided by membership and ideology.[61] Partisan bias rooted in divergent beliefs held by different groups impedes mobilization by making consensus and collective action difficult to achieve. *Ideological Subversion,* commonly known as psychological warfare, is a process through which alternative ideology is used to undermine the ideology of a targeted culture. Perception of reality is altered to such an extent that truth cannot be distinguished from fallacy.[62] Risk and its consequences cannot be fully assessed or understood because factual information is buried in a sea of contradictory information. Truth no longer matters.

Change and Immobility

Intuitive and Categorical Thinking are superficial forms of thought employed in response to changing conditions and circumstances.[63] Gut feelings and hasty judgments shape impressions of circumstances and events. Intuitive thinking involves feeling and sensing, in contrast to rational processing of information, to forge impressions. Categorical thinking compresses information into broad categories to ease processing. When confronted by the threat of risk, individuals relying on intuition and categorization may underestimate the likelihood and ramifications of risk— a circumstance that is potentially fatal in the absence of response to catastrophe.[64] *Cognitive Dissonance* describes the condition of anxiety experienced when truth and belief collide.[65] When confronted with evidence contradictory to personal values and beliefs, individuals may reduce discomfort by avoiding the evidence. Denial, reinterpretation of evidence, and substitution are forms of avoidance behavior that reduce the threat of risk and curtail the need to respond.

Stasis and Immobility

Satisfice, a combination of satisfy and suffice, involves settling for a solution that is "good enough" when an optimal solution is deemed implausible.[66] Using the example of climate change, satisfice would encourage mitigation strategy that is minimally acceptable over an optimal solution because achieving the optimal solution would cost too much in time and resources. The effort expended in mobilization would diminish in proportion to the chosen strategy while exposure to risk would grow in proportion to the strategy. *Normalization* is a process through which ideas and actions falling outside of social norms come to be seen as "normal" in everyday life.[67] In the arena of climate change, normalization would fold extreme conditions (heat waves, flooding, and extreme weather events) into the flow of everyday life. Instead of asking questions about the causes and consequences of climate and acting on information, people would adjust by focusing on safety and personal comfort—moving to higher ground, buying weather-sensitive clothing, and upgrading HVAC technology to acclimate to changing conditions.

Even if one does not fully buy into behavioral dynamics and their relationship to risk, their combined effect suggests that we have been approaching the threat of catastrophic risk through piecemeal solutions instead of coordinated effort. Behavioral dynamics are not single strands of behavior, but a web of behaviors that, when combined with the threat of catastrophe, create a perfect storm. Strategy for mitigation of risk will need to address simultaneously occurring strands of behavior *all at the same time*, not as discrete strands of behavior one at a time.

A Perfect Storm

On October 20, 1991, the captain and crew of the Andrea Gail, a 70-foot fishing vessel working out of Gloucester, Massachusetts left port for the Grand Banks of Newfoundland in a quest for commercially profitable swordfish.[68] Having no luck at the Grand Banks, the Andrea Gail turned east toward the Flemish Cap, filled its hold, and began the 900-mile return journey. Flush with excitement at the prospect of returning home with a big catch and the promise of a big payday, the crew paid little attention to the storm brewing off the coast. A cold front from the east coast of the U.S. carrying a wave of low pressure and a high-pressure ridge from Canada were coming together to create ideal conditions for a massive nor'easter. The meeting of the two fronts over the Atlantic created a swirling mass of wind as air moved between areas of high and low pressure creating 70 mph wind gusts and 30-foot waves.[69] Further out to sea, warm air remnants of Hurricane Grace compressed into a cyclone creating the final element of what was to become a "perfect storm"—a rare combination of circumstances which made the storm unusually powerful. Moving the storm from "danger" to "catastrophe" was inattention of the captain and crew to weather reports and their almost singular focus on returning a profitable catch to home port. The rest of the story is history—the Andrea Gail and its captain and crew were lost to the fury of the storm on October 30, 1991.

What is noteworthy about this account is that catastrophe evolved through a combination of natural conditions and human behavior. Had the captain and crew of the Andrea Gail heeded weather reports and returned home earlier, the ship and crew would not have been lost. Had coastal communities prepared more diligently for calamitous weather, lives would have been saved and storm damage in excess of $200 million would have been minimized. Catastrophic risk is larger in scale and consequence than risk posed by the 1991 perfect storm. Its scale is global and its consequence is the annihilation of intelligent life or permanent curtailment of its potential. Strategy for mitigation of catastrophic risk is different from strategy for assuagement of conventional risk. Catastrophic risk cannot be eliminated through trial and error—there is no opportunity to learn through error. Reactive approaches—let's see what happens and learn from the experience—are unworkable. Mitigation is only possible through coordinated effort directed simultaneously at the causes of risk and human behavior underlying response to risk.

To bring the relationship between risk and behavior closer to home, imagine that you are the CEO of a company located in a small midwestern city besieged by climate challenges that have morphed into a catastrophic threat:

- searing temperatures—40 consecutive days of temperatures in excess of 100 degrees
- extended drought—two years of minimal rainfall
- extreme weather—two weeks of drenching rain and an extended forecast calling for more rain
- flooding—a river 15 feet above flood stage with no sign of abatement
- food and fresh water shortages—transportation arteries and depots are underwater and inaccessible
- economic strain due to farmland destruction and low crop yields
- alarmed citizens divided by age, political affiliation, and ideology
- citizens in denial when confronted with data and scientific evidence of climate change
- impatience edging toward disorder with business and government leaders perceived as incapable of addressing and solving problems
- growing despair among citizens feeling isolated and powerless in a city perceived to be in disorder and out of control

Your city is not alone. Most of the regions in the state and adjacent states are facing the same conditions—underwater, lacking food and fresh water, and trying to calm desperate citizens. The intersection of environmental conditions and behavioral dynamics has elevated risk to the level of catastrophe. Rational and deliberative thought have given way to intuition and the window for consensus and collective action is closing. Who will step up? What role should your company play in mobilizing the community? Is it reasonable to expect that your executive team should understand and act on behavioral dynamics contributing to risk—the human side of risk? What resources can and should your company commit to mitigation? Are you prepared to consider unusual steps to assuage risk and its consequences—for example, expansion of company purpose to embed new goals, reallocation of organizational resources to create new capabilities, alliance with competitors to mitigate risk?

Deepening involvement in catastrophic risk will bring about a change in the orientation of business that is long overdue. Companies leading the way will become navigators in a world in which risk is taking on new meaning. Companies lagging behind will face consequences they helped to create and failed to remediate. To avoid this fate, leaders will need to embrace new roles and ways of thinking. They will also need to possess greater insight into the human side of risk—the topic of the next chapter.

Notes

1 Bulletin of the Atomic Scientists Science and Security Board, *A New Abnormal: It Is Still Two Minutes to Midnight.* Chicago: 2019 Doomsday Clock Statement, January 24, 2019.
2 Knight, F., *Risk, Uncertainty and Profit.* New York: Hart, Schaffner and Marx, 1921.
3 Holton, G., "Defining Risk." *Financial Analysts Journal,* 60(6) (2004): 19–25.
4 The framework for these conceptions of risk is derived from a professional development publication of the Stern School of Business at New York University. See: Chapter 1. *What Is Risk?* New York University. people.stern.nyu.edu/adamodar/pdfiles/valrisk/ch1.pdf.
5 Ibid.
6 Ibid.
7 Ibid.
8 Ibid.
9 Chen, J., "What Is Unsystematic Risk?" *Investopedia,* June 16, 2019.
10 Fontinelle, A., "Systematic Risk." *Investopedia,* December 28, 2018.
11 'Stochastic risk' is a hypothetical construct of risk outside of industry literature on risk. It is adopted and used by the authors to denote the random and episodic nature of catastrophic risk. The term 'stochastic' is used in a wide variety of professional and academic fields to describe events or systems that are unpredictable due to the influence of a random variable. See https:/en.wikipedia.org/wiki/Stochasticprocess.
12 Ortega, R., "Doomsday Clock Is Reset to 100 Seconds Until Midnight, Closest Ever." *American Association for Advancement of Science,* January 23, 2020.
13 Kluger, J., "The End Is Nigh: Doomsday Clock Reaches 100 Seconds to Midnight." *Time,* January 23, 2020.
14 Ibid.
15 Ibid.
16 Ripple, W., Wolf, C., Newsome, T., Galett, M., Alamgir, M., Crist, E., Mahmoud, M., and Laurance, W., "World Scientists' Warning to Humanity: A Second Notice." *BioScience,* 67(12) (November 2017): 1026–1028.
17 Bostrom, N., "Existential Risk Prevention as Global Priority." *Global Policy,* 4(1) (2013): 16.
18 Ibid., 19.
19 Ibid., 16.
20 Ibid., 15.
21 Ibid., 16.

22 World Meteorological Organization, "The State of Greenhouse Gases in the Atmosphere Based on Global Observations Through 2017." *WMO Greenhouse Gas Bulletin*, No. 14, November 22, 2018.

23 Intergovernmental Panel on Climate Change, *IPCC Special Report on Climate Change, Desertification, Land Degradation, Sustainable Land Management, Food Security, and Greenhouse Gas Fluxes in Terrestrial Ecosystems*. Summary for Policy Makers, IPCC, August 7, 2019.

24 Ibid.

25 World Meteorological Organization, *Statement on the State of the Global Climate in 2018*. WMO No. 1233, 2019.

26 Ibid.

27 Intergovernmental Panel on Climate Change, *Special Report on Global Warming of 1.5°C*. Summary for Policy Makers, IPCC, October 8, 2018.

28 Ibid.

29 Ibid.

30 TakePart, "What Is Climate Change?" *Digital News and Lifestyle Magazine*. Participant Media. www.takepart.com/flashcards/what-is-climate-change/index.html. Retrieved: July 10, 2019.

31 Ibid.

32 United States Environmental Protection Agency, *Climate Impacts on Transportation*. EPA Snapshot, January 19, 2017. https://climate change.stloius-mo.gov/climate. Retrieved: June 25, 2019.

33 Intergovernmental Panel on Climate Change, *IPCC Special Report on Climate Change, Desertification, Land Degradation, Sustainable Land Management, Food Security, and Greenhouse Gas Fluxes in Terrestrial Ecosystems*. https://www.ipcc.ch/srcc.

34 Ibid.

35 NJTODAY.NET. "A New Abnormal: It is Still Two Minutes to Midnight." January 24, 2019. njtoday.net/2019/01/24/a-new-abnormal-it-is-still-two-minutes-to-midnight.

36 Nuclear Threat Initiative, "The Nuclear Threat: Despite Progress, the Nuclear Threat Is More Complex and Unpredictable than Ever." *NTI Report*, December 31, 2015. http://nti.org/6455A.

37 Ibid.

38 Krzyzaniak, J., "Project Pluto and the Trouble with Russia's Nuclear-Powered Cruise Missile." *Bulletin of the Atomic Scientists*, August 20, 2019.

39 Nuclear Threat Initiative, *The Nuclear Threat: Despite Progress, the Nuclear Threat Is More Complex and Unpredictable Than Ever*, December 31, 2015. www.nti.org/learn/nuclear/.

40 Gaspar, V. and Garcia-Escribano, M., "Inequality: Fiscal Policy Can Make the Difference." *IMF Blog*, October 11, 2017.

41 Wikipedia, *Social Inequality*. https://enwikipedia.org/wiki/Social_inequality. Retrieved: July 15, 2019.

42 Chappelow, J., "What Is Conflict Theory?" *Investopedia*, May 19, 2019.

43 Ibid.

44 Ibid.

45 Birdsong, N., "The Consequences of Economic Inequality." *Seven Pillars Institute Series on Inequality*, February 5, 2015.

46 The Economist, "The Stark Relationship Between Income Inequality and Crime." June 7, 2018. https://www.economist.com/graphic-detail/2018/06/.

47 Maslow, A., *Motivation and Personality*. New York, NY: Harper & Brothers, 1954.

48 Ibid.

49 Wikipedia has been a particularly helpful source of information on the impact of rogue technology on catastrophic risk. The introduction to rogue technology was taken from an entry on global catastrophic risk in Wikipedia on June 28, 2019, https://en.wikipedia.org/w/imdex.php?title=Global-catastrophic_risk&oldid=905593999.

50 Ibid.

51 Bostrom, N., *Superintelligence: Paths, Dangers and Strategies*. Oxford: Oxford University Press, 2014.

52 Ibid.

53 Ibid.

54 Hawking, S., "AI Will Be 'Either Best or Worst Thing for Humanity'." *The Guardian*, October 19, 2016.

55 Bostrom, *Superintelligence: Paths, Dangers and Strategies*.

56 Weber, T., "Why High-Tech Weather Forecasts Don't Save More Lives." *Time*, March 14, 2019. http://time.com/5551298/weather-forecasts-deaths/?utm.source=time.com&utm_medium. Retrieved: March 20, 2019.

57 Perrin, A. and Duggan, M., "Americans' Internet Access: 2000–2015." *Pew Research Center*, June 26, 2015.

58 The framework for this causal analysis is derived from an article in the *New York Times* authored by Neil Irwin. Reference: Irwin, N., "Could One Problem Cause All the World's Woes." *New York Times*, The Upshot, March 5, 2019.

59 Ibid.

60 Elwell, F., *Emile Durkheim on Anomie*, 2003. www.faculty.rsu.edu/-felwell/Theorists/Essays/Durkheim1.htm. Retrieved: February 3, 2019.

61 Barber, M. and McCarty, N., "Causes and Consequences of Polarization." *American Political Science Association*, 2015. wwwapsanet.org/portals/54/Files/TaskForceReports/Chapter2Mansbridge.pdf.

62 Pham, L., "Ideological Subversion, Psychological War on the United States." *Economics Voodoo*, February 6, 2013.

63 Kunreuther, H., Slovic, P., and Olson, K., "Fast and Slow Thinking in the Face of Catastrophic Risk." Working Paper # 2014-06, *Risk Management and Decision Processes Center, The Wharton School*. University of Pennsylvania, August 2014.

64 De Langhe, B. and Fernbach, P., "The Dangers of Categorical Thinking." *Harvard Business Review*, September–October 2019.

65 Festinger, L., *A Theory of Cognitive Dissonance*. Stanford, CA: Stanford University Press, 1957.

66 Bazerman, M. and Moore, D., *Judgment in Managerial Decision Making*. Hoboken, NJ: Wiley & Sons, 1993.

67 Wikipedia, *Normalization*. https://wikipedia.org/windex.php?title=Normalization_(sociology)&oldid=892692859. Retrieved: August 2, 2019.

68 Redd, W., *The Wreck of the Andrea Gail and the 'Perfect Storm' That Caused It*, July 5, 2018. https://allthatsinteresting.com/andrea-gail.

69 Ibid.

Chapter 2

Deterrents to Action

The frog in boiling water is a metaphor for our capacity to adapt to, and even normalize, abnormal and painful circumstances as they escalate.

Rekha Basu
Correspondent Des Moines Register, *2019*

In 2003, the world watched in horror as the *Columbia* space shuttle broke apart while reentering Earth's atmosphere, killing seven astronauts. An investigation revealed that a large piece of insulating foam had dislodged from the shuttle's external tank during the launch, damaging a wing's leading edge and causing the accident 16 days later.[1] In 2004, a megathrust earthquake on the floor of the Indian Ocean spawned a tsunami with waves up to 100 feet high killing an estimated 227,898 people in 14 countries.[2] The 9/11 Al Qaeda terrorist strike blindsided the U.S. despite piecemeal information in the hands of national security officials regarding Al Qaeda's intentions and plans.

These are examples of ambiguous threats—unpredictable occurrences in time and place but capable of great harm.[3] Some threats are more obvious than others such as the threat of a major earthquake along the San Andreas fault in California, the impact of which could be blunted by retrofitting buildings and installing backup systems. Others are obvious, but the solutions are not thereby setting into motion intensive efforts toward resolution. The most dangerous threats, however, result from the convergence of four conditions: ambiguous warning signs, incomprehensible impact, potentially calamitous consequences, and dysfunctional behavior.[4] In stark contrast to conventional risk, the ambiguity of catastrophe can lull people into a wait-and-see mindset. There is a tendency to neglect or discount risk that one cannot see or comprehend and to avoid events and circumstances that challenge personal beliefs and values—behavior that could have disastrous consequences.

Behavior in response to risk is part and parcel of the business of business. If one believes to the contrary, ponder the following and ask yourself if business can ignore the consequences of inattention to the human side of risk:

- Why do people minimize or avoid challenges associated with risk instead of taking steps to counteract them?
- What are the consequences of avoidance behavior?

- What is the impact of avoidance behavior on society, on communities, on business?
- What is the cost to business of inattention to the human side of risk?

The beginning of an answer to these questions can be found in situational and behavioral dynamics that are both predictable and unpredictable. Unpredictable because catastrophic threats have historically been random events—difficult to predict with any degree of precision. Predictable because much of human behavior in response to risk is a product of social construction—what is known as "socially constructed reality."

Socially Constructed Reality

In socially constructed reality, the way we present ourselves to people is shaped partly by our interactions with others as well as by our life experiences.[5] Sociologists Peter Berger and Thomas Luckmann introduced the concept in 1966 in *The Social Construction of Reality*.[6] They argued that society is created by human interaction, which they called habitualization.[7] Like habits, in general, habitualization describes how any action that is repeated frequently becomes a pattern, which can be repeated in the future in the same way with minimal effort.[8] Our conceptions of what is "real" are determined by our subjective construction of reality rather than objective reality.[9] In the lexicon of risk: *personal conceptions of risk are driven, in large part, by socially determined conceptions of risk*. In this way, risk is not a fact or objective truth but a socially determined conception of reality. In the context of climate change, if a large number of people believe that climate change is a cyclical, naturally occurring event and does not constitute a threat, then climate change is not a threat.

Social construction reduces uncertainty and anxiety by narrowing choice in relationship to circumstances and events to judgments individuals can make knowing that others will judge it in the same way.[10] The result is a set of beliefs that everyone knows and accepts—norms for thought and behavior that make social constructs plausible and acceptable for individuals who might otherwise disagree. These norms "put everything in its right place" by providing explanations for why we do things the way we do and why we hold certain views. Opinions, perceptions, traditions, values, and world views are all socially constructed. They channel individual thought and behavior into patterns that comply with social conceptions. In the lexicon of risk: *Feelings and beliefs in relationship to risk are driven by an innate desire to avoid falling outside of norms governing thought and behavior*. Applied to climate change, individuals with mixed feelings about climate change will avoid discomfort by expressing those feelings in a manner consistent with prevailing opinions and beliefs.

I can relate to the power of social norms on a personal level. In 2016, I was invited to deliver a keynote address to a national organization comprised primarily of college and university executive officers. The address was to focus on challenges facing organizations and strategies for action. An obvious challenge was climate change and the evidence was compelling—climate change was a clear and present danger. One would expect leaders to jump onto a topic of such importance. At least this was early thinking about the presentation—thinking that was scuttled when my attention turned to audience appeal. What would be the "best way" to present ideas about climate change to an audience of college and university leaders?

I mulled over different approaches and convention won out. Irrespective of its importance, climate change is an "inconvenient truth"—it has elements that depress and deflate. How could one deliver an address to an audience touching on catastrophic risk without pulling down the entire room? Further complicating the matter was the circumstantial reality of the occasion. This was a career capstone address to be delivered to an audience of leaders who, by virtue of limited time and resources, were inwardly focused on organizational well-being in contrast to the physical environment. The "norms" surrounding an occasion of this type reduced choice to one option—scrap the content related to climate change and focus on an upbeat view of the future. What should have been a call-to-arms on disruptive change ended in a call for leaders to focus on "sensemaking" as a primary dimension of their work. To this day, I regret the decision to put comfort over uncertainty by acquiescing to social norms.

Risk, Eschewal, and Immobility

Modern-day interpretation of risk has changed as a result of the pandemic and growing evidence of climate change. Catastrophe has entered our vocabulary and it has both objective and socially constructed dimensions. From the standpoint of social construction, we continue to discount risk that is perceived to have a low probability of occurring or has not happened before. Scientific evidence of climate change, however, has added an objective dimension to catastrophic risk. It is capable of observation and its impact can be measured. This is a game changer and it gives rise to questions for organizations and leaders:

- Are there multiple dimensions of risk—the risk itself and human behavior in response to risk?
- What stands in the way of mobilization in response to risk?
- What are the dynamics of thought and behavior underlying response to risk?

The threat posed by climate change is not limited to risk itself. Avoidance behaviors such as denial and normalization compound its effect. *Eschewal*—aversion to accepting, participating in, or partaking of something and *immobility*—a state of motionlessness and inability to move or be moved are core constructs of avoidance behavior. They deter response to risk and obstruct efforts toward mitigation. Mitigation is about more than reduction of carbon emissions. It involves convincing people of the depth and immediacy of risk and mobilizing them toward action. Essentially, mitigation is two-dimensional: it involves countermeasures focused on properties of risk itself and alignment of behavior to counteract risk. Efforts toward mitigation will not be successful unless both dimensions are pursued simultaneously.

Table 2.1 Behaviors Related to Immobility

Behavior	Description
Societally Induced Behavior	
Anomie	Anxiety and isolation that occur when social norms are perceived to have disintegrated or disappeared
Polarization	Active opposition to something or someone resulting from the division of society into sharply contrasting groups holding different opinions or beliefs
Information Overload	Difficulty in understanding an issue or making decisions caused by too much information
Ideological Subversion	Perception of reality is altered to such an extent that despite an abundance of information, truth cannot be distinguished from fallacy

(Continued)

Table 2.1 (Continued)

Behavior	Description
Change-Induced Behavior	
Cognitive Dissonance	Mental discomfort experienced by individuals when confronted with evidence contrary to personal beliefs and values
Intuitive Thinking	Thought related to conditions and events based on simple heuristics and gut feelings causing individuals to pay inadequate attention to the consequences of risk
Categorical Thinking	Loss of capability for deliberative thought through reduction of information into simple categories to make sense of the world
Stasis-Induced Behavior	
Cognitive Complexity	Lack of cognitive capacity to comprehend information and data forming the basis of a threat
Satisfice	Searching for alternatives when an optimal solution is not possible until an acceptability threshold is met
Normalization	Ideas and actions falling outside of social norms come to be seen as "normal" and part of everyday life

Table 2.1 presents categories of behavior associated with immobility in response to risk. Three categories are introduced keyed to the basis of forces driving behavior: *society* (social norms), *change* (forces of change), or *stasis* (preference for the status quo).

Societally Induced Behavior refers to behavior shaped by social conditions such as inequality, polarization, and distrust of authority. Change-Induced Behavior involves behavior in response to rapid change in economic, environmental, technological, and political conditions. Examples include the Great Recession, the consequences of automation, and the onset of climate change. Stasis-Related Behavior refers to behavior undertaken to maintain continuity in the face of change. Examples include resistance to change, routinization of behavior falling outside of norms, and reinterpretation of information to fit existing beliefs and values.

Societally Induced Behavior

In periods of rapid change, social norms do not have the same regulating power as in periods of stability, and individuals are left to their own devices regarding what to believe. This condition is a precursor to *anomie*—the first of four societally induced behaviors influencing response to risk including *polarization, information overload,* and *ideological subversion.*

Anomie

Rudeness and incivility, mass shootings, heated rhetoric over gun control and border security, loss of confidence in government, and other forms of social disorder are manifestations of anomie— a condition that occurs when a society's previously accepted norms and values are perceived to disappear or disintegrate.[11] Anomie is commonly understood to mean normlessness. Popularized by sociologist Emile Durkheim in his influential book *Suicide* (1897), anomie rises out of a mismatch between personal values and societal norms when rapidly changing social attitudes clash with long-standing norms.[12] In individuals, this can lead to an inability to reconcile personal values and beliefs with normative circumstances of the social world—a chaotic occurrence that results in fragmentation of social identity and rejection of societal values.[13]

People differ in how they respond to social change. Some adhere to standing norms or alter behavior and expectations to match the new realities. Others disengage and adopt values and beliefs that diverge from prevailing norms. Feelings of isolation, alienation, powerlessness, and estrangement put this group on the periphery of society. A breakdown in norms holding people together is a prominent feature of complex advanced societies—a circumstance that predisposes them toward mismanagement of risk. When disruptive cycles of behavior are of sufficient force to spawn inertia, response to risk is suppressed.

Polarization

What happens when people react differently to the threat of risk? Do they disagree? Do they work out their differences? Do they reframe the threat to support existing beliefs thereby widening differences between them? Polarization is a reflection of the division of society into groups with sharply different opinions and beliefs.[14] Unlike anomie, it is a function of intense societal engagement fueled by diverging views among groups that become more extreme as evidence is considered. It is an effect of *confirmation bias*—the tendency to search for, interpret, and recall information in a way that affirms one's beliefs.[15] "Hot button" issues that activate emotions commonly elicit this effect. For example, mere thinking about issues such as border security or gun control, without contemplating new or contradictory evidence, can intensify and reinforce the effect of polarization. This effect is further reinforced through repetition when people reiterate and validate each other's beliefs.[16]

Two theories have been advanced to explain how polarization works—social comparison theory and informational influence theory. *Social comparison* theory describes polarization as an outcome of individuals' desire to gain acceptance and be perceived in a favorable way by a group.[17] Newcomers first compare their own ideas with those held by group members, observe and evaluate what the group values and prefers, and then take a position that corresponds to the group position, but slightly more extreme.[18] This can push the entire group toward a more extreme viewpoint or reinforce the stance that best correlates with the views of the group leader.[19] *Informational influence* theory, or persuasive arguments theory, holds that individuals become more convinced of their views when they hear compelling or novel arguments in support of their position.[20] Group members interact on the basis of known information or arguments favoring both sides of an issue but lean toward the side that provides the greatest amount of information or the most persuasive argument.[21] If most or all group members lean in the same direction, new or previously unshared information supporting that direction will be accepted by the group.[22]

The rising popularity of social media platforms such as Facebook, Twitter, and Instagram has enabled people to seek out and share ideas with others who have similar interests and values, thereby intensifying the effects of polarization.[23] Individuals can curate their sources of information and the opinions to which they are exposed and, simultaneously, reinforce personally held views while avoiding information and perspectives with which they disagree.[24] Polarization has been linked to group affiliation and opinion formation on wide-ranging issues including the likelihood and consequences of risk. Research conducted by the Pew Foundation on public views of climate change revealed that perception is closely related to political affiliation and ideology.[25] Wide differences were noted between liberals, conservatives, and moderates regarding the threat of climate change and the credibility of scientists making the case for climate change. These differences reveal the impact of polarization on thought and behavior. It is a key driver of perception, and it has much to do with how people interpret and respond to risk.

Information Overload

Also known as infobesity, infoxication, and information explosion, information overload has been extensively treated in literature and research because of its impact on cognition.[26] Popularized by Alvin Toffler in *Future Shock* (1970), information overload is commonly described as the difficulty involved in understanding an issue and making decisions when too much information is available.[27] Information technology is the primary driver of overload because of its ability to deliver huge quantities of information to a broad audience with relative ease. Its impact has been amplified by the rise of social media and wide-ranging consumption of information through e-mail and spam, instant messages, Tweets, and Facebook.[28]

Information overload has serious implications for management of risk. The growing volume of information surrounding risk factors such as climate change contributes to "processing imbalance"—a circumstance in which people have trouble absorbing and assimilating the information they receive. Shirky (2008) described this problem as one of "filter failure"—a circumstance in which people continually overshare information using multiple platforms.[29] As users consume increasing amounts of information about the onset and consequences of risk through news stories, e-mails, blog posts, Facebook, Tweets, Tumblr posts, and other sources of information, they become their own editors and gatekeepers of information.[30] Cognition is compromised as massive amounts of information are processed and users struggle to discern fact from fallacy, important from unimportant, and relevant from irrelevant information. A consequence can be the contamination of useful information by information that may be inaccurate as illustrated by commonly asked questions: Is climate change real or is it a hoax? I've read that climate change is cyclical—do we really need to worry about it? Information about global warming posted in blogs and news stories is contradictory—what am I supposed to believe?

Ideological Subversion

Known more commonly as psychological warfare, ideological subversion is a dynamic in which perceptions of reality are altered to such an extent that truth cannot be distinguished from fallacy.[31] Truth and factual information cease to matter. Lacking a capacity to discern fact from falsehood, individuals are incapable of making accurate assessments of information and are susceptible to influence from sources they cannot easily judge.

Ideological subversion is an uncomfortable topic to address much less to write about. Referenced primarily in terms of intrigue that may exist between nations, audiences are understandably reluctant to become involved beyond a superficial level with threats to national security posed by foreign governments. Russian interference in the 2016 presidential election is a good example of civilian disposition in relationship to subversion. Irrespective of whether it happened or not, the volume and intensity of misinformation swirling around the presidential candidates was extreme. Who were the purveyors? What was their objective? Was the process part of a long-term strategy or a short-term tactic? For the purpose of illustration, let's assume that something did happen and play out a scenario of subversion underway long before the 2016 election. For a moment, suspend your personal opinion about Russian interference and think about the implications of ideological subversion for a society undergoing rapid change.

In the passage that follows, four stages of ideological subversion are described on the basis of the work of Lan Pham in *Economics Voodoo* (2013).[32] Information describing each stage was obtained through an interview conducted by G. Edward Griffin with a Soviet defector and subversion expert in the 1970s.[33] The reader is cautioned that Pham's account has been abbreviated for clarity and is not verbatim.

> *Demoralization.* It takes 15–20 years to demoralize a nation. This is the minimum number of years required to expose one generation to the ideology of a foreign nation without being counterbalanced by values of the home nation. . . . Most of the activity in this stage involves compiling volumes of information on individuals who are instrumental in creating public opinion—publishers, editors, journalists, actors, educators, professors of political science, members of government, business leaders. Individuals who are receptive to foreign policy are elevated to positions of power through media and public opinion manipulation. Those who refuse are subject to ridicule and character assassination. . . . The demoralization process in the United States is basically complete. Actually, it is over-fulfilled because demoralization now reaches areas which were previously thought to be unreachable. . . . Most is done by Americans to Americans thanks to a lack of moral standards. Exposure to true information does not matter anymore. A person who is demoralized is unable to assess true information. Even if showered with information with authentic proof, with documents, and with pictures, those who are demoralized will refuse to believe.
>
> *Destabilization.* It takes only two to five years to destabilize a nation. The focus of subversion in this stage is no longer opinion leaders, but the structure and functioning of institutions and the extent to which foreign policy has influenced those institutions. What matters are essentials: economy, foreign relations, and defense systems.
>
> *Crisis.* Destabilization leads to crisis—it may take only up to six weeks to the verge of crisis. After crisis with a change of power structure and economy, a period of normalization is entered that may last indefinitely.
>
> *Normalization.* In this phase, false illusions of the 'situation being under control' are promulgated. Everything is not under control, but promises that are part of the illusion say otherwise. Most of the politicians, the media and the educational system train another generation of people who think they are living in peace time. The home nation is in a state of war—undeclared war against the basic principles and foundations of its system.

The progression of ideological subversion illustrates the complex process through which values and beliefs can be undermined by mistruths. Most unnerving is the process and outcome of demoralization—the chilling realization that exposure to facts and true information may not matter anymore. Pham's account is not an isolated piece of journalism based on a 1970's interview. In September 2019, Richard Stengel, Under Secretary of State for Public Diplomacy in the Obama Administration, described the schism between truth and mistruth in a global information war:[34]

> Within a few weeks of being on the job in 2014 [Under Secretary of State for Public Diplomacy], the Russians invaded and then annexed Crimea . . . President Obama and

Secretary of State John Kerry condemned this willful act of aggression and called for sanctions against Russia. I shared their outrage, but I couldn't impose sanctions or call up troops. What I could do was tweet about it . . . so I decided to tweet on my own hoping others would follow. Here's the first: "The unshakable principle guiding events must be that the people of Ukraine determine their own future.

As I started tweeting, I noticed something odd. Within the first few minutes and then for months after, I started getting attacked, often by Russian-sounding Twitter handles. A single tweet would get dozens, sometimes hundreds of comments. I soon started getting hundreds of tweets calling me a fascist propagandist, a hypocrite, and much, much worse. At the same time we observed a wave of social media in the Russian periphery supporting the Russian line on Ukraine, accusing the West of being the source of instability, claiming Ukraine was a part of Russia. Who knew that the Russians were so good at this? We didn't realize or even suspect it at the time, but this tsunami of Russian propaganda and disinformation became a kind of test run for what they did here in the 2016 election.

In many ways, these were the first salvos in the global information war we are living in now. Today, we are all actors in a global information war that is ubiquitous, difficult to comprehend, and taking place at the speed of light. . . . It is a war without limits and boundaries, and one we still don't know how to fight. Governments, nonstate actors and terrorists are creating their own narratives that have nothing to do with reality. These false narratives undermine our democracy and the ability of free people to make intelligent decisions. The disinformationists are aided by the big-platform companies who benefit as much from the sharing of the false as from the true. The bad guys use all the same behavioral and informational tools supplied by Facebook, Google and Twitter. Just as Nike buys information to sell you sneakers, the Russians bought your information to persuade you that America is a mess. Autocrats have learned the same tools once seen as spreading democracy can also undermine it.

Fast forward to the testimony of Fiona Hill, foreign affairs presidential advisor, in the 2019 impeachment hearings for an account of modern-day ideological subversion in American society.[35]

A former White House advisor sharply denounced a 'fictional narrative' embraced by the president and his allies that Ukraine, not Russia, interfered in the 2016 elections, testifying that the claim was a fabrication by Moscow that had harmed the United States. Speaking on the final day of the impeachment hearings, Fiona Hill tied a pressure campaign by the president and some of his top aides to a dangerous effort by Russia to sow political divisions in the United States and undercut American diplomacy. She warned Republicans that a theory that Kyiv undertook a concerted campaign to interfere in the 2016 election—a claim the president pushed repeatedly for Ukraine to investigate—was a 'politically-driven falsehood' that had played into Russia's hands.

In the course of the investigation, I would ask that you please not promote politically-driven falsehoods that so clearly advance Russian interests. . . . These fictions are harmful, even if they are deployed for purely domestic political purposes. . . . The Russians deploy millions of dollars to weaponize our own political opposition research and false narratives. When we are consumed by partisan rancor, we cannot combat these external forces as they seek to divide us against each other, degrade our institutions, and destroy the faith of the American people in our own democracy.

Avoidance of risk is a short step from ideological subversion when the dynamics of subversion are played out. What if a populace showered with data and evidence about the onset and consequences of climate change refused to accept the evidence because of a belief that since the phenomenon had never occurred before, it never would? Time and again, scientific evidence has been waved off by naysayers claiming that climate change is cyclical and would right itself. The most insidious aspect of this behavior is often the result of willful acceptance of fallacious information. If people doubt everything and are susceptible to false information, they cannot see the truth, they cannot engage in sensible discussions about climate change, and they cannot trust one another enough to mobilize in response to risk. A plausible future requires a factual present. Factual information is always available, but if not listened to, it is useless.

Change-Induced Behavior

Social change impacts how people live and work by challenging established norms. It encompasses concepts as broad as a paradigm shift or as narrow as a social cause and is embodied in two schools of thought: *functionalist theory* and *conflict theory*. Functionalists believe that society is largely harmonious with institutions working together to preserve a system. Social change occurs when there is disharmony and institutions move to reestablish equilibrium.[36] Conflict theorists see social change in an entirely different way. Societies are made up of large groups of people and institutions with fundamentally different goals.[37] Conflict between groups is the norm with change dictated by the power of groups to enforce their will. When a group has enough power, it will change society to suit its needs.

Disruption is a common thread in social change irrespective of the lens through which it is viewed. People experience drift when norms undergo change. Drift brings with it the potential for conflict which may alter one's mental state if established and evolving norms are not reconciled. Social change has a decided impact on risk through behavioral states of *cognitive dissonance, intuitive thinking*, and *categorical thinking*.

Cognitive Dissonance

Dissonance theory holds that when confronted with evidence that contradicts beliefs and assumptions, people will resort to defensive tactics to relieve the resulting anxiety.[38] Introduced by Leon Festinger in 1957, cognitive dissonance has been widely used to explain avoidance behavior.[39] The behavior of naysayers, for example, when faced with evidence of climate change is a classic example of tension resolution through avoidance behavior. Naysayers can alleviate the tension by refusing to accept the evidence as part of a belief that climate change is cyclical and natural.[40] They can demand more conclusive evidence or filter evidence by channeling information to conform to belief. They can choose to avoid climate statistics altogether or seek out fellow naysayers to garner support. Choice is a personal matter, but the objective is the same: eliminate or reduce the difference between evidence and belief.

The impact of avoidance behavior does not stop with the mechanics of denial. Naysayers may exacerbate its impact by making blatant claims about the uncertainty of evidence provided by the scientific community—a circumstance that can culminate in a "seepage effect" as scientists qualify research findings in response to constant, and sometimes toxic, public challenges.[41] Naysayer claims affect how scientists speak, and perhaps even think, about their research in a landscape of denial that reinforces doubt and uncertainty. This dynamic was in play during the

Trump administration and may have contributed to a tendency to understate the severity of climate change.[42]

Intuitive Thinking

In research on behavior in the face of natural disasters and mass atrocities, Kunreuther, Slovic, and Olson (2014) coined the term "intuitive thinking" to describe rapid patterns of thought in response to catastrophic events.[43] In *Fast and Slow Thinking in the Face of Catastrophic Risk* (2014), intuitive or "fast thinking" is described as effortless thought based on simple heuristics and gut feelings causing people to underestimate and underreact to the consequences of risk.[44] Intuitive thinking is effective in ordinary situations requiring routine decisions but problematic in relationship to low-probability, high consequence events affording limited opportunity to learn from personal experience.[45] According to Kunreuther, Slovic, and Olson:

> Intuitive assessments of the likelihood of an uncertain event are often based upon the ease with which instances of the occurrence can be recalled or imagined. This *availability bias* is strongly influenced by recent personal experience and can lead to an underestimation of low-probability disasters before they occur, and overestimation afterwards.[46]

Linkages between intuitive thinking and affect in response to catastrophic risk have been modeled through research. *Psychophysical numbing* reflects an insensitivity toward disasters involving large numbers of people with increasing frequency and magnitude evoking a smaller and smaller response.[47] For example, the expression of empathy and support for residents of a city underwater because of repeated episodes of severe weather will be great if it is the first and only city to experience flooding but will diminish as additional communities experience flooding. Psychophysical numbing explains why affect might diminish as growing numbers of people are exposed to risk, but it does not explain generalized apathy toward ongoing catastrophic events following a strong response to victims of a discrete event.[48] A second model, *compassion fade*, describes a tendency for affective feelings and response toward victims of calamitous events to increase at first but then decrease, possibly to the point of collapse, as the number of lives at risk grows larger.[49] According to Kunreuther, Slovic, and Olson: "Intuition comes first in charged circumstances and dominates reasoned judgment unless we make an effort to critique and, if necessary, override our feelings. Left to its own devices, intuition will give way to compassion fade, favoring individual victims and underreacting to catastrophic events."[50]

Categorical Thinking

The human mind is a categorization machine, continually taking in voluminous amounts of information and simplifying and structuring it to make sense of the world.[51] The use of categories to structure information is functional because it facilitates quick decisions about events and conditions. Under more complex circumstances, however, categories can be used inappropriately and lead to erroneous decisions. Categorical thinking can distort perception when it affects how people think about risk. For example, if you were asked "Who is most concerned about climate change, naysayers or advocates" how would you answer? If you answered advocates, technically you are correct. Overall, advocates rate climate change as more important than naysayers do. But some naysayers care more about climate change than advocates do.

A personal example will show how categorical thinking works. Over dinner with a friend in Fall 2019, the conversation turned to atypically warm weather in Maine extending into and through November. I described the prevailing weather pattern as all the more evidence of climate change. The friend, an accomplished professional, said, "Well, you know, climate change is cyclical—the planet moves in warm and cold cycles and this, too, will change." I sat back in my chair and countered the friend's remark with a statement to the effect that I had reviewed a substantial amount of climate change research, and the planet was embedded in the throes of an event that if not countered could be catastrophic. The friend pondered the remark and replied, "Well it is man-made." On the basis of categorical thinking, this friend would be viewed as a naysayer and me as an advocate, but stereotypes mask the overlap between people, amplifying perceived differences among them.[52]

Amplification associated with categorical thinking is especially worrisome in relation to heightened levels of risk facing the nation and the world. Organizations and leaders will struggle with amplification dynamics that make consensus difficult to achieve. Success will hinge, in large part, on creating synergies across groups, but categorical thinking may cause leaders to underestimate how effectively disparate groups are coming together in response to risk. If, for example, leaders do not perform due diligence in preparing the groundwork for synergy because they assume that climate change evidence is so compelling that naysayers will ultimately accept it and that advocates will employ reason and patience in listening to the claims of naysayers, they may be surprised when initiatives falter. Reason may succumb to emotion when belief is amplified by partisan fervor.

Stasis-Related Behavior

Stasis is commonly understood as a state of inactivity or equilibrium. In the domain of risk, it is a preference for the certainty of the status quo in contrast to the uncertainty of risk. When people actively resist change, inaction becomes the operant mode of thought and behavior. The resulting stasis may deter response to risk as evidenced in constructs of *cognitive complexity*, *satisfice*, and *normalization*, which bind people to inaction to maintain the status quo.

Cognitive Complexity

Cognitive complexity is a psychological construct used to describe the extent to which individuals can differentiate and integrate circumstances and events.[53] Individuals with high cognitive complexity think in a multidimensional way. They have the capacity to analyze a situation, discern its constituent parts, and explore connections and possible relationships among the parts.[54] A primary tenet of complexity theory is that the greater the extent to which a circumstance or event can be differentiated and its parts considered in novel relationships, the more enlightened the response and successful the solution.[55]

Cognitive complexity and risk come together in the interplay between perceptual capability and the configuration of risk conditions. Multidimensional thinkers are able to get their arms around complex conditions that are part of risk, whereas others might be stymied by conditions that are beyond their perceptual horizon. Those who are unable to break down and differentiate elements of risk may retreat and become dependent on others whose skills they cannot easily judge. This circumstance is known as *complexity mismatch*, and it is a primary cause of reticence in response to risk.[56]

Satisfice

Introduced by economist Herbert Simon in 1956, satisfice means choosing a solution which is acceptable or reasonable over the optimal solution because reaching the optimal solution would cost more in effort and resources.[57] Simon blended "satisfy" and "suffice" to explain how people behave when circumstances make it difficult to forge an optimal solution. In the world of organizations, decision makers search through available alternatives until an acceptable threshold is reached. In everyday life, people make decisions that fit their comfort zone even if the decisions are less than optimal. Optimal solutions in the complex world we live in require time, effort, and consideration of wide-ranging options—a process that is neither realistic nor cognitively possible for some people.

Satisficing depends in large part on aspiration when choosing among different paths of action. Satisficers will select the first option that meets a given need or the option that meets most of the needs rather than the optimal choice.

> *Illustration:* A homeowner is seeking to lower home energy carbon emissions by reducing drafts and air leaks through caulking and insulation. The best insulation according to performance data is foil-faced fiberglass insulation, but this insulation must be back-ordered and will not be available for six months. The homeowner is in a hurry to install insulation before the onset of winter. A reasonable alternative is plain fiberglass insulation and it is available at a local outlet. Giving in to satisfice, the homeowner chooses to save time and resources by purchasing an acceptable, but less than optimal insulation alternative.

Satisficing is a common behavioral mode in consensus building when a group works toward a solution everyone can agree with even if it may not be optimal.

> *Illustration:* Legislators in a northeastern state have spent months debating strategy and timing of carbon-neutral standards. After months of discourse, they eventually achieve consensus on carbon neutrality by 2050, only to have a legislator speak up and ask if the state has the resources to achieve that standard. When the legislative body reacts unfavorably to the question, it is not because the legislator was wrong to ask, but because the legislature has settled on a standard that is agreeable to all. The time frame is not optimum—from an environmental standpoint, carbon-neutrality by 2035 would be optimal—but the majority agree on one number and this number is sufficient to cap the debate.

The takeaway from these examples is that "optimal" and "acceptable" are entirely different entities. Convenience and comfort may dictate what is "acceptable" but at a cost. In the world of risk, the cost is limited attention to the conditions and circumstances surrounding risk and "good enough" decisions that fall short of optimal solutions.

Normalization

In the winter of 2019, opinion columnist Rekha Basu brought human response to climate change into focus with a simple metaphor:[58]

There is a saying about why a frog in a pot of warm water doesn't try to jump out when the temperature is gradually increased to boiling. If immersed in boiling water from the start, the story goes, the same frog would try to escape. It's a metaphor for our capacity to adapt to and even normalize painful circumstances as they escalate. . . . It was said to be colder in Iowa on Wednesday than in Alaska and some of Antarctica. Crises like this Artic freeze put you into survival mode. You adapt by focusing on getting warm instead of asking why. . . . But what's causing it? Why did the polar vortex break in two and head over the Midwest as reported? Why, if the last four years have been the world's hottest on record, are we experiencing this deep freeze? Where does global warming fit in?

Normalization is the process through which ideas and behavior that fall outside of social norms come to be regarded as "normal."[59] Perceptions of "normal" can change over time as people become accustomed to deviations from routine that are no longer considered deviant despite the fact that they exceed prevailing norms. In a 2017 issue of the *New York Times*, Adam Bear and Joshua Knobe of Yale University, who have studied normalization, wrote that people tend to blur what is "desirable" and what is "average" into a "single undifferentiated judgment of normality."[60] As leaders "continue to do things that once would have been regarded as outlandish," their actions come to be seen as not only more typical but also more normal.[61] Hence, they come to be seen as less problematic and less worthy of outrage. Human perception of normal does not separate the normal from the ideal. As outlandish ideas and behavior become more common through repetition, they become more acceptable.[62]

In the domain of risk, research has shown that normalization occurs through an intuitive process of accommodation and adjustment. Using the example of climate change, extreme temperatures become part of an undifferentiated normality of "hot" or "cold" irrespective of how extreme they are. People adjust by wearing suitable clothing but do not ask why or what's causing the extreme temperatures. A 2018 study by economists at the Vancouver School of Economics analyzed the link between extreme weather and human well-being through the lens of 3.5 billion Facebook and Twitter posts between 2009 and 2016.[62] Using sentiment analysis, the number of positive and negative words contained in each post was counted and then compared to meteorological data for specific locations. The grounding effect of normalization was illustrated through two findings: (1) negative sentiment increased significantly during extreme weather and (2) remarks about extreme weather declined rapidly if people had experienced extreme temperatures in recent years.[63] People adapt to challenging weather patterns and adjust their demeanor to fit prevailing conditions.

Typical of the mindset of adapters to the reality of climate change is the following excerpt from a letter to the editor of the *Arizona Daily Star* in 2019.[64]

Trying to stop global warming is akin to spitting in the face of Mother Nature. After all, we know that the Earth has endured similar cycles of heating followed by periods of cooling for past eons. Humans are known to succeed by depending on their brains and imagination to adopt to a changing world, and thereby not only survive, but thrive. Wouldn't we be wiser to accept that Earth is going through a period of warming and spend our time and effort adapting to that change rather than ineffectively trying to stop it? Heat is energy. Let's use that energy to make changes which will improve our survivability. We should approach the current environmental changes with the attitude that we can adapt to them, which is our natural human recourse.

Inertia Theory

The range of behavior associated with eschewal and immobility in response to risk is almost overwhelming. Will organizations and leaders be able to grasp and act on behavior that is part of the human side of risk? What ties the strands of behavior together? Is there a theoretical perspective—a common thread—that will explain the contribution of behavioral dynamics to risk?

The common thread is *inertia theory*—a theoretical perspective linking immobility to behavioral dynamics specific to change and stasis.[65] Inertia has been used to describe behavior associated with resistance to change.[66] In management and organizational science, *cognitive inertia* describes managerial failure to reevaluate situations and events in the face of change.[67] In sociology, *social inertia* depicts resistance to change as a function of relationship stability in a society or social group.[68] In psychology, the *inertia effect* describes the reluctance of individuals to reduce their confidence in a decision following disconfirming information.[69] The concept of *psychological inertia* has been used to describe the tendency to maintain the status quo.[70] Research studies in medicine and health use the term *patient inertia* to describe the phenomenon of patient adherence to inferior treatment options or failure to initiate treatment even after the diagnosis of a medical problem.[71] Inertia is central to most of the studies of causative factors linked to resistance to change. Irrespective of its application, however, inertia boils down to a preference for the status quo—a desire to maintain equilibrium by either repeating past behavior or avoiding action.

The preference for status quo has been attributed to phenomena of *loss aversion* and *endowment effect*.[72] Individuals tend to weigh the potential loss of departing from the status quo more heavily than they do the potential gain. As a result, they resist change unless the benefits clearly outweigh the risk. Numerous coping behaviors are employed to maintain the status quo. Primary among them is *cognitive dissonance*—denial, substitution, and reinterpretation of evidence. By changing the narrative around evidence contradictory to personal beliefs and assumptions, individuals are able to reconcile differences and quell discomfort. *Intuitive thinking* and *categorical thinking* reinforce the status quo by enabling individuals to gloss over critical aspects of change thereby causing them to pay inadequate attention to risk and its consequences. And stasis maintains the status quo through behavior that softens the disruptive effects of change through suboptimal decisions (*satisfice*) and neutralizes disruptive ideas and actions by making them part of everyday life (*normalization*).

Unquestionably, psychological factors play a major role in preservation of the status quo. Just as prominent, however, are factors embedded in societal conditions which fuel inertia by clouding judgment. Consider, for example, the impact of anxiety on decision-making during the COVID-19 pandemic when social norms guiding interaction changed rapidly and radically (*anomie*); the effect of antipathy rising out of conflict between groups holding sharply contrasting views (*polarization*); the confusion associated with too much information (*information overload*); and the incapacity to distinguish truth from falsehood when perception of reality is altered by misinformation (*ideological subversion*). These socially induced conditions color interpretation of real-world circumstances and events and shape judgment and decision-making. Individuals unable to discern truth and fact from falsehood may withdraw and become dependent on others whose skills they cannot judge. In the world of risk, this would be tantamount to turning over personal responsibility for risk assessment and response to collective opinion.

Organizations, Leaders, and Mobilization

There are many behavioral deterrents to risk response and mobilization. In the world of risk, leaders need to understand and act on behavioral dynamics associated with eschewal and immobility. The urgency for action is real as evidenced in questions about organizational and leader engagement with the human side of risk:

- To what extent are leaders responsible for understanding and acting on behavioral dynamics contributing to risk?
- Are leaders equipped with the skills necessary to manage the human side of risk?
- What must leaders know and do to manage the human side of risk?
- Are leaders willing to make strategic leaps to build organizational capability for managing the human side of risk?

It takes substantial energy and a willingness to look at people, events, and circumstances in a different way to develop robust answers to these questions. The human side of risk has received far too little attention in complex organizations. Moreover, the cognitive framework needed to manage the human element—a fundamental understanding of behavioral dynamics—is not systematically addressed in professional school curricula nor is it a featured element of professional development in complex organizations. The emphasis in leader development is primarily on context—forces inside and outside of organizations that leaders must navigate to achieve organizational and personal success. This is unquestionably an important part of leader development. After all, behavior does not take shape in a vacuum. It is influenced by social forces—the topic in the next section of the book.

Notes

1 Roberto, M., Bohmer, R., and Edmondson, A., "Facing Ambiguous Threats." *Harvard Business Review*, 84(11) (November 2006): 106.
2 Wikipedia, *2004 Indian Ocean Earthquake and Tsunami*, July 25, 2019.
3 Roberto, Bohmer, and Edmondson, "Facing Ambiguous Threats." 107.
4 Ibid.
5 Leeds-Hurwitz, W., "Social Construction of Reality." In Stephen Littlejohn and Karen Foss (eds.), *Encyclopedia of Communication Theory*. Thousand Oaks, CA: Sage Publications, 2009, p. 891. The Leeds-Hurwitz definition of social constructionism was retrieved from Wikipedia on July 30, 2019. https://en.wikipedia.org/w/index.php?title=Social_constructionism&oldid=911633269.
6 Berger, P. and Luckmann, T., *The Social Construction of Reality*. New York: Anchor Books/Knopf Doubleday, 1966.
7 Ibid. Retrieved from Wikipedia on August 4, 2019 from: https://en.wikipedia.org.wiki/The_Social_Construction_of_Reality.
8 Ibid.
9 Searle, J., *The Construction of Social Reality*. New York: Simon and Schuster, 1995.
10 Ibid.
11 Elwell, F., *Emile Durkheim on Anomie*, 2003. http://faculty.rsu.edu/~felwell/Theorists//Essays/Durkheim1.htm. Retrieved: August 10, 2019.
12 Durkheim, E., *Suicide: A Study in Sociology*. New York: The Free Press, 1897.
13 Ibid.
14 Ibid.
15 Plous, S., *The Psychology of Judgment and Decision Making*. New York: McGraw-Hill, 1993, p. 233.

16 Brauer, M., Judd, C., and Gliner, M.D., "The Effects of Repeated Expressions on Attitude Polarization During Group Discussions." *Journal of Personality and Social Psychology*, 68(6) (1995): 1014–1029. https://en.wikipedia.org/w/index.php?title=Group_polarization&oldid=913180419. Retrieved: August 12, 2019.

17 Alvernia University Online, "Group Polarization in Social Psychology." *Psychology*, 2018, May 21. https://online.alvernia.edu/articles/category/psychology/.

18 Ibid.

19 Ibid.

20 https://en.wikipedia.org/w/index.php?title=Group_polarization&oldid=913180419. Retrieved: September 1, 2019.

21 Vinokur, A. and Burnstein, E., "Effects of Partially Shared Persuasive Arguments on Group Induced Shifts: A Problem Solving Approach." *Journal of Personality and Social Psychology*, 29(3) (1974): 305–315. https://en.wikipedia.org/w/index.php?title=Group_polarization&oldid=913180419. Retrieved: September 2, 2019.

22 Ibid.

23 Feilitzen, C., *Influences of Mediated Violence: A Brief Research Summary*. International Clearinghouse on Children, Youth and Media, 2009. https://en.wikipedia.org/w/index.php?title=Group_polarization&oldid=913180419. Retrieved: September 2, 2019.

24 Sunstein, C., "Deliberative Trouble: Why Groups Go to Extremes." *The Yale Law Journal*, 110(1) (2000): 71–119.

25 Motel, S., "Polls Show That Most Americans Believe in Climate Change But Give It Low Priority." *Pew Research Center*, September 23, 2014.

26 https://en.wikipedia.org/windex.php?title=Information_overload&oldid=913082131. Retrieved: September 5, 2019.

27 Toffler, A., *Future Shock*. New York: Random House, 1970.

28 Hemp, P., "Death by Information Overload." *Harvard Business Review*, 87(9) (September 2009).

29 Shirky, C., "It's Not Information Overload. It's Filter Failure." *Web 2.0 Expo*, New York, September 2008. https://en.wikipedia.org/windex.php?title=Information_overload&oldid=913082131. Retrieved: September 5, 2019.

30 Ibid.

31 Pham, L., "Ideological Subversion, Psychological War on the United States." *Economics Voodoo*, February 6, 2013. https://wwweconomicsvoodoo.com/understanding-the-truman-show-part-i-ideological-subversion/. Retrieved: August 15, 2019.

32 Ibid.

33 Ibid.

34 Stengel, R., "We're in the Middle of a Global Information War. Here's What We Need to Do to Win." *Time*, October 7, 2019.

35 Fandos, N. and Shear, M., "A Domestic Political Errand Diverging From U.S. Goals." *New York Times*, November 22, 2019.

36 Crossman, A., "Understanding Functionalist Theory." *Thought Company*, May 4, 2019.

37 Crossman, A., "Understanding Conflict Theory." *Thought Company*, July 3, 2019.

38 Pam M.S., N., "COGNITIVE DISSONANCE (Dissonance Theory)." *Psychology Dictionary.org*, November 28, 2018. https://psychologydictionary.org/cognitive-dissonance-theory/. Retrieved: October 7, 2019.

39 Festinger, L., *A Theory of Cognitive Dissonance*. Palo Alto, CA: Stanford University Press, 1957.

40 Pam M.S., "COGNTIVE DISSONANCE (Dissonance Theory)."

41 Lewandowsky, S., Oreskes, N., Risbey, J., Newell, B., and Smithson, M., "Seepage: Climate Change Denial and Its Effect on the Scientific Community." *Global Environmental Change*, 33(1) (2015): 1–13.

42 Ibid.

43 Kunreuther, H., Slovic, P., and Olson, K., "Fast and Slow Thinking in the Face of Catastrophic Risk." *SSRN Electronic Journal*, August 19, 2014. https://ssrn.com/abstract=2488653.

44 Ibid.

45 Ibid.

46 Ibid.

47 Slovic, P., "'If I Look at the Mass I Will Never Act': Psychic Numbing and Genocide." *Judgment and Decision Making*, 2 (2007): 79–95.

48 Ibid.

49 Vastfjall, D., Slovic, P., Mayorga, M., and Peters, E., "Compassion Fade: Affect and Charity Are Greatest for a Single Child in Need." *PLoS ONE*, 9(6) (2014): e100115.

50 Kunreuther, Slovic, and Olson. *Fast and Slow Thinking in the Face of Catastrophic Risk*.

51 de Langhe, B. and Fernbach, P., "The Dangers of Categorical Thinking." *Harvard Business Review*, 97(5) (2019): 81–91.

52 Ibid.

53 Pervin, L., Cervone, D., and John, O., *Personality: Theory and Research*. Hoboken, NJ: John Wiley & Sons, 2004.

54 Ibid.

55 Ibid.

56 Clarke, R. and Eddy, R., *Warnings: Finding Cassandras to Stop Catastrophes*. New York: HarperCollins, 2017.

57 Simon, H., "Rational Choice and the Structure of the Environment." *Psychological Review*, 63(2) (1956): 129–138.

58 Basa, R., "Frozen Retinas? Cats Under the Hood? Normalize the Polar Vortex Freeze at Your Own Risk." *Des Moines Register*, January 30, 2019.

59 https://en.wikipedia.org/w/index.php?title=Normalization_(sociology)&oldid=892692859. Retrieved: September 8, 2019.

60 Bear, A. and Knobe, J., "The Normalization Trap." *The New York Times*, January 29, 2017.

61 Ibid.

62 Baylis, P., "The Human Cost of Climate Change." *Trek*, University of British Columbia, Spring 2019, p. 10.

63 Ibid.

64 Letter to the Editor. *Arizona Daily Star*, December 6, 2019.

65 https://en.wikipedia.org/w/index.php?title=Social_inertia&oldid=918504867. Retrieved: September 10, 2019.

66 Alos-Ferrer, C., Hugelschafer, S., and Li, J., "Inertia and Decision Making." *Frontiers in Psychology*, 7(169) (2016).

67 Huff, J., Huff, A., and Thomas, H., "Strategic Renewal and the Interaction of Cumulative Stress and Inertia." *Strategic Management Journal*, 13 (1992): 55–75.

68 Bourdieu, P., "The Social Space and the Genesis of Groups." *Theory in Sociology*, 14 (1985): 723–744.

69 Pitz, G. and Reinhold, H., "Payoff Effects in Sequential Decision Making." *Journal of Experimental Psychology*, 77 (1968): 249–257.

70 Gal, D., "A Psychological Law of Inertia and the Illusion of Loss Aversion." *Judgment Decision Making*, 1 (2006): 23–32.

71 Suri, G., Sheppes, G., Schwartz, C., and Gross, J., "Patient Inertia and the Status Quo Bias: When an Inferior Option Is Preferred." *Psychological Science*, 24 (2013): 1763–1769.

72 https://en.wikipedia.org./w/index.php?title=Status_quo_bias&oldid916273609. Retrieved: September 25, 2019.

CHALLENGES AND DETERRENTS

Chapter 3

The Power and Peril of Pandemic

The pandemic is a never-before-seen national economic calamity; history doesn't get bigger than this.

Peggy Noonan
Writer and Author, April 16, 2020

The emergence early in 2020 of the coronavirus created havoc of unimaginable proportion for business. It forced companies into extraordinary measures to protect their employees and maintain operations. Layoffs became standard practice in every industry and many companies, especially those with fragile reserves, were forced into closure. Companies rose and fell on the basis of their ability to scale digital technology and to embrace remote work. COVID-19 was nothing short of a tidal wave that permanently altered how business was conducted, the lives of workers, and the skills required of leaders.

In the wake of pandemic, important questions loom for organizations and for business:

- Are the effects of catastrophe episodic or continuous?
- Is there opportunity in catastrophe? If so, where is it found and pursued?
- What do companies need to do to prepare for and recover from catastrophe?
- How can leaders prepare for a post-catastrophe world in which prevailing assumptions and metrics are no longer relevant?

Episode or Constant?

In the short space of six months, COVID-19 became an all-consuming disaster—so immediate, so intense, and so intrusive as to be palpable. It defied our tendency to deny, to rationalize, or to refute conditions and events that are disruptive—classic forms of avoidance behavior that deter response to risk. As such, it became the embodiment of the three-pronged dynamic driving this book:

- Catastrophic risk is a domain of risk that organizations and leaders will face with greater frequency in the future;

- Avoidance behavior exacerbates the impact and consequences of risk; and
- Business organizations and leaders bear a responsibility for mobilization in response to risk.

A pandemic is different in character than a catastrophe. It is *episodic* in nature with attributes that give it the character of a disaster—a rapidly unfolding event that causes great damage and loss of life.[1] Its duration is relatively short and it is subject to mitigation. COVID-19, for example, moved at warp speed and the destruction it rendered was beyond the imagination. The pages that follow describe the pandemic's course and its effects on people, institutions, and organizations. Of particular importance are changes in the structure and functioning of institutions brought about by the emergence of COVID-19 and the behavioral response of people to *sudden onset risk*. A disaster does not end with alleviation or removal of its immediate potential for harm. Harm is ongoing and life after a disaster is as important, if not more important, than life during a disaster. The chapter closes with planning for life in a post-COVID world—a world in which prevailing assumptions and metrics have been rendered irrelevant.

Anatomy of a Pandemic

A book about catastrophic risk developed in the midst of a disaster is an unfinished work. COVID-19 had no end in sight when this book was written and waiting out the pandemic to finish the book was not an option. Accordingly, this chapter is pinned to a specific point in time—*July 2020*—with the course and consequences of the pandemic pegged to this timepoint. COVID-19 numbers specific to incidence and mortality vary by source and time of day—a circumstance that rendered numbers impossible to report with any degree of precision.

Impact

Unlike an epidemic, a pandemic is a large-scale outbreak of infectious disease leading to a dramatic increase in morbidity and mortality over multiple continents.[2] Pandemics have occurred throughout history but appear to be increasing in frequency as a function of population growth, urbanization, greater demand for animal protein, expansive travel and connectivity between population centers, habitat loss, climate change, and increased interaction between human and animal life.[3] With a global population estimated to reach 9.7 billion by 2050 and with travel and trade steadily intensifying, public health systems have a shorter expanse of time in which to detect and contain a pandemic before it spreads. They also have less time to develop a vaccine and make it universally available.

Numbers

COVID-19 spread throughout the world reaching a level of 14 million cases and 600,000 deaths by July 2020.[4] In the United States, the number of infections rose dramatically and by July the U.S. had become the country with the most COVID-19 confirmed cases in the world with 3.7 million confirmed cases and more than 138,000 coronavirus-related deaths.[5] Table 3.1 presents global and U.S. statistics for confirmed coronavirus cases and deaths as of July 17, 2020. Exact numbers are difficult to validate because confirmed cases and coronavirus-related deaths are subject to change by the hour. The numbers presented are an approximation of the incidence and spread of COVID-19 after its emergence in Wuhan, China, in December 2019.[6]

Table 3.1   Confirmed Cases and COVID-19-Related Deaths

	Global	*United States*
Cumulative Confirmed Cases		
March 21	340,000	2,000
April 30	3,200,000	1,100,000
May 27	5,600,000	1,650,000
June 26	9,200,000	2,350,000
July 17	14,104,033	3,695,469
Cumulative Deaths		
March 21	14,000	471
April 30	233,000	63,000
May 27	352,000	100,000
June 26	511,251	127,251
July17	597,541	140,888

Source: World Health Organization and Johns Hopkins Coronavirus Resource Center

What is remarkable about these numbers is the sheer speed at which COVID-19 spread across the globe, its acceleration in the U.S. between March and July, and clear differences among nations in strategy for managing and mitigating the outbreak. A seven-month timeline of COVID-19 evolution worldwide and in the U.S. reveals the velocity at which COVID-19 spread and differences among nations in managing the outbreak:[7]

Timeline

December 30	*Wuhan Central Hospital physician alerts authorities to the emergence of a SARS-like illness*
January 11	China reports first coronavirus-related death
January 13	Thailand confirms first known coronavirus case outside of China
January 21	CDC confirms first U.S. case in Washington State
January 24	First cases recorded in Europe/Americans told "risk is low"
January 31	Trump Administration declares outbreak a public health emergency
February 1	*U.S. confirms eight COVID-19 cases*
	Outbreak has infected 12,000 people worldwide and killed 250
February 6	First confirmed coronavirus death in the U.S.
February 21	CDC indicates a pandemic is "likely"
February 26	CDC issues warning about the causes and consequences of community spread/Trump appoints vice president to lead national coronavirus task force
March 1	*U.S. confirms 89 cases*
	79,824 cases in China and 1,694 cases in Italy
March 16	Federal guidelines released calling for Americans to avoid social gatherings of more than ten people for 15 days

March 17	Defense Production Act invoked directing industry to produce critical equipment
March 26	U.S. has most cases in the world (83,836) followed by China (81,782) and Italy (80,589)
March 27	Trump signs $2T stimulus package
April 1	*U.S. confirms 213,372 cases and deaths topping 1,000 per day*
April 2	More than 1 million cases confirmed worldwide/6.86 million Americans file first-time jobless claims
April 7	U.S. reports more than 2,000 deaths in a single day/COVID-19 is #1 killer eclipsing heart disease
April 28	U.S. tops 1,000,000 cases/one-third of world's cases
April 29	Economic data indicate that the U.S. economy shrank 4.8 percent in first quarter/steepest decline since 2008 Great Recession
May 1	*U.S. confirms 1,070,032 cases and 63,000 deaths*
May 8	Unemployment at 14.7 percent/U.S. economy loses 20.5 million jobs in April
May 15	Worldwide cases approaching 5 million/worldwide deaths total 300,000
May 18	Widespread reopening of the U.S. businesses
May 29	U.S. withdraws from World Health Organization
June 1	*U.S. confirms 1.8 million cases and 105,099 deaths*
June 9	U.S. economy officially in recession according to National Bureau of Economic Research
June 11	2 million cases and 113,000 coronavirus-related deaths in the U.S.
June 27	U.S. reports record number of daily cases (44,732)
June 30	Global cases reach 10,475,817 and death toll stands at 511,251
	U.S. cases reach 2,627,584 and death toll stands at 127,251
July 1	*U.S. cases at 2.73 million*
July 3	U.S. reports record number of 57,683 daily new cases
	Cases: 2,793,022	Deaths: 129,400
July 9	U.S. reports record number of 65,551 daily new cases
	Cases: 3.1 million	Deaths: 133,195
July 12	U.S. reports record number of 69,000 daily new cases
	Cases: 3,242,073	Deaths: 134,729
July 16	U.S. cases: 3,500,000	U.S. deaths: 137,000
July 22	**U.S. cases: 3,970,671**	**U.S. deaths: 144,173**
	Global cases: 14,951,347	**Global deaths: 616,550**

The timeline tells a story and raises a number of questions. The story is one of the lack of preparation and leadership for a pandemic in high-tech nations seemingly in control of their own destiny. The questions have to do with the behavior and actions of nations, governments, and people confronted by sudden onset risk:

■ Why were nations and governments unprepared for the pandemic?
■ What could governments have done differently to prepare for the pandemic?
■ What practices were employed by nations that effectively managed the pandemic?
■ Where did the United States err in managing COVID-19?

Managing the Pandemic

If polls are to be believed, most people have faith that government understands the gravity of a pandemic and is working to counteract its effects.[8] There is a little doubt, however, that governments throughout the world were ill-prepared for COVID-19. Country after country locked down citizens to slow the spread of the virus and to shield health systems from overwhelming numbers. The lack of protective equipment and supplies put citizens and caregivers at risk, despite repeated calls by scientists for government agencies to stockpile life-saving equipment.

Advanced nations make up a high-tech world. How is it possible that nations and governments were not ready for the pandemic? Pandemics are addressed by regional and national risk registers produced by governments, as well as international registers maintained by non-governmental organizations.[9] These tools highlight the highest impact events that could befall nations including earthquakes, terrorism, influenza, and novel pandemics. Risk registers put information into the hands of government. Why did governments fail to act on warnings of a pandemic, particularly in advanced nations such as the U.S. and Great Britain, which have infrastructure and resources to manage a pandemic?

Tyler and Gluckman (2020) describe a host of reasons underlying lack of preparation.[10]

- *False sense of security.* Policy makers and the public-at-large could not comprehend or accept the magnitude of the problem. Comparable events like the "Spanish flu" are ancient history and outbreaks like SARS, Ebola, and swine flu were contained and subdued with relative ease.
- *Faith in modern medicine.* There is a sense shared by many that modern medicine, at least in advanced countries, can cope with anything a microbiotic can throw at it.
- *Overstated risk.* Skeptical politicians and inflammatory commentators purport that risk analysts and scientists have cried wolf over past viral threats such as swine flu and bird flu and view risk as overstated and dubious.
- *Short-term focus.* Electoral cycles are short and the focus of politicians and government officials is on the here and now. Public policy that requires long-term investment, especially intangibles such as disaster planning, tends to be lower priority.
- *Out of sight/out of mind.* Government attention is directed to events that are underway or have already occurred such as floods and earthquakes. Reward is extended for solution of problems that are manifest, not for problems averted before they become apparent.
- *Information overload.* Risk registers are calculated using voluminous information much of which is not understood. Long lists of hazards and risks reported on scatter graphs linking the likelihood of an event with its impact may lead to an illusion of precision and control that can lull governments into a false sense of security.
- *Political liability.* Risk registers can become politically hazardous if distributed as a guide for action and an event happens for which governments are not prepared to act. Despite their obvious value in developing a common understanding about risk and helping agencies prepare, nations that do not publish registers come under less pressure to act on them.

Nations do not prepare for infectious diseases in the same way they prepare for threats to national security. Would one nation consider issuing a declaration of war against another then conduct an inventory of weapons for use in battle? Yet that is precisely how governments deal with vaccines and treatments for diseases of epidemic potential. Governments are unprepared because of a lack of imagination, a failure to plan and invest, and a lapse in public will. Nations with the vision and wherewithal to protect themselves from a pandemic are not constrained by geography and politics. They frontload investment in pharmaceutical agents, medical equipment and supplies, and continuing research.

Controlling the Contagion

Cyclical contagions like COVID-19 are capable of repetition and rapid movement across borders. Their cyclical nature requires an approach to management keyed to periodic influxes of people needing hospital beds and intensive care. The *Global Health Security Index*, a 2019 report compiled by researchers at the Nuclear Threat Initiative, Johns Hopkins University, and The Economist Intelligence Unit revealed weaknesses in national health security throughout the world.[11] Nations were unable to manage the pandemic because of gaps in preparation including shortfalls in:[12]

- mechanisms for prevention of the emergence or release of pathogens
- epidemic detection and reporting
- rapid response
- health system strength and robustness
- compliance with international norms around disease
- the overall political, economic, and environmental risk environment

To manage a pandemic effectively, nations would need to develop and maintain international commitments and cross-border agreements on health emergency responses and biosafety policies and procedures to guide communications with healthcare agencies and workers.[13] They would need clear plans for emergency response, ample facilities and equipment for treatment of patients and protection of healthcare workers, linkages between public health and security authorities, and established systems for risk communication with the public.[14] They would also need systems for diagnosis and tracking in the early stages of an epidemic: real-time virus detection and reporting systems, strong laboratory systems, a robust epidemiology workforce, and efficient systems for testing and approval of new medical countermeasures.[15] These systems were not in place to the extent needed to manage a global pandemic.

What would it take to stem a pandemic? A May 2020 article in *The New Yorker*, "Why Weren't We Ready for the Coronavirus," described steps taken to manage SARS in 2003 by Tan Tock Seng Hospital, one of Singapore's largest health facilities:[16]

Tan Tock Seng started treating only SARS patients, with sick people diverted to Singapore General. Every suspected or probable case of SARS went into isolation at TTS, and the definition of "suspected or probable" was expanded beyond WHO guidelines to include anyone with a fever or respiratory trouble. All health-care workers suited up with personal protective equipment, including N95 masks, and they were required to check themselves for fever or other symptoms three times a day. Medical staff were also restricted to one institution, so they couldn't carry the virus between hospitals. During risky procedures such as intubating a patient, they wore respirator helmets that pumped in purified air.

Firm measures were also taken to limit the disease's spread in the community. Schools closed and the bodies of those who died of SARS were cremated within twenty-four hours. Investigators traced close contacts of each new SARS patient, also within twenty-four hours, and those contacts were consigned to mandatory self-quarantine. "O.K., you are staying home. There will be a camera we're setting up in your house, and there's a phone. We will call you randomly, and you're expected to turn on the camera and be there." More than eight-hundred people were quarantined. Flout the home quarantine, and you'd be tagged with an electronic tracer, such as an ankle bracelet. Mandatory quarantine brought logistical challenges. "The moment you hold 'em, you own 'em.' You've got to feed these people, see to their health care, make sure they are housed and clothed. Who takes care of them? Who pays for them?" If you're the government ministry enforcing self-quarantine, you do.

Failure of Leadership

On October 24, 2019, 45 days before the world's first suspected case of COVID-19 was announced, the *Global Health Security Index* ranked countries on indicators measuring how effectively a nation could respond to an epidemic.[17] The U.S. was ranked first out of 195 nations.[18] A country that on paper was the best prepared to deal with a pandemic by July 2020 had become the world's biggest failure in tackling COVID-19. With more than 150,000 coronavirus-related deaths at the close of July, the U.S. was home to one-quarter of the world's COVID-19 deaths.[19] What went wrong? Where did the scorecard's metrics fall short?

A simple answer is that the scorecard did not account for the political context in which national policy is formulated and implemented. Early in the Trump presidency, national readiness was downgraded through the elimination of a disease preparedness office established by President Obama after the 2014–2016 Ebola epidemic.[20] Deep cuts were proposed for the Center for Disease Control that led to gutting of the CDC's Public Health Science and Surveillance program.[21] Further compromising national preparedness was a mindset among senior administration officials that the nation was invulnerable—pandemics happened elsewhere in the world, not in the U.S. The virus was a short-term flu-like illness overblown by science.[22] Economic expediency should be the basis of policy, not scientific and medical advice.

The Trump Administration ignored World Health Organization track and trace advice on how to prevent COVID-19 infection and slow transmission. Masks were shunned by leaders, physical distancing directives were not uniformly followed, and public health guidelines were downplayed in favor of economic considerations. Action was delayed on setting up track and trace stations giving the virus free rein to spread in the early days of contagion. Worse yet, national policy on testing, social distancing, and use of face masks was not forthcoming and responsibility for managing the pandemic shifted to the states. A July 19, 2020, *New York Times* article detailed the actions of a small group of White House aides to shift responsibility for leading the fight against the pandemic from the White House to the states.[23] Referred to as "state authority handoff," it was the catalyst for what would simultaneously become a catastrophic policy blunder and an attempt to escape blame for a crisis that had engulfed the country.

> Over a critical period beginning in mid-April, President Trump and his team convinced themselves that the outbreak was fading, that they had given state governments all the resources they needed to contain its remaining "embers" and that it was time to ease up the lockdown. In doing so, he was ignoring warnings that the numbers continue to drop only if social distancing was kept in place, rushing instead to restart the economy and tend to his battered re-election hopes. . . . A sharp pivot soon followed, with consequences that continue to plague the country today as the virus surges anew. Even as a chorus of state officials and health experts warned that the pandemic was far from under control, Mr. Trump went, in a matter of days, from proclaiming that he alone

had the authority to decide when the economy would reopen to pushing that responsibility onto the states. The government issued detailed reopening guidelines, but almost immediately, Mr. Trump began criticizing Democratic governors who did not "liberate" their states. Mr. Trump's bet that the crisis would fade away proved wrong. An examination of the shift in approach in April and its aftermath shows that the approach he embraced was not just a misjudgment. Instead, it was a deliberate strategy that he would stick doggedly to as evidence mounted that, in the absence of strong leadership from the White House, the virus would continue to infect and kill large numbers of Americans. . . . The number of new cases has now surged far higher than the previous peak of more than 36,000 a day in mid-April. On July 16, there were more than 75,000 confirmed new cases, a record.

Retrospective analysis reveals that the president was warned early on about the potential for a pandemic, but that internal divisions, lack of planning, and blind faith in his own instincts led to a failure to provide critically needed leadership.[24]

Resistance and Resurgence

Facing growing pressure from the federal government, business owners, and a restless populace, the U.S. economy began to reopen on a state-by-state basis in May 2020. It was premature. The absence of a national lockdown policy and resistance to mask usage, social distancing, and stay-in-place orders led to an alarming post-Memorial Day surge of COVID-19.[25] People continued to go about their daily business of shopping, traveling, and socializing with friends as if a pandemic did not exist. In spite of repeated warnings from health authorities, many Americans flaunted basic precautions and refused to wear masks or social distance. In so doing, they threw caution to the wind prompting questions about their concern for safeguarding health.

Research offers insights into behavior that affects well-being.[26] Medical advice is resisted because of a belief in invulnerability—a virus can't infect me and if it does, I will recover. Media reports indicating that older adults to be most at risk for contracting the virus fueled a false sense of invulnerability among younger adults. For some, mask wearing morphed into a political and cultural statement about individual rights. Freedom of expression is a right and the requirement to wear a mask is discriminatory.[27] A mask could also be seen as a statement of group affiliation—a form of in-group expression.[28] Adding fuel to the fire was advice from health authorities that understated health risks and misstated the benefits of wearing a mask. Mask advice kept changing and evolving data indicated that most of the people contracting the virus recovered from it. Confusing information and resistance to health advisories powered a virus that would not quit—undeterred by boundaries of time and place, age and social standing, and political pressure.

Risk and Eschewal

Eschewal—the tendency to forgo or deter response to risk—cuts to the heart of citizen resistance to health advisories to reduce exposure to COVID-19. Eschewal alters the capacity of individuals to comprehend and respond effectively to risk by channeling perception.[29] When people are challenged by information contradictory to personal values and beliefs—for example, unwelcome information from health authorities regarding the importance of social distancing and mask wearing—a convenient way out is to disregard the information. Words such as "I am not going to wear a mask because it violates my right of expression" were commonly heard at the height of the pandemic.

Unwelcome information can be circumvented by intuition—a gut reaction to risk without conscious reasoning. "Psychosocial numbing" helps to explain why people suppress affect in relationship to catastrophe and disregard information designed to protect personal safety.[30] As the number of people impacted by the pandemic grew, the novelty of the crisis subsided and people routinized behavior. Intuition and impulse began to dominate reason and distorted the impact of the pandemic. For some, it was as if the pandemic did not exist.

Impact on Institutions

Midway through the pandemic, investors, government officials, and economic forecasters anticipated a V-shaped recovery. Recovery would take root in late summer 2020 and accelerate in the Fall as the virus receded, restrictions on commerce loosened, and consumers reverted to more normal spending patterns.[31] It did not happen. The failure to suppress a resurgence of confirmed infections, the continuing threat of government lockdowns, and uncertain federal support for businesses and unemployed workers extinguished hope for a rapid recovery. Business activity plunged in late summer because of renewed virus fears, stalled consumer spending, and curtailment of business investment. A McKinsey report on global economic sentiment in July 2020 revealed growing discomfort among North American executives about the condition of national economies and potential scenarios for COVID-19 recovery.[32] The recovery scenarios most frequently cited by business leaders were those calling for vigilance and caution:

■ partially effective public health and economic policy interventions leading to a slow return to pre-crisis levels of GDP, income, and corporate earnings
■ public health interventions that are effective, but fail to prevent virus reoccurrences, thereby blunting the ability of economic policy interventions to bring recovery to pre-crisis levels

The combination of renewed lockdowns imposed by states, the continuing threat of virus resurgence, and slowed consumer spending turned hopes for a V-shaped economic recovery into a reversal. Schools were in danger of remaining closed, the federal government continued to be short of testing and tracing capacity that economists warned was necessary to restore consumer confidence, and lawmakers failed to build bipartisan strategy to put Americans back to work and kids back in school. Education became a key sticking point of the nation's response to COVID-19. Without in-person schooling, the economy would remain stalled with working parents lacking crucial support to return to work.[33]

Education

K-12 Schools. More than 1.2 billion children were displaced from classrooms around the world at the height of the pandemic.[34] The pandemic was a double-edged sword for schools: an obstacle to overcome in early childhood development but an opportunity to rethink K-12 education in institutions with entrenched organizational practices and outmoded classrooms. COVID-19 became a catalyst for educational institutions worldwide to search for innovative solutions. Teaching changed overnight from teacher-centered instruction focused on rote learning and memorization to remote instruction via digital platforms. Prior to COVID-19, educational technology was accelerating at a rapid rate with global technology investment reaching $18.6 billion (US) in 2019 and the market for online education projected to reach $350 billion by 2025.[35] Whether in language apps, virtual tutoring, video conferencing tools, or online learning software, e-learning surged as a result of COVID-19.

The widespread closing of schools did more than bring advanced technology to learning. It brought into public view inequities of access and opportunity long prominent in the lives of impoverished families and children. In the words of Paul Reville, Professor at the Harvard Graduate School of Education:[36]

> Suddenly, we saw front page stories and lead editorials on topics like uneven Internet and technology access, food insecurity, and limited access to physical and mental health services. It's as though a tidal wave has pulled back the ocean to reveal the ocean floor and the uncomfortable realities of life below the surface . . . The coronavirus crisis with its attendant school closings has exposed the underlying flaw in our overreliance on the institution of schooling to create the equal opportunity society we aspire to.

Schools reopened remotely and with hybrid learning models in Fall 2020 with widely varying thresholds for delivery of instruction. Governors in some states pushed aggressively to reopen schools with in-person classes despite worsening COVID-19 numbers.[37] The fusion of education and politics met resistance—teachers rebelled and unions challenged the authority of state officials to make policy decisions for local education. Politicization of schooling and lack of funding limited the ability of schools to provide an environment necessary to maximize learning. Individualized learning was shelved in favor of group instruction, and a growing emotional toll was exacted on children in families ill-equipped to support learning. A McKinsey study conducted at the height of the pandemic projected the average student would fall behind seven months if schools remained closed until 2021—a number that grew to nine months for Latinos and ten months for Black students.[38] Closed schools were costly for parents. Working parents with kids at home had no choice but to stay home and take care of their children—a circumstance that put jobs and income in jeopardy.

School systems struggling to meet student needs under the continuing threat of COVID-19 were urged to rethink norms and strategies for public education. The school schedule and calendar were singled out for reform with hybrid delivery models and the year-round calendar and daily schedule redesigned around student needs.[39] Schools in Denmark established a model for classroom instruction that drew worldwide attention.[39] Danish schools broke students between the ages of 2 and 12 into groups of 12—called "protective bubbles" or "microgroups"—that arrived at school at staggered times, ate lunch separately, and had their own zones on the playground.[40] Students weren't forced to wear masks but were required to follow rigorous handwashing protocols. Desks were socially distanced, and classes were held outside when possible. Parents were not allowed on school property. Teachers who were at greater risk of COVID-19 infection were permitted to teach from home. Ten weeks after elementary schools reopened, coronavirus-related cases in Denmark were trending down.

Colleges and Universities

COVID-19 turned teaching and learning upside down as campuses were forced to convert to online-only courses while working to stabilize enrollment and finances. The immediate challenge facing many institutions was cash flow. When colleges closed, auxiliary revenues left campus with departing students and unbudgeted distance learning expenses surfaced immediately. Further complicating cash flow was the uncertainty surrounding fall enrollment. Students stopping out because of dissatisfaction with distance learning or because of inability to afford tuition put institutions in an enrollment crunch. Colleges and universities responded by paring back non-essential expenditures, dipping into endowment funds, and enacting cost-cutting measures including cutting pay and benefits and furloughing faculty and staff.[41] For institutions operating from a deficit position prior to the pandemic, the combination of short-term unanticipated expenditures and long-term enrollment declines threatened solvency, in some cases, forcing closures and mergers.

The transition to distance delivery impelled residential institutions to flip a tradition-based campus delivery model. The change to online learning and virtual services was especially difficult for colleges emphasizing an intimate learning experience and individualized services. Students and families balked at paying high-touch residential college tuition for a low-touch college experience—a circumstance that further complicated enrollment planning and brought financially strapped institutions to the edge of insolvency.

Health

The coronavirus threw the relationship between health providers and patients into disarray and led to remarkable changes in health care. Virtual health revolutionized the delivery of health services, supply chains were reorganized for greater efficiency, and technology-fueled advances in diagnostics and treatment.[42] Concerns about the spread of COVID-19 pushed healthcare providers to minimize in-person contact with patients. Standard visits for screening and check-ups were eliminated or conducted via technology, planned elective surgeries were canceled, and routine vaccinations and immunizations for children were suspended.[43] The upshot of the virus was a wait list for primary health services that put people on hold until the coronavirus caseload diminished to a point where full service could be restored.

Heralded for more than a decade as the next great advance in healthcare delivery, but with minimal evidence of adoption, virtual health became the go-to model for health delivery. The pandemic pushed providers, patients, and payers over the tipping point into widespread adoption beyond traditional methods. Advanced technology was used to deliver service to high-risk patients—most commonly through telecommunication. A 2020 report by McKinsey & Company profiled a range of options for virtual healthcare delivery:[44]

Telehealth

- *Synchronous:* Live two-way audiovisual interaction between patients and providers and providers and providers (video conference visits and review of patient profile)
- *Asynchronous:* Provider to patient and provider to provider transmission of patient information and patient history via e-mail and text
- *Remote Patient Monitoring:* Collection of electronic personal health/medical data which is transmitted for review by a remote provider

Digital Therapeutics

- *Replacement Therapies:* Evidence-based therapeutic interventions that leverage software to prevent, manage, or treat a medical condition in lieu of conventional treatments (e.g., pharmaceuticals)

- **Treatment Optimization:** Digital techniques optimizing medication and extending the value of pharmaceutical treatments (e.g., monitoring side effects of medication)

Care Navigation

- **Patient Self-Directed Care:** Patients accessing their own health information via website with secure 24-hour access
- **E-Triage:** Tools that provide support in searching for and scheduling appropriate care based on symptoms and conditions as well as price and quality of providers

The pandemic accelerated primary care delivery through virtual technologies while simultaneously pushing healthcare providers to shift health care to non-traditional settings as a means to contain rising costs and serve more patients.[45] Rising costs and equipment shortages were acute at the peak of the pandemic. Protective gear and supplies and available beds consistently ran low during surge periods—a calamitous circumstance in a healthcare system in which routine supply and demand made one of the three hospital beds available on a normal day.[46] Medical centers in hard-hit areas such as New York City and King County, Washington, crept dangerously close to capacity. Health providers were overwhelmed as extended time in health facilities put staff at risk of becoming infected and passing the virus on to their families.

COVID-19 brought the financial plight of hospitals and the relationship between wealth and health into sharp relief. Midway through 2020, hospital margins were projected to shrink to –7 percent without government support with half of all hospitals operating in the red.[47] Hospitals closed in 2020 with margins ranging from –1 percent to –11 percent depending on location, the number of COVID-19 cases, and government support.[48] Numbers describing the wealth divide were even more telling. Prior to the pandemic, research showed that the wealthiest 1 percent of Americans could expect to live more than a decade longer than the poorest 1 percent.[49] COVID-19 accentuated the gap between people on different sides of the wealth divide. Those occupying white-collar jobs had advantages of ready access to health advisories and flexible work arrangements. Those occupying service-related jobs had to be physically on site to collect a paycheck, thereby risking infection. Vulnerable populations on the lower end of the wealth divide were least able to stock up on groceries, prescription medication, and other supplies. They were also least able to shelter in secure housing and to own a car or have transportation to health facilities.

Business

The world is confused and frightened. COVID-19 infections are on the rise across the U.S. and around the world, even in countries that once thought they had contained the virus. The outlook for the next year is at best uncertain; countries are rushing to produce and distribute vaccines at breakneck speeds, some opting to bypass critical phase trials. Meanwhile, unemployment numbers remain dizzyingly high, even as the U.S. stock market continues to defy gravity. We're headed into a global depression—a period of economic misery that few living people have experienced.[50]

Ian Bremmer, President
Eurasia Group, August 6, 2020

COVID-19 wiped out five years of U.S. economic growth in a three-month market contraction during the second quarter of 2020—the most devastating quarterly contraction on record.[51] Gross domestic product fell 9.5 percent as consumers cut back spending, businesses pared investment, and global trade dried up.[52] The collapse was more than twice as large as in the Great Recession in 2007–2008 but occurred in a fraction of the time. Hopes for a V-shaped recovery—a scenario in which scientists conquered COVID-19 and everybody went back to work—vanished with rising infection rates as the virus resurged in nations throughout the world. The global nature of the virus, its resurgence despite unparalleled efforts to control it, and its lingering negative effects altered business and consumer behavior on a large scale.

Supply Chain Disruption

Many manufacturing firms rely on imported products and raw materials as well as sales in China to meet financial goals. Originating in China, the virus quarantined a large number of workers and led to partial or full shutdowns of plants and factories throughout the country. The slowdown in economic activity significantly impacted production and profitability of global companies and was especially severe for companies reliant on intermediate goods from China and unable to switch sourcing.[53] Small- and medium-sized companies working with lean capital sustained losses that threatened long-term survival.

Changing Consumer Behavior

Consumer spending declined sharply following the onset of COVID-19. Consumers under shelter-in-place orders dramatically reduced discretionary spending with grave consequences for industries such as restaurants and hotels, salons, apparel and footwear, accessories, travel, and out-of-home entertainment.[54] Consumers continued to shop, but shopping turned selective. Scarcity and panic buying drove many to strip store shelves of staple products as quickly as they were restocked. The combination of reduced demand for some products and increased demand for others led to supply and demand shock—a condition in which market factors simultaneously reduce the capacity of the economy to produce goods and services at given prices and reduce consumers' ability or willingness to purchase goods and services at given prices.[55]

COVID-19 forced consumers to change buying behavior in a way that would happen only under the most extreme conditions. In a consumer society, goods and services are expected to be continuously available. In the environment of scarcity created by the pandemic, products were not always available and consumers could not readily get what they wanted from stores. Nor could they partake of leisure-related services in the manner to which they were accustomed. Consumption patterns changed as consumers with limited means had little choice but to reduce spending. Spending on in-person services such as travel, restaurants, and entertainment was curbed and redirected toward essentials such as housing, groceries, and transportation.[56] The impact on service industries was disastrous with many suffering losses that would never be recovered.

Business Meltdown

COVID-19 brought many well-known brands to the edge of bankruptcy and pushed some over the edge. The travel industry was deeply impacted as hotel rooms stood empty. Airlines hollowed out their workforce and tourism destinations disappeared from the map. Conferences, expos, sporting events, and large venues as well as cultural establishments such as galleries and museums were abruptly shut down as were personal services such as hairdressers, gyms, and taxis. Important industries such as the car, truck, and electronic industries closed in the early stages of the outbreak and reopened with entirely different operating models. Small businesses were especially hard hit with many lacking sufficient cash or credit to function beyond 60 days without federal relief.[57]

With business revenue falling precipitously, economic pain rippled through the economy. In the finance sector, commercial real estate owners incurring huge losses were unable to make debt payments to banks and other lenders. Banks short on capital found themselves in a weakened financial position to lend. Businesses unable to borrow or access new lines of credit languished in red ink. The promise of profitability following reopening did not materialize as consumers, fearful of contracting the virus, avoided physical stores and large gathering places. Spending lagged behind projections as the pandemic continued to peak in some markets and resurfaced in others. Amidst continuing uncertainty, companies sought opportunities wherever and however they could find them. Agile business models were adopted and sales were fast ramped from offline to online channels—a move that permanently altered the buying behavior of consumers and the sales models of companies.[58]

While some businesses struggled, others thrived. Internet businesses—particularly those related to online entertainment, food delivery, online shopping, online education, and solutions for remote work—experienced record growth and profits.[59] Consumption patterns changed with takeout, snacks, alcohol, and cleaning products high on the list of desirables. In anticipation of a resurgence of COVID-19, consumers turned protective.[60] Food, equipment, and medications were stockpiled and backup sources for staple products were identified—a marked shift in what people bought and how they bought. The impact on business was uneven with some companies left in the cold, others treading water, and vital industry businesses raking in profits.

Massive Unemployment

Over 20 million Americans lost their jobs following the outbreak of COVID-19.[61] The labor participation rate dropped to 60.2 percent and unemployment rose from 6.2 million to 20.5 million between February and May 2020.[62] In February, the unemployment rate stood at 3.8 percent—among the lowest on record in the post-World War II era—and more than tripled to 14.7 percent in May.[63] This rise put the number of unemployed workers due to COVID-19 well beyond its peak during the Great Recession, when the number of unemployed rose by 8.8 million.

Unemployment among all groups of workers rose sharply during the downturn, but some worker groups were more adversely affected than others. Unemployment rates for women, minority workers, and workers without a high school diploma exceeded that of men.[64] Overrepresentation of women and minorities in the leisure and hospitality sectors accounted for much of the unemployment rate. Workers in all but one age group saw unemployment climb into double digits during the viral outbreak. The unemployment rate among young adults (16–24) was especially severe—more than double the rate of workers 35 and older.[65] The concentration of young adults in service occupations subject to social distancing and government-ordered shutdowns put this group at continuing risk for job loss.

Growth of E-Commerce

COVID-19 rerouted purchasing from direct store buying to online shopping. According to data from IBM's U.S. Retail Index, the pandemic accelerated the shift from physical stores to digital shopping by roughly five years.[66] In the first quarter of 2020, department store sales and sales of "non-essential" retailers declined by 25 percent. This ballooned to 75 percent in the second quarter. By the close of 2020, department store sales had declined by 60 percent and e-commerce sales had grown by nearly 20 percent. In sharp contrast, retail e-commerce reached $211.5 billion in the second quarter of 2020—up 32 percent from the first quarter and 45 percent year over year.[67]

Changing Employee Dynamics

Many office workers found themselves forced to work from home to reduce the spread of the virus. For some, remote work would become permanent, while for others the post-COVID office to which they would return would be unlike the pre-COVID office they left. Companies quickly figured out how to go remote in serving customers and clients. From telemedicine in hospitals to remote learning in schools and colleges and streaming fitness classes, every industry accelerated its digital transformation.[68] The transition to remote work changed the conception of when and how work is carried out, how communication is conducted, and how performance is evaluated. Companies learned that time spent on individual tasks and getting work done is not readily measurable in a virtual work setting—output and the value of work are the key performance metrics.[69] The standard "nine to five" work day gave way to flex time—workers would allocate time to work when and how it met personal needs.

Office space was redistributed through retrofitting of common areas including improved ventilation, larger conference rooms, new kitchen protocol, one-way pathways, and reduced capacity in elevators.[70] Personal safety became the mantra for office design through tools such as hands-free technology and advanced air filtration systems. Open space, close seating designs, and recirculating air systems were discontinued. Sensors were installed to avoid contact with high-touch surfaces including elevator buttons, doors, light switches, coffee machines, and microwaves.[71] Bathrooms and office furniture were disinfected daily, and cough and sneeze guards were installed at desk stations. Temperature registration and masks became standard in the workplace. Staggered office hours with small groups of employees going into an office at any one time were used to regulate social distancing. Over time, remote work, or working in an office ceased to be a binary choice with companies providing employees with the opportunity to do both.[72]

Government

As the number of coronavirus cases continued to grow, government agencies searched for ways to minimize in-person interaction. Services that put employees and the general public at risk of contracting the virus were suspended or cut back.[73] Federal offices remained open with telework opportunities extended to eligible agencies and employees. In states and localities, in-person legal proceedings were suspended, public meetings were streamed online, operating hours were reduced, customer flow was regulated, and government business was conducted virtually.[74]

State and local governments were confronted by severe cash shortfalls. Expenditure budgets built in better economic times could not be supported by diminished sales tax proceeds and property tax collections. Data published by the National Association of Counties revealed that the full extent of fiscal damage to U.S. counties caused by the coronavirus:[75]

- $144 billion in lost revenue (not including revenue loss or delay due to property tax disruptions) and $30 billion in COVID-19 response costs through FY 2021
- $54 billion in property tax revenue at risk in states that had not collected any or all property tax in 2020
- a reduction of nearly one-quarter (24 percent) in the 2021 operating budgets of small counties due to declining revenues and rising costs

Revenue streams supporting county services were flat-lined and prospects for future revenue growth were limited as most of the counties lacked authority to raise additional funds to balance deficits. Charges and fees, sales tax and gross receipts, income taxes and license fees—collectively accounting for 42 percent of all county-generated revenue—were sidetracked by the pandemic.[76] The combination of declining revenue and rising COVID-related expenditures for health and hospital systems, justice and public safety services, human services, technology infrastructure, and education put counties on precarious financial footing entering 2021. With limited options for raising additional revenue, state and local governments were forced to delay the full impact of revenue shortfalls by selling off assets, using rainy-day funds, and reallocating budgetary resources.[77]

Preparing for a Post-COVID World

It is increasingly clear our era will be defined by a fundamental schism: the period before COVID-19 and the new normal that will emerge in the post-viral era: the 'next normal.' In this unprecedented new reality, we will witness a dramatic restructuring of the economic and social order in which business and society have traditionally operated. And in the near future, we will see the beginning of discussion and debate about what the next normal could entail and how sharply its contours will diverge from those that previously shaped our lives.[78]

Kevin Sneader and Shubham Singhal
McKinsey & Company

If there is one big takeaway from our national response to the COVID-19 outbreak, it is that we were slow in preparing for the virus, slow in reacting to its spread, slow in putting lockdowns and safety measures into place, slow in adhering to safety guidelines, and slow in planning and mobilizing for a post-COVID world. The one exception was the economic policy response as the federal government moved with unprecedented speed to approve funds to cushion the impact of lockdowns on communities and businesses. Policy was consumed, however, by the number of issues simultaneously impacting communities, companies, and workers that produced a shock unprecedented in scale.

In closing, this chapter addresses the elephant in the room—a question facing leaders in every industry, every company, and every organization: *What will it take to prepare for a post-COVID world—a world in which prevailing assumptions and metrics have been rendered irrelevant?* There is no easy answer to this question, but there are actions that can be taken to position organizations for optimal performance. These actions fall into three domains—intelligence, imagination, and ideation—and they extend from outbreak of the virus to a new normal. They were formulated through a synthesis of strategy reports prepared and published by McKinsey & Company in 2020.[79]

Intelligence

Decision-making in a COVID-19 world was and is extraordinarily difficult. Information about the pandemic provided contradictory signals to leaders culminating in decisions that were not always in the best interest of companies. Yet companies do not have the luxury of waiting out a pandemic. Choices have to be made and a course of action determined even under the most uncertain of conditions. Deep information about the course of the pandemic and its impact on business are important. Companies seeking to create opportunity out of adversity would be well advised to ask the following questions:[80]

Virus Spread

- What is the rate of change (increase or decrease) in the number of infections?
- How quickly have state and local policy makers moved to put public safety measures into effect to counteract the virus?

- How closely has the public adhered to safety precautions to limit exposure to COVID-19?
- How much time has passed between outbreak of the virus and public adherence to safety precautions?
- How stringently are public safety measures enforced?

Impact on Consumer Demand

- Which customer markets are most adversely affected by the virus?
- How deep are the reductions in demand for our product or service?
- How long is the downturn likely to last?
- Will there be a recession following reduction in demand?
- What factors could contribute to a recession following reduction in demand?

Scenarios for Recovery

- What are the potential scenarios for recovery?
- How far off is mass distribution of a vaccine?
- What proportion of the population has to be vaccinated to achieve herd immunity?
- How long will it take to achieve herd immunity?
- What is the likelihood of a virus resurgence?
- What is the level of preparedness of public health systems for a virus resurgence?

Deep information gathered in relationship to these questions will enable companies to create multiple scenarios for recovery and settle on a planning track and set of assumptions to guide strategy going forward. Information is available from multiple sources: the rate of change in infections, traffic congestion and reduction in restaurant bookings as an indicator of adherence to public health guidelines, speed of government intervention, late payments and credit defaults as an indicator of recessionary impact following demand reduction, the progress of vaccine rollout, and federal guidelines for vaccine distribution and administration.[81] These are not perfect metrics, but they are reasonable early indicators of the course and consequences of COVID-19 and can be used as a basis for decision-making.

Imagination

However, hard companies work to acquire intelligence and the leverage it provides, it is meaningless unless used to reimagine business in a post-COVID world. In the grip of COVID-19, companies were forced to work in new ways—faster, smarter, leaner, and with greater fluidity. Much of their progress can be attributed to a shift in operating models. Sharpened goals, shorter strategy cycles, rapid decision-making, streamlined manufacturing processes, modified ways of working, and widescale adoption of digital technology.[82] In a crisis, what matters becomes clear very quickly. Companies that adapt effectively have a strong sense of identity.[83] Leaders and workers have a clear sense of purpose and a common performance culture. They know what is important beyond shareholder value and what must be done to emerge stronger from crisis. Reimagining company goals and operations through a new business model is not an option—it is essential to company well-being in a post-COVID world.

Reimagination was speed dialed in companies with small nimble teams knowledgeable about company strategy and operations.[84] Companies with simplified organizational structures, digital platforms, and interconnected teams were best positioned to transform their operating model coming out of crisis.[85] In these companies, circuits were wired to make swift decisions working with just-in-time intelligence keyed to specific factors:[86]

- company purpose in a post-COVID world
- evolving customer needs and engagement preferences
- new product and service development
- health and safety requisites for customers and employees
- new ways of working for employees
- incentives and roadblocks to innovation
- new approaches to partnering and collaboration
- digital solutions and adoption
- supply chain strategy.

A simple example related to company purpose illustrates the transformative effect of reimagination. Grocery stores responding to the changing needs and priorities of customers in crisis mode morphed from competing over market share to "feeding the nation."[87] Logistics services moved from parcel delivery to critical national infrastructure. Broadband moved from comparison site commodity to connectivity lifeline. Companies broadening their purpose to the common good would be hard-pressed to revert to a pre-COVID business model when customers have bought into a new virtuosity. The balance between "traditional" (profit and market share) and "evolving" (virtuosity and customer value) business purpose is difficult to maintain much less to achieve. In a post-COVID world, the reward of being able to successfully develop and manage a dual-purpose business model makes the challenge of reimagination all the more important.

Ideation

Ideation—building ideas from scratch for real-world application—is an integral part of preparing for business in a post-COVID world. Important as they are, intelligence and reimagination are useless without ideas to guide and power change. During a crisis, ideation does not begin with randomly generated thought. Ideas are reverse engineered to fit parameters of a crisis and its impact on business.[88] Impact is clearly defined using information about the crisis—its progression, its consequences, and its scenarios for recovery. Once the scope of impact is understood, teams can crowdsource potential ideas and pare down to one idea or set of ideas that can serve as the basis of a new operating model.

Streetify—a UK-based e-commerce platform launched directly after the COVID-19 outbreak—offers an excellent illustration of how ideation works.[89] With shoppers unable to shop in person at local stores following the coronavirus outbreak, a team led by Streetify founder Thuong Mai brainstormed ideas to help consumers connect with local stores without leaving home. The team landed on the idea of a technology app to bring stores into the homes of shoppers.[90] Using the app and website, shoppers were able to choose the street they wished to visit and scroll left or right to "walk" up and down. They were shown virtual storefronts and could click on any store to enter its Streetify website. Once inside the "store," consumers could see all of the special offers, deals, and promotions that had been gathered from deal sites such as Groupon and Rakuten. Business owners could also put messages in their virtual storefront windows, announcing deals, delivery options, in-stock goods, and more.

Moving from idea to initiation is never easy. A crisis can work to the advantage of staff tasked with the challenge of convincing decision makers to think differently about the way a company is doing business. A business case describing the impact and consequences of the pandemic would be essential as would be an analysis of changes to the current operating model, advantages and disadvantages of a new model, and short- and long-term impact of the model on market position and company resources. This is where leadership and vision come in. Leaders who cannot clearly define what they want to accomplish through a new operating model cannot expect others to participate meaningfully in its adoption.

Plan for a Different World

COVID-19 has been unlike any crisis the modern world has faced. Change of unparalleled magnitude has challenged the capabilities of organizations and leaders in every industry. A March 2020 article in *Politico* described a tapestry of change involving a loss of innocence and reluctance to act stemming from the realization that calamities thought only to happen elsewhere can also happen here.[91] Questions were raised that pushed buttons: Could it be that the comfort of being in the presence of others will be replaced by comfort in solitude? Could it be that a new form of patriotism will emerge—not patriotism attached to the military but patriotism attached to sacrifice and service? Will the wave of political and cultural polarization that has gripped the nation be broken by the pandemic—shattered by a "common enemy" driving people to look past their differences? Will science and expertise once again reign supreme? Will investment in the public good—especially health—flourish with the help of digital tools? Will universal family care become an integral part of the post-COVID economy? Will trust in institutions, government, and democratic values rekindle? Will a new civic federalism emerge—a sense of solidarity among citizens collectively facing the enormous challenges ahead? Will our understanding of change assume a different form as our realization of what is possible changes?

Far-fetched ideas? Perhaps, but if some achieve fruition, the implications for business will be stunning. While companies today face challenges of revenue disruption, liquidity, changing customer and employee, and needs—operating challenges that can be overcome with sound management—companies tomorrow will face existential challenges that alter organizational purpose and business strategy. Changes of this magnitude will require imaginative planning for a very different world and sustained strong leadership. Bain & Company management consultant Hernan Saenz captured the essence of business in a post-COVID world:[92]

> The human suffering now is evident to everyone. Every stakeholder is going to come out of this crisis with an even stronger agenda to define a new world. Investors will direct their investments toward companies that both make money and do good. Consumers and employees will punish companies that do not have sustainable goals and outcomes. A far more positive world will emerge.

Only by working creatively and with imagination can business hope to surmount the risk landscape of the present—resolving the pandemic—and the risk landscape of the future—climate change. COVID-19 will be resolved. A vaccine will be developed that simultaneously provides immunity and circumvents the need for behavioral change. Climate change is a threat unfolding over decades that will require behavioral change potentially beyond human capacity. Mobilizing response to a looming catastrophe that can only be resolved through behavioral change is the next great frontier for business.

Notes

1 Nies, M. and McEwen, M. "Disaster Characteristics and Management Stages." *Bartleby Research*, https://bartleby.com/essay/Disaster, Retrieved: July 2, 2020.

2 Porta, M. (ed.), *Dictionary of Epidemiology*. Oxford: Oxford University Press, 2008, p. 179. Retrieved: May 22, 2020.

3 Senthiligam, M., "Seven Reasons We're More at Risk than Ever of a Global Pandemic." *CNN Health*, April 10, 2017. Retrieved: May 25, 2020.

4 Linnane, C., "Coronavirus Update: U.S. Reports Another Record Case Tally for a Single Day While Global Cases Top 14 Million." *Market Watch*, July 18, 2020. Retrieved: August 5, 2020.

5 World Health Organization, *WHO Coronavirus Disease (COVID-19) Dashboard*, July 14, 2020. Retrieved: August 11, 2020.

6 Table 3.1 is derived from cumulative statistics reporting confirmed COVID-19 cases and deaths published by the World Health Organization and Johns Hopkins Coronavirus Resource Center as of July 17, 2020. Statistics are approximate due to nuances of timing, methodology and data reporting.

7 Events and statistics in this timeline were drawn from a report published by *USA Today* on June 23, 2020. The full citation: Hauck, G., Gelles, K., Bravo, V., and Thorson, M., "Five Months In: A Timeline of How the Coronavirus Outbreak Began, and How It Has Unfolded in the U.S. So Far." *USA Today*, June 23, 2020. Retrieved: July 20, 2020.

8 Tyler, C. and Gluckman, P., "Coronavirus: Governments Knew a Pandemic Was a Threat—Here's Why They Weren't Better Prepared." *The Conversation*, April 27, 2020. Retrieved: June 12, 2020.

9 Ibid.

10 Ibid.

11 GHS Index, "2019 Global Health Security Index." Retrieved: July 17, 2020.

12 Kiersz, A., "The 20 Countries in the World Best Prepared for an Epidemic Like Coronavirus Still Aren't All That Ready." *Business Insider*, March 11, 2020. Retrieved: June 11, 2020.

13 Ibid.

14 Ibid.

15 Ibid.

16 Quammen, D., "Why Weren't We Ready for the Coronavirus?" *The New Yorker*, May 4, 2020.

17 GHS Index, "2019 Global Health Security Index."

18 Ibid.

19 Hauck, Gelles, Bravo, and Thorson, "Five Months In."

20 Reichman, D., "Trump Disbanded NSC Pandemic Unit That Experts Had Praised." *Associated Press*, March 14, 2020. Retrieved: July 22, 2020.

21 Doucleef, M., "Trump Proposes Deep Cuts in Detecting Disease Outbreaks Worldwide." Goats and Soda, *National Public Radio*, February 12, 2018. Retrieved: July 15, 2020.

22 Danner, C., "Trump Officials Altered CDC's Weekly COVID-19 Reports to Protect the President." *Intelligencer*, September 13, 2020. Retrieved: September 20, 2020.

23 Shear, M., Weiland, N., Lipton, E., Haberman, M., and Sanger, D., "Push to Pass Off Response to Virus Deepened a Crisis." *New York Times*, July 19, 2020.

24 Woodward, R., *Rage*. New York: Simon and Schuster, September 15, 2020.

25 Pell, S., Buckner, C., and Dupree, J., "Coronavirus Hospitalizations Rise Sharply in Several States Following Memorial Day." *The Washington Post*, June 20, 2020.

26 Whitbourne, S., "Why Do Some People Think They're Invulnerable to COVID-19? *Psychology Today*, April 4, 2020. Retrieved: August 22, 2020.

27 Lee, B., "Top 10 Excuses Offered for Not Wearing Masks Despite COVID_19 Coronavirus." *Forbes*, May 25, 2020. Retrieved: September 5, 2020.

28 Ibid.

29 Scott, E., "Avoidance Coping and Why It Creates Additional Stress." *VeryWellMind*, September 17, 2020. Retrieved: September 22, 2020.

30 Kunreuther, H., Slovic, P., and Olson, K. "Fast and Slow Thinking in the Face of Catastrophic Risk." August 19, 2014. SSRN: https://ssrn.com/abstract=2488653.

31 Ranasinghe, D. and Carvalho, R., "Coronavirus: 5 Predictions for How the Economy Might Recover." *World Economic Forum*, April 14, 2020. Retrieved: August 12, 2020.

32 FitzGerald, A., Singer, V., and Smit, S., "The Coronavirus Effect on Global Economic Sentiment." Report, *McKinsey & Company*, July 27, 2020.

33 Roberts, P., "For Many Families, School Online Means Tough Choices in the Coronavirus-Battered Economy." *The Seattle Times*, September 3, 2020. Retrieved: September 12, 2020.

34 Li, L. and Lalani, F., "The COVID-19 Pandemic Has Changed Education Forever. This Is How." *World Economic Forum*, April 29, 2020. Retrieved: August 25, 2020.

35 Ibid.

36 Reville, P., "Coronavirus Gives Us an Opportunity to Rethink K-12 Education." *Boston Globe*, April 9, 2020.

37 Associated Press, "Iowa Governor's Push to Reopen Schools Descends into Chaos." August 19, 2020. Retrieved: September 8, 2020.

38 Dorn, E., Hancock, B., Sarakatsannis, J., and Viruleg, V., "COVID-19 and Student Learning in the United States: The Hurt Could Last a Lifetime." *McKinsey & Company*, June 1, 2020. Retrieved: August 28, 2020.

39 Reville, P., "Coronavirus Gives Us an Opportunity to Rethink K-12 Education." April 9, 2020.

40 Orange, R., "Split Classes, Outdoor Lessons: What Denmark Can Teach England About Reopening Schools After COVID-19." *The Guardian*, May 17, 2020.

41 DePietro, A., "Here's a Look at the Impact of Coronavirus (COVID-19) on Colleges and Universities in the U.S." *Forbes*, April 30, 2020. Retrieved: September 5, 2020.

42 Fowkes, J., Fross, C., Gilbert, G., and Harris, A., "Virtual Health: A Look at the Next Frontier of Care Delivery." *McKinsey & Company*, June 11, 2020. Retrieved: September 10. 2020.

43 Cohut, M., "How the Pandemic Has Affected Primary Healthcare Around the World." *Medical News Today*, May 15, 2020. Retrieved: September 10, 2020.

44 Fowkes, Fross, Gilbert, and Harris, "Virtual Health: A Look at the Next Frontier of Health Delivery."

45 Rogal, B., "Healthcare Real Estate Moves to Non-Traditional Settings." *Globe.St.com*, May 5, 2020. Retrieved: September 1, 2020.

46 Ducharme, J., "Coronavirus Will Have Long-Lasting Impacts on the U.S. Healthcare System—and the Poorest Will Suffer Most." *Time*, March 26, 2020.

47 American Hospital Association, "New AHA Analysis Shows COVID-19's Dramatic Impact on Financial Health of Hospitals and Health Systems." *AHA News*, July 21, 2020. Retrieved: September 6, 2020.

48 Ibid.

49 Ducharme, J., "Coronavirus Will Have Long-Lasting Impacts on the U.S. Healthcare System—and the Poorest Will Suffer Most." March 26, 2020.

50 Bremmer, I., "The Next Global Depression Is Coming and Optimism Won't Slow It Down." *Time*, August 6, 2020.

51 Mutikani, L., "COVID-19 Crushes U.S. Economy in Second Quarter; Rising Virus Cases Loom Over Recovery." *U.S. News and World Report*, July 30, 2020.

52 Ibid.

53 Globe Newswire, "Impact of COVID-19 on the World's Logistics Market: Post-Pandemic Growth Opportunity Assessment Report 2020." *Yahoo!Finance*, June 29, 2020. Retrieved: August 25, 2020.

54 Donthu, N., "Effects of COVID-19 on Business and Research." *Journal of Business Research* (September 2020): 284–289.

55 Brinca, P., Duarte, J., and Castro, M., "Is the COVID-19 Pandemic a Supply or Demand Shock?" Economic Synopsis, *Federal Reserve Bank*, May 20, 2020. Retrieved: August 27, 2020.

56 Ahora, N., Robinson, K., Charm, T., Ortega, M., Staack, Y., Whitehead, S., and Yamakawa, N., "Consumer Sentiment and Behavior Continue to Reflect the Uncertainty of the COVID-19 Crisis." *McKinsey & Company*, July 8, 2020. Retrieved: September 1, 2020.

57 Guinn, J., "Survey: COVID-19 Impact on Small Businesses." *MSN The Blueprint*, July 20, 2020. Retrieved: September 6, 2020.

58 Azim-Khan, T., "The Future of Retail: How COVID-19 Continues to Transform E-commerce." *Royal Bank of Canada*, Undated. Retrieved: September 8, 2020.

59 Blue, A., "COVID-19 Has Changed Consumer Behavior. What Does It Mean for the Future?" *Phys. Org News*, April 24, 2020. Retrieved: September 8, 2020.

60 Ibid.

61 Davidson, P., "Unemployment Soars to 14.7%, Job Losses Reach 20.5 Million in April as Coronavirus Spreads." *USA Today*, May 8, 2020.

62 Ibid.

63 Ibid.

64 Mueller, E., "Women, Minorities Disproportionately Reliant on Jobless Aid, Data Shows." *Politico*, July 9, 2020. Retrieved: September 5, 2020.

65 Collins, L., "How COVID-19 Dimmed Generation Z's Plans and Confidence." *Deseret News*, July 1, 2020. Retrieved: September 6, 2020.

66 Pastore, A., "IBM's 2020 U.S. Retail Index Shows Rapid Acceleration of Retail Trends." *Yahoo!News*, August 25, 2020. Retrieved: September 6, 2020.

67 Wilson, M., "E-commerce Sales Jumped Nearly 40% in Second Quarter, Says U.S. Census Bureau." *Chain Store Age*, August 18, 2020. Retrieved: September 8, 2020.

68 Marr, B., "How the COVID-19 Pandemic Is Fast-Tracking Digital Transformation in Companies." *Forbes*, March 17, 2020.

69 Schrage, M., "Rethinking Performance Management for Post-Pandemic Success. *Sloan Management Review*, June 1, 2020.

70 Hamilton Place Strategies, "Reimagining Work in the Era of COVID-19." *WeWork*, June 16, 2020. Retrieved: September 10, 2020.

71 Roth, R., "Life After COVID-19: How Can We Work in an Office Again." *Reference*, August 9, 2020. Retrieved: September 11, 2020.

72 Lowe, R., "IPE RE Conference: The Future of Remote Working and the Office Is Not Binary." *IPE RA Magazine*, September 17, 2020. Retrieved: September 21, 2020.

73 National Association of Chief State Administrators, *COVID-19 Government Operations National Briefing*, March 30, 2020. Retrieved: September 9, 2020.

74 Ibid.

75 National Association of Counties, *Executive Summary. Analysis of the Fiscal Impact of COVID-19 on Counties*, May 2020. Retrieved: September 10, 2020.

76 Ibid.

77 Dorfhuber, C., O'Leary, J., and Agarwal, S., "Surviving the Pandemic Budget Shortfalls: A Playbook for State and Local Governments." *Deloitte*, September 9, 2020. Retrieved: September 18, 2020.

78 Sneader, K. and Singhal, S., "Beyond Coronavirus: The Path to the Next Normal." *McKinsey & Company*, March 23, 2020.

79 Beginning in March 2020 following the outbreak of COVID-19, McKinsey & Company published a series of briefing notes under the working title *Coronavirus: Leading through the Crisis*. These insightful notes examined scenarios for business recovery from the coronavirus and served as the basis for business strategy in a post-COVID world.

80 Mysore, M., Singhal, S, and Brown, S., "Inside the Strategy Room." *McKinsey & Company*, April 2, 2020. Retrieved: September 12, 2020.

81 Ibid.

82 Sneader, K. and Sternfels, B., "From Surviving to Thriving: Reimagining the Post-COVID Return." *McKinsey & Company*, May 1, 2020. Retrieved: September 10, 2020.

83 Ibid.

84 Ibid.

85 Deloitte, "Reimaging Operating Models of the Future to Survive." Retrieved: September 18, 2020.

86 Sneader, K. and Sternfels, B., "From Surviving to Thriving: Reimagining the Post-COVID Return." May 1, 2020.

87 Whitmore, E., Patel, B., and Easterbrook, J., "Key Theme 2: Reimagining the Business Model—How to Thrive in the Post-COVID World." *Moorhouse Consulting*. Retrieved: September 11, 2020.

88 Martin, S., "Adaptive Ideation During a Crisis." *B2C Business 2 Community*, April 1, 2020. Retrieved: September 15, 2020.

89 Springwise, "7 Innovative Business Ideas in Response to Coronavirus." April 15, 2020. Retrieved: September 20, 2020.
90 Ibid.
91 The Friday Cover, "Coronavirus Will Change the World Permanently. Here's How." *Politico*, March 19, 2020. Retrieved: September 21, 2020.
92 Endresen, J., "Plan Now for a New, Post-COVID-19 World, Urges Top Bain Executive Hernan Saenz III, MBA/MILR '98." *Cornell: SC Johnson College of Business*, April 21, 2020. Retrieved: September 23, 2020.

Chapter 4

Climate Change: Default, Mitigation, or Adaptation?

Climate change could lead to a collapse of our civilization and the extinction of much of the natural world.

David Attenborough
Natural historian, 2018

Greta Thunberg, the young climate crisis activist, opened the United Nations Climate Action Summit on September 23, 2019, with a condemnation of world leaders for failing to take strong measures to combat climate change:[1]

How dare you! This is all wrong. I shouldn't be up here. I should be back in school on the other side of the ocean. Yet you all come to us young people for hope. How dare you! You have stolen my dreams and my childhood with your empty words. And yet I'm one of the lucky ones. People are suffering. People are dying. Entire ecosystems are collapsing. We are in the beginning of a mass extinction. And all you can talk about is money and fairy tales of eternal economic growth. How dare you! Adults keep saying we owe it to the young people to give them hope. But I don't want your hope. I want you to panic. We are watching you. If you choose to fail us, we will never forgive you. How dare you continue to look away and come here saying you are doing enough when the politics and solutions needed are still nowhere in sight. You say you 'hear' us and that you understand the urgency. But no matter how sad and angry I am, I don't want to believe that. Because if you fully understood the situation and still kept on failing to act, then you would be evil. And I refuse to believe that.

Extreme temperatures, rising sea levels, more frequent and intense weather events, flooding, prolonged drought, wildfires, food and water shortages, insect-borne disease—climate is now changing faster than at any point in human civilization. In its 2019 climate assessment report, the United Nations Environment Programme (UNEP) called for immediate and sustained action to limit the magnitude and rate of greenhouse gas emissions.[2] Global greenhouse gas emissions have grown by

1.5 percent every year over the last decade despite repeated warnings from scientists, to lower emissions to levels called for in the 2015 Paris Agreement.[3] If the world is to avoid the worst effects of climate change, including intense droughts, stronger storms, and widespread hunger by midcentury, the opposite must happen. Emissions must decline by 7.6 percent every year between 2020 and 2030 to halt global warming.[4] Alden Meyer, director of policy and strategy at the Union of Concerned Scientists, puts the catastrophe into words: "We are sleepwalking toward a climate catastrophe and must wake up and take urgent action."[5] Even if governing bodies fulfill their pledges under the Paris Agreement—and many are not on track to do so—most of the countries are headed in the wrong direction. A 2019 analysis examining the volume of coal, oil, and natural gas that the world's nations expect to produce and sell through 2030 revealed an emissions gap significantly beyond current projections. If all of the fossil fuels planned for extraction are burned, global temperatures are projected to rise 5.8 degrees by 2100 bringing wide-ranging and increasingly destructive climate impacts.[6]

Scientific evidence of cause and effect has moved climate change beyond possibility to the intelligible world of certainty. Thousands of studies conducted by researchers around the world have documented changes in surface, atmospheric, and ocean temperatures; the effect of global warming on glaciers and snow cover; and the impact of rising sea levels and acidification on marine life and coastal communities.[7] Climate change is no longer an inconvenient truth; it is a looming catastrophe for vulnerable populations and global ecosystems. Resources that we value and depend on—water, energy, transportation, wildlife, agriculture, and ecosystems—are subject to their effects. It is risk of unprecedented magnitude that will require energy, resources, and commitment for resolution—if resolution is possible.

How did we arrive at the threshold of climate catastrophe and what does it mean for business? Understanding cause and effect is a necessary first step. Analysis begins with a series of questions for business organizations and leaders:

- What will happen to a society when its baseline conditions ultimately depend on climate and weather?
- How will life and work need to change to counteract the worst effects of climate change?
- What influence will climate change have on business—purpose, strategy and resources, and architecture?
- Will climate change reshape the role, skill requisites, and preparation of leaders?
- What role can companies and leaders play in mobilizing response to climate change?

Footprint of Climate Change

Climate change is ground zero for catastrophic risk in this book. It is a topic of unparalleled complexity requiring extensive information to build understanding of its effects and consequences. The pages that follow present detailed information and data about climate change that may test the patience of the reader. Accordingly, the reader is advised to peruse the chapter as a sweep of information about climate change and avoid getting stuck in narrow corners of information and data.

What Is Climate Change?

"Climate change" refers to a transition in climate that persists over a sustained period of time. The World Meteorological Organization defines this period as 30 years.[8] Changes in climate result from natural causes and human activities. Scientific evidence, however, points to carbon emissions as the primary cause of climate change. Carbon dioxide, methane, nitrous oxide, and fluorinated gases generated by human activity have been rising since the start of the Industrial Revolution and have reached a level detrimental to air, land, and oceans. The Fifth Report of the Intergovernmental Panel on Climate Change (IPCC) issued in 2014 stated that surface temperature by the end of the 21st century is likely to exceed pre-industrial levels by 1.5°C and may well rise 2°C beyond the pre-industrial temperature average.[9] Even if emissions were eliminated overnight, warming would be irreversible because CO_2 takes hundreds of years to break down.[10] Given the current rate of carbon dioxide buildup and the projected trajectory of global warming, we are in dangerous uncharted waters.

There is a social impact of climate change beyond its physical impact. In environmentally challenged regions, food and water are becoming insufficient to meet demand, conflict is escalating because of competition for scarce resources, and involuntary migration is on the rise. In established economies, life and work are changing to reduce carbon emissions. New technologies and jobs are emerging; investment is accelerating in renewable energy and energy storage techniques; electric cars and mass transit are becoming preferred modes of transportation; and innovative policies for water conservation, agriculture, and carbon pricing are being pushed by governments. Government action alone, however, will not be enough to mobilize people and communities in response to climate change. Strategy to curb carbon emissions and adapt citizens to new ways of living, and working will need to be embraced by organizations and leaders.

Table 4.1 presents a compendium of indicators used to measure and monitor the effects of climate change.

Table 4.1   Climate Change Indicators

Atmosphere	Oceans	Land
* CO_2 concentration	* sea level	* agriculture
* surface air temperature	* ocean temperature	* land resources
* heat waves	* ocean acidity	* water resources
* extreme weather	* marine life	* biodiversity
* precipitation	* coral reef degradation	* soil degradation
* particulate	* extent of Arctic sea ice	* water and food supply

Climate changes associated with these indicators are chronicled by data highlights presented in the *Climate Science Special Report* issued by the U.S. Global Change Research Program (USGCRP) in 2018.[11]

- Annual average *surface air temperature* increased by 1.8°F (1.0°C) between 1901 and 2016—the warmest period in the history of modern civilization.[12] The last three years have been the warmest years on record for the planet. Over the next three decades, annual average temperatures are expected to rise 2.5°F for the continental United States if CO_2 emissions continue on their current trajectory.[13]
- Global average *sea level* has risen 7–8 inches since 1900 with almost half of the rise occurring since 1993—a rate of rise that is greater than during any preceding century in 2,800 years.[14] Global average sea levels are expected to continue to rise by several inches in the next 15 years and by 1–4 feet by 2100.[15] A rise of as much as 8 feet by 2100 cannot be ruled out.
- Records show that *carbon dioxide* (CO_2) *concentrations* in the atmosphere rose from 325 parts per million (ppm) in 1972 to 407 ppm in 2018—a level that last occurred millions

of years ago when global average temperatures and sea level were significantly higher than today.[16] CO_2 emissions will need to decline by nearly half by 2030 and reach net zero by 2050 to limit global warming to 1.5°C and avoid the worst effects of climate change. If global energy demand continues to grow and be met primarily by fossil fuels, atmospheric CO_2 will likely exceed 900 ppm by the end of the century with catastrophic results.[17]

■ *Precipitation* is increasing in frequency, intensity, and volume globally and is expected to continue to increase with rising temperatures. Warmer air holds more water vapor, and each degree of warming increases the capacity of air to retain water vapor by 4 percent.[18] Air with elevated levels of water vapor produces more intense precipitation events as evidenced in records documenting the percentage of annual rainfall in the form of heavy precipitation. Heavy precipitation accounted for a significantly higher percentage of total annual rainfall in the 15-year period 1986–2016 compared to the six-decade average for 1901–1960.[19]

These illustrations offer palpable evidence of the ongoing effects of climate change. There are episodic effects, however, that impact the way people live and what they must do to maintain quality of life. Consider, for example, the growing incidence of large-scale *wildfires* and habitat displacement as regional ecosystems are altered by climate change. Think about water resources that can no longer be taken for granted because early *spring melt* and reduced *snowpack* in western states fail to replenish hydrological reserves. Consider the possibility of *long-term drought* brought on by extended heat waves and minimal change in water resource management policies and practices.[20] And consider the effect of *soil depletion* on agricultural production and food supply.[21] Soil depletion results from excessive rainfall, flooding, and drought—a triad of occurrences that impact health through diminished food supply, rising incidence of malnutrition, and reduction in immunity to infectious disease.[22]

Atmosphere

The climate in New York City in 60 years could feel like Arkansas now. Chicago could seem like Kansas City and Tucson could feel like Hermosillo, Sonora if global warming continues at its current pace. In 2080, Raleigh, North Carolina, could feel more like Florida's capital, Tallahassee, and Washington, DC, could have a climate more akin to the Mississippi Delta according to a study conducted and released by the Center for Environmental Sciences at the University of Maryland.[23]

A research team examined 12 different variables for 540 U.S. and Canadian cities under two climate change scenarios to chart the way the future would look for each city given continued global warming. Climatically speaking, the 540 cities on average moved 528 miles south if carbon emissions continued to rise and 319 miles if carbon emissions were reduced.[24] In southeastern Maine, a homeowner planning a major landscaping project for a private residence would be advised to plant shrubs and trees native to Maryland and Virginia; a farmer would plant seed crops in late March and count on a 6-month growing season; and a family planning a beach vacation would expect to be swimming in 70-degree water by June. On a personal level, the "new normal" would be the hottest day one may have experienced in a lifetime becoming a typical summer day by the middle of the century if we continue on our current path.

Naysayers argue that warming is cyclical and part of naturally occurring variations in climate. What sets recent warming apart in the geologic sweep of time, however, is the sudden rise of temperatures and its clear correlation with increasing levels of greenhouse gases. The consequences of warming are evident in heat waves in Australia and Europe, drought conditions and flooding in Midwestern states, shrinking Arctic ice and glaciers, and rising seas. Warming is also linked to increasingly severe weather events—more violent hurricanes and tornadoes, severe thunderstorms, and excessive rainfall. In May 2019, 12 consecutive days of destructive storms spawned hundreds of tornadoes from Texas to Ohio leaving in their wake a score of ravaged communities and millions of people who had faced peril.

CO_2 *Emissions*

The magnitude of climate change beyond the next few decades will depend primarily on the amount of carbon dioxide emitted globally. Ancient air bubbles trapped in polar ice caps enable scientists to step back in time and see what Earth's atmosphere and climate were like in the distant past. They reveal that the level of CO_2 in the atmosphere at this time is higher than at any time in the last 400,000 years.[25] During ice ages, CO_2 levels were about 200 ppm, and, during warmer interglacial periods, they hovered around 280 ppm.[26] In the 1960s, the global growth rate of atmospheric carbon dioxide was roughly 0.6 ppm per year; in the past decade, it approximated 2.3 ppm per year.[27] Overall, the annual rate of increase in atmospheric carbon dioxide over the past 60 years has been 100 times faster than its natural increase at any period in history.[28] In 2013, CO_2 levels passed 400 ppm for the first time in recorded history.[29]

Why does atmospheric CO_2 matter? In *Climate Change: Atmospheric Carbon Dioxide*, science analyst, Rebecca Lindsey, provided a description of atmospheric CO_2 that can be readily understood by lay audiences.[30] "Carbon dioxide absorbs heat. Warmed by sunlight, the Earth's land and sea surfaces continuously radiate thermal infrared energy. CO_2 absorbs the heat and releases it gradually over time. Without this natural greenhouse effect, Earth's average temperature would be below freezing instead of close to 60°F. Increases in carbon dioxide and other greenhouse gases, however, have tipped Earth's energy budget out of balance, trapping additional heat and raising Earth's average temperature." Carbon dioxide concentrations are rising mostly because of fossil fuels that humans are burning for energy. Fossil fuels such as coal and oil contain carbon that plants have pulled out of the atmosphere through photosynthesis over millions of years. Humans are returning that carbon to the atmosphere in just a few hundred years.[31]

Trees, plants, and soil absorb CO_2 and are an important component of strategy for mitigation of atmospheric carbon. Reforestation is essential but insufficient in and of itself to neutralize carbon emissions. It is most effective when combined with mitigation strategies such as land use; however, vast expanses of land are in a state of desertification because of misuse. United Nations climate scientists believe CO_2 emissions could be stabilized by converting carbon into biomass through return of half of the 5 billion acres of unproductive land worldwide to pasture, food crops, and trees.[32] Reforestation and soil trapping methodologies could be combined to buy 15–20 years of time to adopt carbon-neutral technologies. Scientists have determined that 2.5 billion acres of land capable of storing 200 gigatons of carbon could be reforested worldwide without shrinking land occupied by cities and farms.[33]

Temperatures and Heat Waves

Global annual averaged temperatures are expected to continue to rise over this century and beyond. Without significant reductions in emission of greenhouse gases, the increase in annual average temperatures relative to pre-industrial times could reach 9°F (5°C) or more by the end of the century.[34] With significant reduction in these emissions, the global annually averaged temperature rise could be limited to 3.6°F (2°C) or less.[35] To stop global warming, CO_2 emissions need to be substantially reduced, not just stabilized. Even if we were to stabilize greenhouse gas emissions at today's rates, carbon dioxide levels would continue to rise because we currently emit more CO_2 into the atmosphere than natural processes like photosynthesis and ocean absorption can remove. CO_2 deposits would continue to exceed natural "withdrawals," and temperatures would continue to rise.[36]

Global average surface air temperature increased by 1.8°F (1.0°C) between 1900 and 2015, and warming caused by rising atmospheric CO_2 elevated global temperature in the 20th century have established this century as the warmest period recorded on Earth in over 2000 years.[37] Warming has continued in the new millennium with 18 of the 19 warmest years on record for the planet occurring since 2001.[38] Rising temperatures, however, are only part of the equation. Of growing concern are life-threatening heat waves which have become more frequent and intense since the 1960s through a multiplier effect produced by changes in the jet stream. What would appear to be a relatively small rise in temperature—a 1°centigrade temperature rise, for example—can lead to a tenfold increase in the frequency of 100-degree days.[39] Since the 1960s, the number of heat waves has risen from an average of two per year to nearly six per year in 2020, and the time span in which heat waves can be expected to occur is 45 days longer than it was in the 60s.[40]

Extreme Weather

Extreme weather can affect water quality and supply, agricultural productivity, infrastructure, and ecosystems. Events such as hurricanes, tornadoes, and winter storms have become more frequent and intense in recent years and are expected to continue to increase and worsen. The intensity and frequency of precipitation have also changed with widespread increases in heavy precipitation even in locations where the overall rainfall volume has decreased.[41] Heavy downpours are increasing nationally, especially over the last five decades.[42] A greater percentage of precipitation now comes in the form of intense single-day events rising from an average of ten events per year in the 1960s to 40 events per year in the 2000s.[43]

The mechanism driving extreme weather is well understood. Warmer air contains more water vapor than cooler air. As temperature rises, moisture is infused into cooler upper air causing unstable air to spin faster and making more moisture available to storm systems.[44] This is the generator that fuels extreme weather events such as hurricanes, tornadoes, and thunderstorms. Atlantic hurricanes have substantially increased in frequency and intensity (Category 4 and 5) since the early 1980s.[45] The recent increase in activity is linked to higher sea surface temperatures which are influenced, in part, by emission of heat-trapping gases.[46] Winter storms have also increased in frequency and intensity since the 1950s, and there has been an upward trend in the number and severity of tornadoes and thunderstorms causing large financial losses.[47] By late century, scientific models, on average, project an increase in the number of extreme weather events in a climate warming to a level that will challenge human capacity to adapt.[48]

Air Particulate

Although they may seem to be different issues, air quality and climate change are closely linked. Air pollution is measured by the presence of substances and particles in the air that are hazardous to organisms. The main sources of atmospheric contamination are ozone gases, sulfur oxides, nitrogen oxides, benzopyrene, and particulate matter. These gases result from burning of fossil fuels, industrial processes, forest fires, aerosol use, and radiation.[49] As particulate matter is circulated around the globe by the jet stream, it settles on and darkens ice and snow, leading to less sunlight reflected into space and contributing to global warming.[50]

Aerosols—to be phased out worldwide under the Montreal Protocol—influence climate in several ways: by scattering and absorbing radiation, by cloud formation, and by deposition on snow and ice-covered surfaces that reflect light.[51] There are billions of tiny bits of solids and liquids floating in the atmosphere and thousands of aerosols in each cubic centimeter of air. The smaller and lighter the aerosol particle, the longer it will stay in the air. Larger particles settle to the ground by gravity in a matter of hours, whereas smaller particles can stay in atmosphere for weeks and are mostly removed by precipitation. Aerosols affect climate by helping clouds form which alter climate by scattering and absorbing sunlight.[52]

Data collected at the height of the coronavirus pandemic suggest a link between air pollution in vulnerable cities, particulate matter, and COVID-19. When Massachusetts released town-by-town coronavirus infection rates in April 2020, towns that topped the list were densely populated and had high concentrations of minority, low-income residents.[53] Each had high rates of asthma and environmentally related respiratory disorders, in part, because of pollution. Further evidence of the link between air pollution and COVID-19 came from a nationwide study in 2020 by Harvard researchers which found that long-term exposure to air pollution increased the risk of dying from COVID-19.[54] Cities with high pollution rates attributed to years of industrial impact have some of the worst public health statistics in the nation—a circumstance that may have predisposed residents to higher incidence of COVID-19.

Oceans

Oceans occupy two-thirds of the planet's surface and host unique ecosystems and species. We know that oceans are rising, warming, and becoming more acidic. We also know that oceans have absorbed more than 90 percent of the possible increase in heat content caused by greenhouse gas warming since the mid-20th century.[55] The cumulative effect of humans on oceans and the interplay between oceans and the atmosphere is unknown, but this relationship is a vital component of warming and acidification.

Sea Level

Two factors contribute to sea-level rise. Ocean water expands as it warms resulting in thermal expansion which accounts for 70–75 percent of sea-level rise.[56] Melting land-based ice in glaciers and ice sheets due to global warming also contributes to sea-level rise but to a lesser extent than thermal expansion. NASA satellite data, for example, reveal that Greenland's ice sheet lost about 255 billion metric tons of ice a year between 2003 and 2016 with the rate of loss accelerating during that period.[57] Global mean sea level has risen by 7–8 inches since 1900 with almost half of the rise occurring since 1993.[58] Using the year 2000 as a baseline, projections indicate that global mean sea level is likely to rise 3.6–7.2 inches (9–18 cm) between 2000 and 2030, 6–14.4 inches (15–38 cm) by 2050, and 1–4.3 feet (30–130 cm) by 2100.[59] The lower end of the range for sea-level rise represents continuation of the rate of sea-level rise over the last quarter century. The upper end of the range assumes rapid mass loss from the Antarctic ice sheet.

U.S. Global Change Research Program data indicate that almost all U.S. coastlines are experiencing greater than average sea-level rise as a result of Antarctic ice loss and melting of land-based ice in glaciers.[60] The number of tidal floods each year has increased five- to ten-fold since the 1960s in vulnerable Atlantic and Gulf Coast cities.[61] Tidal flooding associated with coastal storms such as hurricanes and Nor'easters is projected to grow in frequency and extent throughout the century.[62] High-intensity North Atlantic hurricanes increase the probability of extreme flooding along most of the Atlantic and Gulf Coast states beyond what would be projected based solely on sea-level rise.[63] Increasingly powerful storms push seawater inland over ground devoid of fresh water flowing outward. This allows seawater to claim new territory and renders land unusable.[64] The result is a loss of coastal property and rising costs for repair and insurance which are burdensome to taxpayers and regional economies. Response options for sea-level rise run a continuum from *prevention*—curb sea-level rise by reducing atmospheric CO_2—to *protection*—safeguard land and property by constructing barriers and restricting development to higher ground.

Ocean Temperature

Ocean heat content has increased at all depths since the 1960s and surface waters have warmed by 1.3°F from 1900 to 2016.[65] The temperature of the Antarctic Southern Ocean rose by 0.17°C between the 1950s and 1980s, nearly twice the rate of the world's oceans as a whole.[66] A global increase in average sea temperature of 4.9°F (+/–1.3°F) is projected by 2100.[67]

Warming reduces the ability of oceans to absorb CO_2 and affects ecosystems. It also impacts mixing of warm and cold currents in the North Atlantic Ocean—a key driver of the world's climate. This is known as the Atlantic Meridional Overturning Circulation of which the Gulf Stream is one component.[68] Scientists describe the Atlantic Meridional as a giant ocean conveyor belt that moves water from Greenland south beyond the tip of Africa into the Indian Ocean.[69] Warm, salty water near the surface moves north and mixes with cold, fresh water. As the water cools and sinks, it drives ocean circulation that is critical to the global climate—in particular, the location of droughts and frequency of hurricanes. It also stores heat-trapping CO_2 deep in the ocean. The potential slowing of the Atlantic Meridional as a result of rising ocean heat content could have a dramatic effect on climate as the ocean absorbs less heat and CO_2 from the atmosphere.[70]

Ocean Acidity, Marine Life, and Coral Reef Degradation

The world's oceans currently absorb more than a quarter of the CO_2 emitted to the atmosphere from human activity, increasing their acidity and creating detrimental conditions for marine ecosystems.[71] When carbon dioxide dissolves in seawater, oxygen is depleted and water becomes more acidic. In the past 200 years alone, ocean water has become 30 percent more acidic—faster than any known change in ocean chemistry in 50 million years.[72] Rapid change in ocean chemistry does not give marine life evolving over millions of years in an ocean with stable acidity much time to adapt. The world's oceans are projected to lose one-sixth of fish and marine life by the end of the century if climate change continues on its current path. With every 1.8°F of ocean warming, the total mass of marine life is projected to drop by 5 percent based on computer models developed by marine biologists.[73] Beyond lost biodiversity, acidification has the potential to cause serious problems for sea-related economies and global food security as human population continues to grow over the century.

A more acidic ocean will not destroy all marine life, but the 30 percent rise in acidity already recorded will limit *coral growth* by corroding existing coral structures while simultaneously retarding the growth of new coral.[74] The weakening that results could make reefs vulnerable to erosion. *Fish stocks* will be affected through the intake of carbonic acid which puts physical structure into overdrive to bring body chemistry into line with changing acidity.[75] To balance chemistry with acidity, fish burn extra energy to excrete excess acid through gills, kidneys, and intestines thereby reducing the energy required for digestion and reproduction. In more acidic water, *shellfish* experience shell weakening as magnesium calcite used for shell building diminishes in acidic water increasing the chance of being crushed or eaten.[76] These organisms provide food and habitat for many forms of marine life and their diminution will significantly impact the food chain.

Extent of Arctic Sea Ice

Decline in Arctic sea ice is arguably the most dramatic evidence of the effect of global warming on ocean systems. Sea ice extent is a measure of the surface area of the ocean covered by sea ice. Rising air and ocean temperatures diminish the extent of sea ice reflecting the sun's radiation and simultaneously increase the area of dark ocean surface that absorbs it.[77] This albedo affect results in a continuing cycle of sea ice melt and ocean warming.[78] Snow-covered sea ice absorbs only about 20 percent of the solar radiation that reaches it, whereas ice-free ocean surface absorbs over 90 percent.[79] A warmer ocean melts ice from below and releases heat back into the atmosphere before the ocean refreezes in the winter. The result over time is less sea ice and a warmer climate.

Temperatures in the Arctic are currently climbing two to three times faster than the global average. With 2.7 million square miles of Arctic sea ice in 1979 and 1.8 million square miles in 2018, Arctic sea ice has declined by more than 30 percent over four decades.[80] At this rate, projections indicate that the Arctic could be virtually ice-free during summers by the middle of this century. An ice-free Arctic in summer has ushered in a geopolitical scramble among nations, governments, and business for the Arctic's rich reserve of resources. The Arctic contains an estimated 30 percent of the world's undiscovered gas, 13 percent of undiscovered oil, and 20 percent of liquefied natural gas.[81] It is filled with rare-earth minerals essential for cell phones and solar technology. The opportunity for economic benefit is enormous especially with the increased feasibility of new shipping routes. Imagine connecting the Atlantic and Pacific by sailing the Northwest Passage over Canada and Alaska or by taking the Northern Sea route running above Russia. Lloyds of London has recognized the potential benefit of an ice-free Arctic with an estimate that "investment in the Arctic could reach $100 billion within 10 years."[82]

With opportunity comes adversity. The changing Arctic will be consequential because of its impact on Earth's climate, bountiful resources that will generate tension among nations, and meteorological conditions that will marginalize the benefit of investment.[83] There is a rush underway among nations to claim territory with Russia, the United States, Canada, Denmark, and Norway all vying for territorial control. Airfields are being built and restored, hydrometeorological services are being developed, and maritime capabilities and military defenses are being built up to advance the interests of nations. As the Arctic ice cap retreats, shipping lanes are opening that trading nations hope could rival, or at least complement, conventional routes during summer months. Russia is investing billions in Arctic infrastructure to develop a "Suez of the North" connecting the Atlantic to the Pacific across the rim of Siberia.[84] Daunting challenges confront shipping companies, however, as harsh environmental conditions make navigation difficult.

Land

Wildfires are ravaging California, heavy rain is flooding communities across the country, and drought has withered and killed off crops in the heartland. Rising temperatures affect the timing and volume of rainfall, snowmelt and evaporation, and soil moisture. They also affect the frequency of drought and flooding, disease outbreaks, severe storms, forest fires, atmospheric composition and air quality, and land use. Warmer summer temperatures have not only lengthened growing seasons but also extended summer drought stress and vulnerability to insect-borne disease. Changes in precipitation and the size of storms have impacted moisture availability to plants, the extent of snowpack and snowmelt, flooding, and water quality. The impact of climate change on land is not as clearly defined as its impact on atmosphere and oceans. What is known, however, is articulated in research reports issued by the National Center for Atmospheric Research (NCAR) under the auspices of the U.S. Climate Change Science Program (CCSP).[85] Additional data are available in assessment reports prepared and issued by the NCAR based on extensive review of relevant scientific literature, measurements and data collected, and published by U.S. government agencies.[86]

Agriculture

Weather and climate factors such as temperature, precipitation, CO_2 concentrations, and water availability directly impact the vitality of plants, pasture and rangeland, and livestock. For any agricultural commodity, variation in yield is related to growing season weather and the presence of weather-related factors such as insects, disease, and weeds. Data aggregated and published by the United States Environmental Protection Agency and the NCAR indicate that:[87]

- Agriculture is highly dependent on climate. Increases in temperature and carbon dioxide can increase crop yields, but to realize this benefit, nutrient levels, soil moisture, and water availability must be adequate. Changes in the frequency and severity of droughts and floods pose challenges to farmers and threaten food security.[88]
- Higher CO_2 affects crop yields. Elevated CO_2 levels can increase plant growth, but changing temperatures, ozone, and water and nutrient constraints may counteract increases in yield.[89] If temperature exceeds a crop's optimal level or sufficient water and nutrients are not available, yield increases may be reduced or reversed.
- Extreme temperature and precipitation, especially floods and droughts, can harm crops and reduce yields. High nighttime and warm winter temperatures in 2010 and 2012 affected corn yields in the Midwest, and premature budding caused a $220 million loss in the Michigan cherry yield in 2012.[90]
- Weeds, pests, and fungi thrive in warmer temperatures and wetter climates. The range and distribution of weeds and pests are likely to increase with climate change—a challenge for farmers growing crops previously unexposed to new weed and pest species.[91]
- Rising CO_2 can stimulate plant growth, but it also reduces the nutritional value of most crops by reducing concentrations of protein and essential minerals in plant species, a potential threat to human health.[92]

Climate change will increase the likelihood of drought in many parts of the United States in the decades ahead. Regions of the U.S.—particularly the Southwest—will see increased heat, changing rainfall patterns, and less snowpack. Droughts unfold through rising temperatures that increase evaporation from soil, making periodic droughts worse than they would be under cooler conditions.

They lengthen and persist through a "feedback loop" where excessively dry soils and diminished plant cover suppress rainfall in already dry areas.[93] This condition makes the U.S. historically susceptible to drought as evidenced in the Dust Bowl of the 1930s, the drought of the 1950s and, most recently, the droughts of 2011 and 2012. At the peak of the 2012 drought, a remarkable 81 percent of the contiguous United States was under abnormally dry conditions.[94] Beyond its impact on crops and livestock, drought affects transportation through water levels that cannot support commercial river traffic and energy production from industrial facilities that require cooling water to maintain safe operation.

Land Resources

Climate strongly influences forest sustenance and the frequency and magnitude of forest fires, insect outbreaks, and tree mortality. Plant and animal species in arid ecosystems are especially vulnerable to changes in temperature and rainfall. Data aggregated and published by the NCAR reveal that:[95]

- Climate change has increased the size and number of forest fires, insect outbreaks, and tree mortality in the West, Southwest, and Alaska and will continue to do so.
- Higher temperatures, increased drought, and more intense thunderstorms have increased erosion that will lead to invasion of exotic grass species in arid lands.
- Climate change in arid lands will create physical conditions conducive to the proliferation of exotic grasses, thus increasing the frequency and severity of wildfires.
- Changes in temperature and precipitation are likely to decrease the cover of vegetation protecting the ground surface from wind and water erosion.
- Stream temperatures are likely to increase and water volume decrease with direct and indirect effects on aquatic ecosystems.

The impact of climate on land is most visible through forest fires, storms, and severe drought which impact public safety and land use. According to National Interagency Fire Center data, the extent of land area burned by wildfires each year has steadily increased. Of the ten years with the largest acreage burned, nine have occurred since 2000, including 8 million acres of forest in the U.S. (roughly the size of Maryland) and $1.8 billion in damages in 2011.[96] Climate change is projected to increase the intensity and frequency of wildfires in southwestern and western states and usher in a new normal—life interrupted by power outages and fire lines drawn around homes. The threat of wildfires also means pop-up assistance centers, sprinkler systems, and do-it-yourself actions to combat fire—trimming vegetation and creating defensible space around homes.

Water Resources

Plants, animals, and ecosystems are susceptible to variations in the supply and quality of water, both of which are sensitive to climate change. Not only do weather- and human-related factors play into water supply and quality, but also scientific evidence reveals that climate change has influenced water-related variables that contribute to floods.[97] Floods have brought destruction to every state and nearly every county in the continental United States and are projected to worsen in the decade ahead. Sea-level rise and extreme weather will increase land area designated as "floodplain" by approximately 45 percent by the end of the century and upward of 41 million U.S. residents will be at risk from flooding caused by heavy rainfall, melting snow, and ice jams.[98] Shallow floods (also known as "high tide" floods) caused by seawater washing over roads into storm drains are becoming increasingly common as are flash floods triggered by heavy precipitation and alterations to land including dams, levees, and reservoirs.

Climate change increases flood risk through heavy precipitation, more frequent hurricanes, and higher seas. A warmer atmosphere holds and dumps more water. As the country has heated up, it has also become wetter with the eastern half of the U.S. experiencing the heaviest precipitation.[99] In the Northeast, the most extreme storms generate roughly 27 percent more moisture than they did a century ago.[100] Heavy precipitation events are projected to increase through the 21st century to a level that could approach three times the historical average, and the frequency of strong hurricanes is expected to increase through this century.[101] In the Atlantic basin, an 80 percent increase in the frequency of category 4 and 5 hurricanes is projected over the next 80 years.[102] More intense storms are predicted with tomorrow's hurricanes expected to pack as much as 37 percent more precipitation near their center and about 20 percent more precipitation on their periphery.[103] Stronger storms produce turbulent winds that combine with rising seas and high tide to inundate low-lying coastal regions. Damage caused by storm surges, heavy precipitation, and high winds is projected to total $54 billion annually (equivalent to 0.3 percent of the nation's gross domestic product) according to a 2019 report issued by the Congressional Budget Office.[104]

Biodiversity

Climate change is generally evaluated in terms of how it will affect people—temperature extremes, droughts and flooding, and sea-level rise impacting cities, homes, and the global economy. But perhaps the most significant effects of a global warming will be on plants, animals and birds, and marine life. Biodiversity—the number and range of living species—is expected to decline as the climate warms, resulting in negative impacts on global ecosystems and, ultimately, humankind. Biodiversity is important because of its contribution to the functioning of ecosystems and because it is difficult to recover once eroded. Among the habitats most severely affected are corals in shallow waters experiencing bleaching as a result of rising ocean temperatures and Arctic wildlife losing habitat because of shrinking ice caps.

Analysis of scientific data on the ecological consequences of climate change reveals that nearly 60 percent of more than 1500 species studied have undergone shifts in distribution over a 140-year time frame.[105] Among the more noteworthy changes are:[106]

■ rapid rates of warming in the Arctic have dramatically reduced ice cover that provides habitat for animal life and biomes supporting a food chain including algae, invertebrates, birds, fish, and marine mammals.

■ expansion of the territory species inhabit in response to increasing temperatures.

■ change in the distribution of plants and animals that impacts the entire food chain relying on them for sustenance.

■ change in weather patterns that alters when seasons begin throwing plant and animal species out of balance and altering hibernation, migration, germination, and reproduction patterns.

■ growing risk of disease, pathogens, and parasites with serious ramifications for human health and agriculture.

The most obvious consequence of biodiversity loss is large-scale extinction of species and wildlife. The rate of extinction is one thousand times higher than that evidenced in fossil records, and the forecast extinction rate is more than ten times the current rate.[107] Extinction and decline in biodiversity will lead to reduction of ecosystem functions such as purification of air and water, climate stabilization, and the generation of soil and vegetation.

Soil Degradation

The world's soils store more carbon than the planet's biomass and atmosphere combined. This includes soil organic carbon, microbes and fungi, and invertebrates as well as root matter and decomposing vegetation. Loss of soil organic carbon, erosion, and salinization and acidification are principal causes of land degradation. When land is degraded, soil carbon is released into the atmosphere, along with nitrous oxide, making degradation one of the largest contributors to climate change. Small increases in global soil organic carbon have a high impact on the global carbon cycle and on atmospheric concentration of CO_2. An increase of just 1 percent of the carbon stocks in the top meter of soils would be higher than the amount corresponding to annual CO_2 emissions from fossil fuel burning.[108] An estimated two-thirds of all terrestrial carbon stores from soils and vegetation have been lost since the 19th century through degradation.[109]

Soils enhance CO_2 uptake from the atmosphere through a carbon cycle that transfers heat from soil to the atmosphere through plant growth, decomposition, and rainfall. When the carbon cycle is disrupted through soil degradation, carbon dioxide uptake from the atmosphere is reduced and the consequence is desertification of land which exacerbates the effect of climate change. When wetlands are lost, water storage is lost; when forests are lost, absorptive capacity is lost; when absorptive capacity is lost, land is rendered incapable of productive use because of runoff during rainfall. These conditions, combined with exploitation of land beyond its productive capacity through unsustainable management practices, accelerate the process of degradation. Vulnerable populations are placed at risk due to insufficient food and water which, in turn, increases demand on productive land—a primary cause of desertification and the loss of agricultural land. Global warming has intensified this cycle and millions are now living on land with diminished or declining productivity.

Recent estimates of the global loss of ecosystem function due to land degradation and desertification are between $6.3 trillion and $10.6 trillion (US) annually.[110] Managing land sustainably results in lower carbon emissions and greater carbon capture. A number of practices can be used to increase carbon in soil including reforestation, fallowing land, fertility enhancement through organic means and agro chemicals, integrated erosion control, conservation agriculture, water conservation and harvesting, diversification of ecosystems in landscapes, and sustainable pasture management through managed herd mobility.[111] Other practices include treating soil-based approaches to climate change mitigation as integral to global and national policy, promoting awareness, and ensuring that soil organic carbon is fully accounted for as an indicator of the benefits of sustainable land management.

Water and Food Supply

Water is the primary medium through which people will feel the effects of climate change. We depend on a reliable, clean supply of water to sustain health, agriculture, energy production, navigation, recreation, and manufacturing. These uses put pressure on water resources that combined with climate-induced events such as flooding and droughts make water availability less predictable. Higher temperatures and extreme weather change the water cycle by altering the distribution of rainfall, river flows, and groundwater. The water cycle is a delicate balance of precipitation, evaporation, and steps in between that affect supply and availability. Warmer temperatures increase the rate of evaporation into the atmosphere and elevate the atmosphere's capacity to hold water—an occurrence leading to drought in some areas and excess precipitation in others.

Change in the water cycle is most evident in patterns of precipitation. Over the past 50 years, the amount of rain falling in heavy precipitation events has increased for most of the United States.[112] Warming temperatures cause more precipitation to fall as rain rather than snow and cause snow to begin melting earlier in the year. This alters the timing of streamflow in rivers that are fed by mountains serving as headwaters to rivers and freshwater sources. When snow and ice collect on mountaintops, the snowmelt releases water slowly to streams, rivers, and reservoirs throughout the spring and summer. When rain falls on mountaintops during winter months, water runs off quickly and fills up reservoirs to capacity which can result in excess water runoff that cannot be stored. Rain flowing faster than melting snow can reduce soil moisture and groundwater recharge causing freshwater shortages in areas that rely on meltwater as their primary freshwater source.

The changing global water cycle has resulted in the increased likelihood of more intense weather events, droughts, and water fouled by algal blooms. Precipitation extremes in the form of lengthy dry spells interspersed with brief but heavy precipitation events and flooding cause runoff which results in water and soil loss. Water warmed by rising temperatures spawns harmful algal blooms in rivers, lakes, and oceans. Naturally occurring algal blooms supercharged by nutrient pollution and worsened by drought and deluge cycles act as toxic fuel for blooms propelled by heavy precipitation into rivers. These blooms can produce toxins that threaten health and the economy by polluting drinking water, hampering tourism, and damaging aquatic life. The combination of drought, extreme precipitation, and algal blooms has a significant effect on infrastructure and agricultural planning as standing assumptions about climate and precipitation upon which decisions are made for infrastructure projects such as dams and reservoirs are rendered unreliable for predictive planning.

Food Supply

Crops, livestock, and seafood produced in the United States contributed more than $200 billion to the economy in 2009 and volume will surpass $300 billion in 2020.[113] When food service and other agriculture-related industries are included, the agriculture and food sectors contributed more than $1.05 trillion to the gross domestic product in 2017.[114] Agriculture, fisheries, and food supply are highly dependent on climate. Increases in temperature and CO_2 can increase crop yields but to realize these benefits, nutrient levels, soil moisture, water availability, and other conditions must be met. Changes in the frequency and severity of droughts and floods caused by climate change counter crop yield gains and threaten food supply. Warmer temperatures also induce change in the habitat ranges of fish and shellfish species. Overall, climate change disrupts food security and supply by making it more difficult to grow crops, raise animals, and catch fish in the same ways and same places as we have done in the past.

In a 2017 snapshot report, the Environmental Protection Agency issued a series of data points regarding climate impacts on agriculture and food supply based on research findings:[115]

Impacts on Crops

- Higher CO_2 levels have differential effects on crop yields. Elevated CO_2 levels can increase plant growth; however, factors such as changing temperatures, ozone, and water and nutrient constraints may counteract potential increases in yield. If temperature exceeds a crop's optimal level and if sufficient water and nutrients are not available, yield increases may be reduced or reversed.[116]

▪ Extreme weather—soaring temperature, heavy precipitation, floods, and droughts—can harm crops and reduce yields. Drought is an ongoing challenge in areas where rising temperatures cause soils to become drier. Water runs off dry soil in heavy precipitation events thereby further enhancing drought conditions.[117]

▪ Weeds, pests, and fungi thrive under warmer temperatures, wetter conditions, and increased CO_2 levels. Currently, U.S. farmers spend more than $11 billion per year to control weeds, which compete with crops for light, water, and nutrients.[118] The range and distribution of weeds and pests are likely to increase with climate change.

▪ By reducing concentrations of protein and essential minerals in plants, rising CO_2 reduces the nutritional value of most of the food crops. Combined with increased pesticide use, the effect of CO_2 on the nutritional value of crops represents a potential threat to human health.[119]

Impacts on Livestock

▪ Americans consume more than 36 million metric tons of meat and poultry annually. Heat stress associated with climate change directly affects animals by increasing vulnerability to disease and reducing fertility and milk production. In 2011, exposure to high-temperature events caused over $1 billion in heat-related losses to agricultural producers.[120]

▪ Climate change may increase the prevalence of parasites and diseases that affect livestock. Earlier onset of spring and warmer winters could allow some parasites and pathogens to survive. Changing veterinary practices, including increased use of parasiticides to maintain livestock health, could increase the risk of pesticides entering the food chain.[121]

Impacts on Fisheries

▪ American fishermen catch or harvest $5 million metric tons of fish and shellfish each year.[122] Fisheries already face multiple challenges including overfishing and water pollution. Rising temperatures will affect the distribution of species as well as the timing of reproduction and migration.

▪ Marine disease outbreaks have been linked with changing climate. Warmer temperatures have caused disease in coral, eelgrass, and abalone.[123] Aquatic species preferring cold lakes, streams, and oceans migrate to lower temperature waters thereby changing species distribution.

Climate impact on crops, livestock, and fisheries is supported by research, but its principal impact is on food security. Rising temperature, changing precipitation patterns, extreme weather events, and reduction in water availability reduce agricultural productivity and elevate food prices. Disruption in food production, distribution, and transport will have a significant impact not only on food security and quality but also on food access. The food transportation and distribution system in the United States moves large volumes of grain crops by water. Extreme weather events affecting waterways leave few, if any, alternative pathways for transport. In 2012, historically high temperatures and a shortage of rain produced a severe drought followed by flooding in the Mississippi River watershed, which brought transcontinental shipping to a crawl. Significant food and economic losses resulted due to reduction in barge traffic and the volume of goods carried. Climate-induced change in food supply is an intensifying concern of business, government, and the health industry because of the threat it poses to well-being and national security.

Default, Mitigation, or Adaptation?

The effect of climate change on people is far-reaching—how they live and work, their comfort and safety, their mobility, where they live, what they eat and drink, and much more. Its impact is evident in almost every sector of society—the economy, agriculture, health, energy, transportation, infrastructure, food security, water supply, and ecosystems. It affects some groups more than others—particularly populations located in vulnerable areas, those living in poverty, older adults and young children, and immigrant communities. Cities and coastal communities are uniquely sensitive to their impact—especially those subject to extreme weather. And professions and industries closely linked to weather and climate—tourism, commerce, and agriculture—are impacted.

A sampling of societal impacts associated with climate change leaves little to the imagination. Health and well-being will be compromised through more frequent and intense extreme weather events, decreased air quality, and diseases transmitted by insects, food, and water. Climate disruptions to agriculture—crop loss, changes in the nutritional quality of foods, soil erosion, and land degradation—will become more severe over this century and will diminish the nation's food supply. Surface and groundwater supplies in some regions will diminish and water quality will be affected. Prolonged periods of high temperatures accompanied by drought will further deplete soil moisture and contribute to conditions that lead to longer fire seasons, larger wildfires, and flooding following extreme weather events. Sea level will continue to rise and will cause storm surge damage and flooding in coastal communities. Extreme heat, sea-level rise, and extreme downpours will damage infrastructures such as roads, rail lines, airports, port facilities, energy infrastructure, and military bases. The capacity of ecosystems to buffer impacts of extreme events will be challenged as well as their ability to shield population centers from harm.

A 2020 report by the McKinsey Global Institute, *Climate Risk and Response: Physical Hazards and Socioeconomic Impacts*, identified important areas of climate change impact:[124]

- socioeconomic impacts of climate change will affect human well-being as well as physical and natural capital as system thresholds are breached
- risk recognition brought forward by financial markets will bear consequences for capital allocation and insurance
- countries and regions with lower per capita GDP will be more at risk from climate change
- systematic risk management, accelerating adaptation, and decarbonization will be needed to address climate risk

The McKinsey Report depicts a climate future that will swell the number and size of regions affected by substantial physical impacts. This will have a direct effect on livability and workability, food systems, physical assets, infrastructure, and natural capital. As temperature and humidity increase, by 2030, millions could live in regions experiencing heat waves that exceed the threshold of survivability. Climate risk will have an economic impact by making long-duration borrowing unavailable and increasing insurance cost and reducing terminal values—occurrences that could trigger capital reallocation and asset repricing. Facing climate calamity, decision makers would have little choice but to translate climate science impacts into potential physical and financial damages through systematic risk management and robust modeling extending beyond the limitations of past data.

Mitigation or Adaptation?

When it comes to countering climate change, two approaches are at work in policy and practice: mitigation and adaptation. Mitigation involves actions to reduce greenhouse gas emissions, while adaptation refers to actions to reduce vulnerability to the negative effects of climate change.[125]

Adaptation can help manage risk although it will prove costly for vulnerable regions and entail hard choices. In whatever form—seawalls, cooling shelters, or drought-resistant crops—adaptation will require calculated and collective attention, particularly about where and when to invest versus retreat. While adaptation is urgent, climate science indicates that further warming and risk escalation can only be stopped through mitigation—zero net greenhouse gas emissions.

Early thinking on greenhouse gas emissions focused on adaptation as a reasonable course of action. As the pace of emissions accelerated over the past decade, however, mitigation has drawn increased attention as an essential course of action. In 2018, the global average concentration of CO_2 reached 407.8 ppm and the heating effect of the atmosphere rose to a level 43 percent stronger than 1990—the highest levels in recorded history.[126] Change at this velocity will not be slowed or diminished by piecemeal efforts toward solution. More will be necessary and the "more" involves reduction of greenhouse gas in the atmosphere and adaptation to change already in the pipeline. Mitigation and adaptation will need to work hand in hand to curb the negative effects of climate change.

Adaptation

Actions for countering climate change are highlighted in Figure 4.1 on a continuum ranging from adaptation to mitigation. Adaptation is accomplished through reduction in greenhouse gases using low-carbon technologies—primarily reduction of energy waste and switching to low-carbon sources of energy. Cities and municipalities are the front line of adaptation—a process made more difficult by the absence of national or international climate policy. Faced with the reality of having to address and resolve climate problems on their own, municipalities adjust by building flood defenses to combat sea-level encroachment, developing emergency plans for heat waves and high temperatures, installing water-permeable pavement to control floods and stormwater, redesigning buildings and infrastructure to withstand extreme weather events, and upgrading systems for water storage.[127]

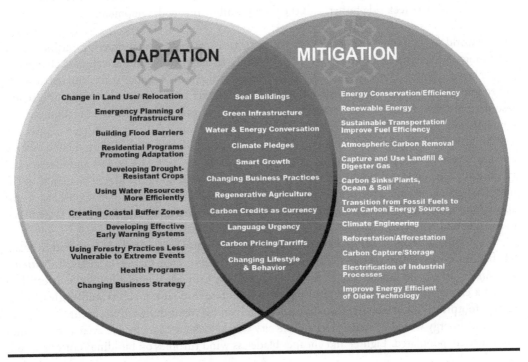

Figure 4.1   Tactics for Response to Climate Change.

Governments at local and regional levels are getting better at adaptation. Assessment reports issued by the United Nations IPCC indicate that climate change is starting to be factored into development plans for managing disasters and their associated risks, protecting coastlines and combatting sea-level encroachment, managing land and forests, planning for reduced water availability, developing resilient crop varieties, and protecting energy and public infrastructure.[128] Recognizing that global warming is a crisis of imminent danger, local governments and climate advocates are calling for greater urgency in language and action to produce the level of mobilization required to curtail it. Examples of local and regional action include:

■ Economic development plans in Fresno, California, are aligned with principles of the Green New Deal. Zoning code and transportation infrastructure have been reconstructed to lower its carbon footprint and its development strategy has been altered to address environmental problems.[129]

■ New York City passed a sweeping resolution in 2019 calling for an "immediate emergency mobilization to restore a safe climate." Los Angeles established a Climate Emergency Mobilization Department enabling city agencies and the public to take coordinated action against planet-warming emissions.[130]

■ Coastal cities are mobilizing to protect infrastructure against sea-level rise. New York City is considering an artificial land extension to the southern tip of Manhattan to protect against storm surges, and Boston is studying barrier harbor construction to repel rising tidewaters.[131]

■ Vulnerable cities are learning to say "no." Squeezed between the clamor for new housing and relentless flooding fueled by climate change, Virginia Beach has rejected developer proposals for construction of housing on floodplain—an action upheld in court.[132]

■ Nashville has implemented a voluntary program to purchase homes at fair market value in flood-prone areas.[133] Once homeowners move out, their homes are razed, the land becomes an absorbent creek side buffer, and the City prohibits future development.

On the world stage, nations are developing policy to measure well-being differently, businesses are redefining performance and value, and cities are being reimagined to embrace climate change. In 2019, New Zealand became the first nation to drop gross domestic product as its primary measure of economic success in favor of national well-being.[134] Apart from schools, hospitals, and roads, resources are distributed according to their impact on five national priorities: contribution to a low emission economy, mental health, child well-being, the inequalities of indigenous people, and building a nation adapted to the digital age. In the business world, environmental, social, and governance issues are becoming increasingly important for corporate leaders and investors.[135] Historically a secondary concern, ESG and the role it plays in tackling the urgent challenge of climate change has become a top priority for corporate leaders. Corporations are being held accountable by shareholders for ESG performance; in response, they are ramping up internal systems for measuring and reporting ESG.

What will cities of the future look like? By 2050, the world's population is expected to reach 9.8 billion. Nearly 70 percent—6.7 billion people—are projected to live in cities.[136] *National Geographic* asked the architectural and urban planning firm Skidmore, Owings & Merrill to design a city of the future.[137] The resulting design centered on sustainability and mitigation of carbon footprint. Water resources would be protected and systems designed to capture, treat, and use them. Energy would be renewable and the city would become more livable even as it becomes more densely populated. Lighter and cheaper bladeless wind turbines on building rooftops would provide supplemental energy. Food would be locally produced through vertically planted crops and underground farming. Waste would become a resource to produce energy, alternative material, and potable water. Mobility would be improved through high-speed rail and remotely controlled drones powerful enough to transport people. Infrastructure would be carbon-neutral and the economy would be automated and on-line.

Mitigation

Limiting human emission of greenhouse gases (GHG) is an essential first step in mitigation of global warming. Mitigation can also be achieved by removing carbon from the atmosphere, increasing the capacity of carbon sinks, and switching to low-carbon sources of energy. Other frequently discussed methods include increasing vehicular fuel economy, lifestyle changes, and changing business and land use practices. Futurists working with creative energy have proposed sci-fi stopgaps including a giant parasol hovering high in orbit to block the sun, pumping excess carbon dioxide deep underground for indefinite storage, or spraying sulfur dioxide into the atmosphere to form clouds that artificially cool the Earth. As global warming becomes more dire and nations falter on decreasing emissions, technological fixes known as geoengineering are garnering attention to buy time for nations to move away from burning fossil fuels.

Fossil Fuel Phase-Out

Greenhouse gas emissions are due primarily to fossil fuels and phase out in favor of renewable energy is essential. Electricity is included in the category of renewable energy along with heat generated from solar, wind, ocean, hydropower, biomass, geothermal resources, and biofuel sources. Renewable energy replaces fossil fuels in three areas: power generation, hot water/space heating, and transport fuels. Countries with favorable geography, geology, and weather are favorably suited to economic exploitation of renewable energy sources and already acquire most of their energy from renewables. Wind power provides a significant amount of electricity in some regions, and solar water heating is making a growing contribution to fossil fuel reduction in many countries. The use of biomass for heating and direct geothermal heating is growing as well.

Demand-Side Management

The Fifth Assessment Report of the IPCC strongly emphasized the potential of behavioral, lifestyle, and cultural changes to reduce carbon emissions.[138] High-consumption lifestyles have an environmental impact significantly beyond the comparatively low impact of "greening"—washing clothes in cold water, recycling, upgrading light bulbs, and so forth. Public discourse on reduction of carbon footprint overwhelmingly focuses on low-impact behavior with almost no mention of high-impact behavior in mainstream media and government publications.[139] High-impact behavior involves life-altering changes: eating a plant-based diet, using public transportation, reducing energy use, and switching fuels for energy and mobility. Energy efficiency and conservation are especially important. International Energy Agency estimates indicate that reduction of energy use through conservation and improved energy efficiency in buildings, industrial practices, and transportation could reduce the world's energy needs in 2050 by one-third and contribute significantly to reduction in greenhouse gas emissions.[140]

Carbon Sinks and Removal

A carbon sink is a natural or artificial reservoir such as a forest that accumulates and stores carbon-containing chemical compounds for an indefinite period.[141] Carbon dioxide removal involves permanent removal of CO_2 from the atmosphere through direct air capture and storing in geologic formations underground.[142] Reforestation and afforestation are primary methods for sequestering CO_2. Research by Crowther et al. indicates that there is sufficient land worldwide to plant an additional 1.2 trillion trees—a number that would cancel out the last ten years of CO_2 emissions.[143] With intensive agriculture and urbanization, there is enough available farmland that if reforested could offset years of carbon emissions. Restoring the world's 8.7 billion acres of grasslands would store CO_2 from the air in plant material and increase the carbon content of soils by 1 percent—a process that would offset nearly 12 years of CO_2 emissions.[144]

Agricultural Practices and Land Management

The use of agriculture practices that minimize carbon emissions and meet society's food and textile needs without compromising the ability of future generations to meet their own needs is known as regenerative agriculture.[145] Regenerative processes include conservation tillage, rotation and cover crops, limitation of physical disturbance, and minimizing the use of chemicals. A 2015 study found that farming can deplete soil carbon and render soil incapable of supporting plant life; however, the study also showed that conservation farming can protect carbon in soils and repair damage over time.[146] The relationship between soil and carbon can best be described as dualistic. On the one hand, soils account for about half of agricultural greenhouse gas emissions in the United States, while, on the other hand, carbon retention is essential to soil health.[147] Accordingly, one of the most important projects for reduction in greenhouse gas emissions is sequestration of carbon from the atmosphere through agroforestry—a land use practice in which trees and shrubs are grown around or among crops and pastureland.

Societal Controls

Another approach to mitigation drawing close attention is transforming carbon into a form of currency by taxing emissions and introducing tradeable "personal carbon credits." An emissions tax on greenhouse gas emissions requires individual emitters to pay a fee or tax for every ton of greenhouse gas emitted into the atmosphere.[148] Most of the taxes associated with emissions are levied on energy products and motor vehicles leaving non-transport sectors such as agriculture untaxed—a practice that limits the impact of taxation on emissions. Personal carbon credits would be designed to motivate individuals to reduce their carbon footprint through the way they live. Each citizen would receive a free annual quota of carbon that could be used to travel, purchase food, and travel less often on personal business.[149] This practice would have variable benefits according to age, socioeconomic status, and income. Adults living at poverty level and old age pensioners traveling less often would benefit because they could enhance purchasing power by cashing in unused carbon credits.

New Roles for Organizations and Leaders

Climate change is much more than an environmental challenge. It is inextricably linked to business and will significantly impact business performance moving forward. Central to its impact on business are fundamental questions facing companies and leaders: How will climate change affect the future of business? What is the cost of inaction on climate change? How can companies prepare for and adapt to climate change? What are the resource requirements of different climate change strategies? What role can business play in helping communities overcome the effects of climate change? Unknowns are many and they pose daunting challenges to companies and leaders. Primary among them is the question of strategy: Should companies focus on the future and mitigate risk by reducing greenhouse gas emissions or conserve ongoing resources and expend them on moderating the effects of climate change?

The answer to this question depends on the extent to which climate change will affect business operations and performance, the cost-benefits of preparing for climate change, and corporate responsibility to markets and communities.

Effect of Climate Change on Business

Renewable Energy, a clean energy journal, has identified prominent ways in which climate change will affect business. Among them are the following:[150]

- *Rising insurance costs.* Extreme weather events will increase the cost of insurance. Higher risk equals more claims equals higher premiums. As risk increases, so do costs associated with managing risk and premiums which are passed on to business.
- *Changes in resource availability and cost.* Extreme weather events have the potential to disrupt supply chains making resource and material acquisition more difficult. Severe drought may cause a shortage of crops used for food, apparel, and other products and rising cost of energy and transportation could make the expense of moving goods prohibitive.
- *Changing demand.* Demand will shift as climate changes. As global temperatures rise, for example, demand for heating oil will decline as well as demand for winter goods. Consumers will prioritize sustainability in the products they buy, shifting demand toward environmentally friendly goods.
- *Changing regulations.* Regulations aimed at mitigating and preventing pollution will significantly impact businesses. Companies that produce high levels of emissions will need to invest substantial resources into upgrading facilities to reduce, capture, or eliminate emissions.
- *New energy programs and policies.* Businesses working with cap and trade programs are legally allowed a set level of emissions. Companies emitting more than their legal limit must purchase extra credits while those keeping their emissions below their legal threshold can sell their excess credits to other companies. Depending on emission patterning, cap and trade programs can be either an expense or a source of extra revenue.
- *Harsher working conditions.* As temperatures rise and weather patterns change, working conditions may become more challenging. Jobs that require physical labor will become more difficult, and costs will rise to offset burgeoning health and safety risks.
- *Increased public pressure.* As the public becomes more accepting of climate change as fact, consumers will increasingly look for products that are sustainably produced or at least have a smaller environmental impact than comparable products. Companies will be expected to become socially and environmentally responsible and take steps to reduce their carbon footprint.

Among the significant impacts of climate change on business will be destabilization of financial markets and changing skill requirements for employees.[151] Frequent and volatile weather events increase risk for providers of financial products who have little choice but to incorporate climate risk into their portfolios. Extreme weather conditions will impact the ability of borrowers to acquire loans, home mortgages, and insurance due to higher service costs associated with borrowing. In the employee arena, despite growing evidence of climate change, employees lack training in incorporating climate patterns into planning and operations. The civil engineering profession illustrates the depth of the problem.[152] Civil engineers are trained to anticipate periodic small amounts of rain—not massive inundations followed by prolonged drought. Industry systems are out of sync with climate conditions and workforce skills have not shifted to address the gap. The most desired skills are technology-based—cloud computing, marketing, and web architecture. In the same way that technology has transformed today's workforce, climate change will transform tomorrow's workforce.

Preparing for Climate Change

Leading companies are mobilizing to reduce carbon emissions and become more resilient to climate impacts. Internally, they are seeking a deeper understanding of the risks and opportunities of a changing climate and taking steps to reduce their carbon footprint (emissions from production) and handprint (emissions from the sale and use of their products). Externally, they are engaging suppliers, customers, key stakeholders, and policy makers in mitigation strategy and publicly reporting emissions and energy-usage data, climate-related risks, and management strategies. Companies are demonstrating their commitment to climate action by partnering with other companies and stakeholders on solutions and publicly supporting policies like the Paris Agreement. Basic steps that companies are taking, or should take, to prepare for climate change are described succinctly by Emily Folk in *The Environmental Magazine* and a blog published by the *Center for Climate and Energy Solutions*.[153]

■ *Create a climate action plan.* A company-wide climate action plan and associated plans for business units are the first step in preparing for climate change. Although plan components vary by type of business, every company must make decisions related to process, climate targets, and market strategy.

■ *Develop goals and targets.* Climate targets are variable among companies depending on product, policy environment, and business model. Some companies base targets on reduction of greenhouse gas emissions and others on energy use; some establish targets that are absolute while others employ elastic targets; and some focus on operational efficiency and others on sustainability. Irrespective of their basis, climate targets make good business sense. Greenhouse gas targets save money for companies through reduction in energy use and enhance their reputation with customers, shareholders, and prospective employees.

■ *Improve energy efficiency.* Energy efficiency has emerged as a key component of corporate climate change strategies. Companies that develop efficiency strategies encompassing internal operations, supply chains, and products and services quickly see energy use in a new light. When calculating their carbon footprint, they typically find that energy consumption accounts for a large portion of their measurable emission impact—a finding that makes energy efficiency a sustainability imperative.

■ *Commit to internal carbon pricing.* Companies that assign a monetary value to CO_2 emissions factor carbon values into investment decisions and establish a baseline for analysis of strategy alternatives ranging from emissions reduction to low-carbon climate-resilience in operations and products.

■ *Outsource services and diversify suppliers.* To remain viable, companies have no choice but to maintain continuity of operation during climate crisis. Many brands continue to operate through partnerships with third-party companies serving customers through web commerce. Similarly, partnerships with a broad array of suppliers ensure operational continuity by enabling companies to procure production resources during extreme weather events.

- *Determine best ways to protect assets.* Once companies understand the scope and scale of risk involved in climate change, it is essential to protect assets and minimize financial loss. Many businesses possess millions of dollars in products, supplies, and assets. The best method of protecting them is awareness of the most likely risks. Companies should pinpoint and evaluate which environmental risks threaten their assets and plan accordingly.

- *Incorporate risk assessment into stakeholder documents.* Leaders would do well to be mindful of stakeholder expectations regarding climate readiness. They can start by describing climate-related actions a company has taken to reduce vulnerability to extreme weather events and demonstrate to stakeholders that it is protected against threats. At a minimum, transparency with stakeholders about climate preparedness should provide a rationale for continued affiliation with a company over the long term.

- *Innovative finance.* Some companies are preparing for climate change by financing environmental projects through green bonds or sustainability bonds. Green bonds act as vehicle for investors seeking to put capital into projects that address climate change and drive innovation and development of low-carbon products. Green bonds can be issued by a corporate bank or government entity. The debt insurance provided by investors removes the need for companies to tap into limited credit lines or cash reserves to fund renewable or energy efficiency projects.

- *Crisis response plan.* A primary step companies should take in preparation for climate threats is to have a well-defined response plan. A recent AT&T survey revealed that a majority (62 percent) of companies do not have a plan for reaction to climate change events.[154] Companies would do well prepare for the inevitability of climate challenges by conducting vulnerability assessments and developing concrete action plans. Preparedness is essential for minimizing damage and the time required to restore normal operations after a crisis.

Social and Environmental Responsibility

On August 19, 2019, the Business Roundtable issued an open letter titled "Statement on the Purpose of a Corporation" that extended the business model of corporations to a purpose beyond profit.[155] Sandwiched between the title and the signatures of 181 top executives was a one-page declaration that ended as follows: "Each of our stakeholders is essential. We commit to deliver value to all of them, for the future success of our companies, our communities, and our country."[156] This statement explicitly countered the world view of Milton Friedman (1970) that the "business of business is business, and the sole focus of the CEO is to maximize the profits of business."[157]

Despite growing attention to climate change and its economic impact, many if not most of the corporate boardrooms are grappling with how to embed a viable climate strategy into their business models. The carbon tax is a strategy backed by a growing number of businesses as a solution to climate change. The thinking behind the tax is simple. Companies pay for what they pollute and face rapidly increasing costs if targets are not met. Companies supporting the tax represent a broad coalition, from oil giants like ExxonMobil to tech behemoths like Microsoft, major environmental groups like Conservation International, and a range of economists and political leaders.

Strategy for managing the effects and consequences of climate change, however, is vastly more complex than a carbon tax or conventional business strategy. A knotty challenge facing corporate leaders lies in how to build strategy of sufficient breadth to address the complexity, scale, and systemic nature of climate change. The impact of climate change—whether through the disruptions it causes or policy to avert it—will play out over a horizon that far exceeds the typical business planning cycle. There is the matter of obligation to investors, customers, and especially the communities that businesses serve. Investors will expect leaders and boards to take ownership of climate change by ensuring that risks and opportunities are systematically embedded in plans and business operations. Customers will expect to do business with companies that care about the environment. Communities will expect companies to take an active role in responding to climate change. Mobilization, however, is not a standard element of the business playbook. It will require new thinking and approaches to leadership and governance to bridge the divide between traditional business practices, climate science, investor expectations, and community engagement. As yet, guidance to assist corporate leaders and boards in understanding and acting on climate change in partnership with communities is negligible.

A Challenge

Climate change affects the economic and social structure of communities already exposed to a range of stressors. Extreme weather and climate-related impacts put essential systems at risk including water resources, food production and distribution, energy and transportation, public health, and security. For companies and leaders slow to prepare for the impact and consequences of climate change, I offer a challenge:

> Put yourself in the position of CEO of a for-profit company in a mid-size midwestern city on the eastern bank of the Mississippi River. Your company is a primary employer and for years has operated on the basis of profit, market reputation, and financial stability. Over the past couple of years, conditions have changed dramatically and the city and region are enmeshed in a climate challenge that has morphed into a catastrophe:
>
> - *soaring temperatures and extended drought* —60 consecutive days of temperatures exceeding 100 degrees following two years of minimal rainfall
> - *extreme weather* —two weeks of drenching rainfall on a daily basis
> - *runoff and flooding* —a river 10 feet above flood stage and land under 2–4 feet of water 50 miles in every direction
> - *disrupted systems* —water, energy, transportation, health services, and food resources that are inaccessible to all but the most affluent citizens
> - *alarmed citizens* —citizens divided by age, income, political affiliation, ideology, and access to essential systems edging toward panic
> - *emergency help interrupted* —emergency help suspended because transportation arteries in the western portion of the state are closed
>
> Your company has long been a pillar of economic stability for the city and its citizens. Now, however, it is being looked to for something entirely different—leadership for mobilization in response to a crisis of catastrophic proportion. Long-standing company benchmarks of profit, market reputation, and financial stability are irrelevant. What matters now are the actions your company will take to help the community in a time of crisis. Is climate risk part of your company's strategic plan? Does your company have a crisis response plan? Are resources and leadership capability in place to respond to the crisis? What steps will your company take to help the community and mobilize it to action?

Notes

1 "Transcript: Greta Thuneberg's Speech at the U.N. Climate Action Summit." *National Public Radio*, September 23, 2019.

2 UNEP, "Emissions Gap Report 2019." *Executive Summary*. United Nations Environment Programme. Nairobi, 2019.

3 "Paris Climate Accord Marks Shift Toward Low-Carbon Economy." *Globe and Mail*. Toronto, Canada, December 14, 2015. Retrieved: October 12, 2019.

4 UNEP, "Emissions Gap Report 2019."

5 Rice, D., "Sleepwalking Toward Climate Catastrophe: World Must Slash Emissions Immediately, UN Report Says." *USA TODAY*, November 26, 2019.

6 Leahy, S., "Fossil Fuel Production Plans Shred Paris Agreement." *WUWT Watt's Up With That?*, November 22, 2019. https://wattsupwiththat.com/2019/11/22fossil-fuel-production-plans-shred-paris.

7 Intergovernmental Panel on Climate Change, "IPCC Special Report on Global Warming of 1.5°C." *Summary for Policymakers*, October 8, 2018.

8 Arguez, A. and Vose, R., "The Definition of the Standard WMO Climate Normal." *World Meteorological Society*, June 2011, p. 699.

9 Intergovernmental Panel on Climate Change, "AR5 Synthesis Report: Climate Change 2014." October, 2014.

10 Ibid.

11 USGCRP, *Impacts, Risks and Adaptation in the United States: Fourth National Climate Assessment, Volume II* (D.R. Reidmiller, C.W. Avery, D.R. Easterling, K.E. Kunkel, K.L.M. Lewis, T.K. Maycock, and B.C. Stewart (eds.)). Washington, DC: U.S. Global Change Research Program, 2018, 1515pp. https://doi.org/10.7930/NCA4.

12 Ibid.

13 Ibid.

14 Ibid.

15 Ibid.

16 Ibid.

17 Ibid.

18 Ibid.

19 Ibid.

20 Institute of Medicine (US) Forum on Microbial Threats, "Global Climate Change and Extreme Weather Events: Understanding the Contributions to Infectious Disease Emergence." *Workshop Summary*. Washington, DC: National Academies Press, 2008.

21 Ibid.

22 Ibid.

23 Fitzpatrick, M. and Dunn, R., "Contemporary Climatic Analogs for 540 North American Urban Areas in the Late 21st Century." *Nature Communications*, University of Maryland Center for Environmental Science, February 12, 2019.

24 Ibid.

25 Lindsey, R., "Climate Change: Atmospheric Carbon Dioxide." *NOAA Climate.gov*, September 19, 2019.

26 Ibid.

27 Ibid.

28 Ibid.

29 American Meteorological Society, "State of the Climate." *Bulletin of the American Meteorological Society*, September, 2019.

30 Lindsey, "Climate Change: Atmospheric Carbon Dioxide."

31 Ibid.

32 Majende, A and. Parija, P., "These U.N. Climate Scientists Think They Can Halt Global Warming for $300 Billion. Here's How." *Time*, October 24, 2019.

33 Ibid.

34 U.N. World Meteorological Organization, "Global Temperatures on Track for 3–5C Rise by 2100." *Environment*, November 29, 2018.

35 Gramling, C., "Half a Degree Can Make a World of Difference." *Science and Society*, October 18, 2018.

36 Intergovernmental Panel on Climate Change, "Chapter 10: Global Climate Projections." In S. Solomon, D. Qin, M. Manning, Z. Chen, M. Marquis, K.B. Averyt, M. Tignor, and H.L. Miller (eds.), *Climate Change 2007: The Physical Science Basis. Contribution of Working Group I to the Fourth Assessment Report of the Intergovernmental Panel on Climate Change.* Cambridge, UK and New York: Cambridge University Press, 2007.

37 Lindsey, R. and Dahlman, L., "Climate Change: Global Temperature." *NOAA Climate.gov*, September 19, 2019.

38 Schwartz, J. and Popovich, N., "2018 Continues Warming Trend as 4th Hottest Year Since 1980." *New York Times*, February 7, 2019.

39 Pierre-Louis, K., "Heat Waves in the Age of Climate Change: Longer, More Frequent and More Dangerous." *New York Times*, July 19, 2019.

40 U.S. Global Change Research Program, "U.S. Heat Wave Frequency and Length Are Increasing." *Global Change.gov*. Retrieved: August 15, 2019.

41 U.S. Global Change Research Program, "2014 National Climate Assessment." *Global Change.gov*. Retrieved: August 18, 2019.

42 Ibid.

43 Ibid.

44 Kunkel, K.E. et al., "Monitoring and Understanding Trends in Extreme Storms: State of Knowledge." *Bulletin of the American Meteorological Society*, 94 (2013). https://doi.org/10.1175/BAMS-D-11-00262.1.

45 Zhang, R. and Delworth, T.L., "A New Method for Attributing Climate Variations Over the Atlantic Hurricane Basin's Main Development Region." *Geophysical Research Letters*, 36 (2009): 5. https://doi.org/10.1029/2009GL037260.

46 U.S. Global Change Research Program, "2014 National Climate Assessment."

47 Ibid.

48 Ibid.

49 Acciona, "The Link Between Climate Change and Air Pollution." *Sustainability for All*. Retrieved: November 2, 2019.

50 United Nations Environment Programme, "Air Pollution in the Form of Particulate Matter." www.unenvironment.org/news-and-stories/story/taller-plants-warming-artic-could-speed-climate-change. Retrieved: October 30, 2019.

51 Ibid.

52 Ibid.

53 Greenberg, Z., "Pollution May Be a COVID Catalyst." *The Boston Globe*, April 30, 2020.

54 Ibid.

55 Bindoff, N.L. et al., "Ch. 5: Observations: Oceanic Climate Change and Sea Level." http://archive.ipcc,ch/publications_and_data/ar4/wg1/en/ch5.html. Retrieved: October 5, 2019.

56 Albritton, et al., "Technical Summary." www.grida.no/climate/ipcc_tar/wg1/010.htm. Box 2: "What Causes Sea Level to Change?" In IPCC TAR WG1 2007.

57 Engdahl, M., "Greenland Ice Loss Much Faster Than Expected." *European Space Agency Report*, October 12, 2019.

58 USGCRP, *2017: Climate Science Special Report: Fourth National Climate Assessment, Volume I* (Wuebbles, D.J., D.W. Fahey, K.A. Hibbard, D.J. Dokken, B.C. Stewart, and T.K. Maycock (eds.)). Washington, DC: U.S. Global Change Research Program, 2017, 470pp. https://doi.org/10.7930J0J964J6.

59 Ibid.

60 Ibid.

61 Ibid.

62 Ibid.

63 Ibid.

64 Velasquez-Manoff, M., "Stands of Lonely Trees Trace the Insidious Rise of the Sea." *New York Times*, October 9, 2019.

65 USGCRP, *2017: Climate Science Special Report: Fourth Annual Climate Assessment, Volume I*.

66 Purkey, S. et al., "Warming in Deep Southern Ocean Linked to Sea-Level Rise." *Live Science*, September 10, 2010. Retrieved: October 15, 2019.

67 USGCRP, *2017: Climate Science Special Report: Fourth Annual Climate Assessment, Volume I*.

68 Ibid.

69 Fecht, S., "Changes in Ocean 'Conveyor Belt' Foretold Abrupt Climate Changes by Four Centuries." *State of the Planet*. Earth Institute/Columbia University, March 20, 2019. Retrieved: July 5, 2019.

70 Ibid.

71 USGCRP, *2017: Climate Science Special Report: Fourth Annual Climate Assessment, Volume I*.

72 NOAA Ocean Acidification Program, "Ocean Acidification." *Smithsonian*, April 2018. Retrieved: July 20, 2019.

73 Borenstein, S., "Study: One-Sixth of Sea Life May Be Lost to Warming in This Century." *The Associated Press*, July 11, 2019. Retrieved: September 7, 2019.

74 NOAA Ocean Acidification Program, "Ocean Acidification." *Smithsonian*, April, 2018. Retrieved: July 20, 2019.

75 Ibid.

76 Ibid.

77 Lightie, K., "Solar Energy, Albedo, and the Polar Regions." *Energy and the Polar Environment*. Ohio State University, October, 2008. Retrieved: October 28, 2019.

78 Shell, K., "The Albedo Effect and Global Warming." *Real Climate*, October 23, 2016. Retrieved: October 21, 2019.

79 Ibid.

80 National Oceanic and Atmospheric Administration, "Why Is Arctic Sea Ice Melting Faster Than Predicted? NOAA Probing Arctic Pollution." *Science Daily*, April 9, 2008. Retrieved: November 1, 2019.

81 Masters, J., "The Thawing Arctic: Risks and Opportunities." *Council on Foreign Relations*, December 16, 2013. Retrieved: November 12, 2019.

82 Ibid.

83 Ibid.

84 Ibid.

85 Backlund, P., A. Janetos, D. Schimel, J. Hatfield, M. Ryan, S. Archer, and D. Lettenmaier, 2008. *The Effects of Climate Change on Agriculture, Land Resources, Water Resources, and Biodiversity*. Executive Summary. A Report by the U.S. Climate Change Science Program and the Subcommittee on Global Change Research. Washington, DC, pp. 1–10.

86 Ibid.

87 United States Environmental Protection Agency, "Climate Impacts on Agriculture and Food Supply." *Climate Change Impacts*, January 19, 2017.

88 USGCRP (2014). Ziska, L. et al. "Chapter 7: Food Safety, Nutrition and Distribution." In *The Impacts of Climate Change on Human Health in the United States: A Scientific Assessment*. Washington, DC: U.S. Global Change Research Program, 2016, pp. 189–216.

89 United States Environmental Protection Agency, January 19, 2017.

90 USGCRP (2014). Hatfield, J. et al. "Chapter 6: Agriculture." In J.M. Melillo, Terese Richmond, and G.W. Yohe (eds.), *Climate Change Impacts in the United States: The Third National Climate Assessment*. Washington, DC: U.S. Global Change Research Program, 2014, pp. 150–174.

91 Ibid.

92 USGCRP (2014) Ziska, L. et al., pp. 189–216.

93 Center for Climate and Energy Solutions, "Drought and Climate Change." *U.S. Drought Monitor*, November 5, 2019.

94 Ibid.

95 Backlund, P. et al., *The Effects of Climate Change on Agriculture, Land Resources, Water Resources, and Biodiversity*, pp. 7–8.

96 National Interagency Fire Center, "Total Wildland Fires and Acres (1926–2018)." *National Interagency Coordination Center.* www.nifc.gov. Retrieved: November 3, 2019.

97 Wehner, M., J. Arnold, T. Knutson, K. Kunkel, and A. Legrande. "Droughts, Floods and Wildfires." In Wuebbles, D., D. Fahey, K. Hibbard, D. Dokken, B. Stewart, and T. Maycock (eds.), *Climate Science Special Report: Fourth National Climate Assessment, Volume I.* Washington, DC: U.S. Global Change Research Program, 2017, pp. 231–256.

98 Denchak, M., "Flooding and Climate Change: Everything You Need to Know." *National Resources Defense Council*, April 10, 2019. Retrieved: November 15, 2019.

99 Ibid.

100 Ibid.

101 Ibid.

102 Ibid.

103 Ibid.

104 Congressional Budget Office, "Expected Costs of Damage from Hurricane Winds and Storm-Related Flooding." April, 2019. www.cbo.gov/publication/55019. Retrieved: November 19, 2019.

105 Backlund, P. et al., *The Effects of Climate Change on Agriculture, Land Resources, Water Resources, and Biodiversity*, pp. 9–10.

106 Ibid.

107 Dell'Amore, C., "Species Extinction Happening 1000 Times Faster Because of Humans?" *National Geographic*, May 30, 2014. Retrieved: November 20, 2019.

108 International Union for Conservation of Nature, "Land Degradation and Climate Change." *Issues Brief*, November 2015. Retrieved: November 25, 2019.

109 Ibid.

110 United Nations University, "World Loses Trillions of Dollars of Nature's Benefits Each Year Due to Land Degradation." *Science Daily*, September 15, 2015. Retrieved: November 21, 2019.

111 The Nature Conservancy, "The Soil Science Imperative." January 24, 2019. Retrieved: November 22, 2019.

112 Backlund, P. et al., *The Effects of Climate Change on Agriculture, Land Resources, Water Resources, and Biodiversity*, p. 8.

113 Karl, T., J. Melillo, and T. Peterson (eds.), "Global Climate Change Impacts in the United States." In *United States Global Change Research Program.* New York: Cambridge University Press, 2009.

114 United States Department of Agriculture Economic Research Service, "What is Agriculture's Share of the Overall U.S. Economy?" September 20, 2019. Retrieved: October 30, 2019.

115 United States Environmental Protection Agency, "Climate Impacts on Agriculture and Food Supply." January 19, 2017. Retrieved: December 2, 2019.

116 Hatfield, J. et al., "Ch. 6: Agriculture." pp. 150–174.

117 Ibid.

118 Ibid.

119 Ziska, L. et al., "Ch. 7: Food Safety, Nutrition and Distribution." pp. 189–216.

120 Hatfield, J. et al., "Ch.6: Agriculture." pp. 150–174.

121 Backlund, P. et al., *The Effects of Climate Change on Agriculture, Land Resources, Water Resources, and Biodiversity*, pp. 6–8.

122 NOAA, *Fisheries in the United States, 2014.* NOAA Current Fishery Statistics No. 2014. National Marine Fisheries Service, 2014.

123 United States Environmental Protection Agency, "Climate Impacts on Agriculture and Food Supply." January 19, 2017. Retrieved: December 2, 2019.

124 Woetzel, J., Pinner, D., Samandari, H., Engel, H., Krishnan, M., Boland, B., and Powis, C., "Climate Risk and Response: Physical Hazards and Socioeconomic Impacts." *McKinsey Global Institute*, January, 2020.

125 National Aeronautics and Space Administration, "Responding to Climate Change: Mitigation and Adaptation." Retrieved: December 12, 2019.

126 World Meteorological Organization, "Greenhouse Gas Concentrations in Atmosphere Reach Yet Another High." *WMO Greenhouse Gas Bulletin*, November 25, 2019. Retrieved: December 4, 2019.

127 National Aeronautics and Space Administration, "Responding to Climate Change: Mitigation and Adaptation."

128 Ibid.

129 Gili, E., "With Calif. Cap and Trade Funds, a City Plagued by Pollution Plans Swift Transformation." *Energy News Network*, July 8, 2019. Retrieved: December 7, 2019.

130 Barnard, A., "A 'Climate Emergency' was Declared in New York City. Will that Change Anything?" *New York Times*, July 5, 2019.

131 Abell, D., "As Seas Rise a City Mulls a Massive Sea Barrier Across Boston Harbor." *Boston Globe*, February 18, 2017.

132 Flavelle, C. and Schwartz, J., "As Climate Risk Grows, Cities Test a Tough Strategy: Saying 'No' to Developers." *New York Times*, November 19, 2019.

133 Schwartz, J., "As Floods Keep Coming, Cities Pay Residents to Move." *New York Times*, July 6, 2019.

134 Ellsmoor, J., "New Zealand Ditches GDP for Happiness and Well-Being." *Forbes*, July 11, 2019.

135 Ibid.

136 Kunzig, R., "Cities of the Future." *National Geographic Magazine*, April 2019.

137 Ibid.

138 Intergovernmental Panel on Climate Change, "AR5 Synthesis Report: Climate Change 2024."

139 Ibid.

140 Perkins, S., "The Best Way to Reduce Your Carbon Footprint Is One the Government Isn't Telling You About." *Science*, July 11, 2017.

141 Greentumble, "Why Are Carbon Sinks Important?" November 6, 2016. Retrieved: December 12, 2019.

142 Cho, R., "Can Removing Carbon from the Atmosphere Save Us from Climate Catastrophe?" *Earth Institute/Columbia University*, November 27, 2018. Retrieved: December 12, 2019.

143 Fischetti, M., "Massive Forest Restoration Could Greatly Slow Global Warming." *Scientific American*, July 4, 2019.

144 Lal, R., "Sequestering Carbon in Soils of Arid Ecosystems." June 17, 2009. https://doi.org/10.1002/ldr.934 Retrieved: December 14, 2019.

145 The Chalkboard, "Regenerative Agriculture: The Farming Practice That Could Save the World." October 17, 2019. Retrieved: December 15, 2019.

146 Papanicolaou, N., Wacha, K., Abban, B., Wilson, C., Hatfield, J., Stanier, C., and Filley, T., "Conservation Farming Shown to Protect Carbon in Soil." *Journal of Geophysical Research: Biogeosciences*, 120(11) (2015): 2375–2401.

147 Environmental Protection Agency, "Agriculture: Sources of Greenhouse Gas Emissions by Sector." 2019. www.epa.gov/ghgemissions/global-greenhouse-gas-emissions-data. Retrieved: December 12, 219.

148 Congressional Budget Office, "Impose a Tax on Emissions of Greenhouse Gasses." Washington, DC, December 8, 2016. Retrieved: December 16, 2019.

149 Wikipedia, "Personal Carbon Credits." December 11, 2019. Retrieved: December 20, 2019.

150 Folk, E., "How Climate Change Will Affect Businesses." *Renewable Energy Magazine*, December 18, 2019. Retrieved: December 20, 2019.

151 Davenport, Coral, "Climate Change Poses Risks to Markets, Regulator Warns." *New York Times*, June 12, 2019.

152 Ruggeri, A., "How Climate Change Will Transform Business and the Workforce." *BBC Future*, July 9, 2017. Retrieved: December 20, 2019.

153 Folk, E., "How Businesses Can Prepare for Climate Change-Related Disasters." *The Environmental Magazine*, July 15, 2019. Retrieved: December 20, 2019.

154 AT&T, "AT&T Survey Finds That Most Companies View Climate Change as a Priority, But Have Not Yet Evaluated the Risks." Retrieved: February 8, 2020.

155 Gartenberg, C. and Serafeim, G., "181 Top CEOs Have Realized Companies Need a Purpose Beyond Profit." *Harvard Business Review*, August 20, 2019. Retrieved: December 20, 2019.

156 Ibid.

157 Ibid.

Chapter 5

Social Inequality

A nation will not survive morally or economically when so few have so much while so many have so little.

Bernie Sanders
U.S. Senator and politician, 2019

A growing body of research on inequality reveals mounting evidence of a decline in America's vaunted economic mobility. Where one starts on the socioeconomic ladder is increasingly likely where one will end up. In a society historically built on fair play and justice, individuals ideally will have equal access to opportunity and should benefit from their own toil. When access is unequal, resources are distributed unevenly and reward does not follow effort. The result is displacement from a preferred state depriving people of social and cultural identity and of aspiration. For society, the cost is a loss of economic mobility and productivity. For business, it is a loss of human capital—the knowledge, skills, and personal attributes needed to achieve goals and produce economic value. Access to human capital through equal opportunity is not only good business—it is essential for business success. As an essential, it brings important questions into focus: *What is the evidence and impact of social inequality? What is the cost to business of a lack of commitment to social equality?* and *What would business look like with a full commitment to equality and human rights?* Answering these questions is the aim of this chapter.

Growing Inequality

Data documenting social inequality reveal a stunning disparity in income, wealth, and opportunity between groups based on age, gender, and race and ethnicity. To appreciate the magnitude of the dilemma, put yourself in the position of CEO of a company located in a depressed community:

> *One in three residents is 65 or older, half of the residents are Black or Latino, women constitute the majority of the labor pool, and one in four residents is living at or below poverty level. Median household income for Black families is $28,500 while for white*

families it is $58,000. The 65 and older age group is the fastest growing age group in the community but its employment rate is half that of other age groups. Inside your company, employee data reveal gross disparities in representation, income, and wealth: Women are over-represented in lower-tier clerical jobs, they earn 81 cents for every dollar a male employee makes, and they earn $10,000 less annually than men in equivalent jobs. Black and Latino employees earn on average $7,500 less than white employees in equivalent jobs. Older workers—despite their large number in the community—represent only 5 percent of company employees.

Your company espouses commitment to human rights in its marketing and policy statements but its demographics and business operations indicate otherwise. Its workforce is not representative of the community and it has repeatedly passed over older workers when hiring. It has an on-the-job training program for low-income families, but the program is underfunded and serves small numbers. The executive team is talking about hiring more women and older workers but talk has yet to move to action. Given the disparity between community and company demographics, compensation for men and women, and income for different racial and ethnic groups, how can your company claim a commitment to human rights?

The Data

In January 2020, the United Nations Department of Economic and Social Affairs chronicled historically high levels of inequality that could exacerbate divisions and retard economic and social development.[1] According to the UN researchers, "more than two thirds of the world's population today reside in countries where inequality has grown." Key findings indicate:[2]

- Inequality is rising in countries that saw inequality decline in recent decades.
- Highly unequal societies make it more difficult to break out of the cycle of poverty and marginalize opportunity for economic and social development.
- Technological innovation, climate change, urbanization, and international migration exacerbate the effects of inequality.
- Inequality erodes trust in government by concentrating influence among those who are better off.
- Growing inequality benefits the wealthiest through tax codes favorable to high-income taxpayers without a concomitant benefit to low- and middle-income taxpayers.
- In developing countries, children in the poorest households, and those in the most disadvantaged ethnic groups, experience slower progress in secondary school attendance than those from wealthier families.
- Climate change is not uniform among nations; the world's poorest countries are more deeply impacted by global warming.
- Policies designed to counter climate change may increase inequality in developing countries.
- Technology breakthroughs have increased inequality by opening new opportunities for highly skilled workers and diminishing opportunity for low-skilled workers in routine labor-intensive jobs.

There is a consensus in literature and research that inequality tends to *reduce the pace and durability of growth*. World Bank studies indicate that when markets are imperfect, inequalities in power and wealth lead to wasted production potential and the formation of institutions that perpetuate inequality.[3] Inequality has been found to *subvert social cohesion*. Studies indicate that the presence of horizontal inequality among identity groups is likely to increase the risk of social and political conflict.[4] Inequality *undermines social justice and human rights.* It also places enormous pressure on communities buckling under the strain of an economic system oriented toward consumerism and unprecedented concentrations of power and wealth.[5] Finally, inequality has *devastating health impacts* which result in massive costs for health systems in unequal countries. Overall levels of health are far worse in economically depressed societies—life expectancy is shorter and rates of adult mortality, infant mortality, mental illness, and obesity are higher in poor nations.[6]

Displacement

Displacement occurs when resources are distributed unevenly among people on the basis of power, race and ethnicity, age and gender, orientation, prestige, and social class.[7] Root causes of displacement are:

- *Membership:* disparity in social position associated with age, gender, race and ethnicity, and sexual orientation.
- *Income and Wealth:* disparity based on what an individual can earn on a daily or monthly basis contributing to annual income and wealth.
- *Life Circumstance:* disparity in opportunity which improves or diminishes life quality.
- *Political Influence:* disparity brought about by access to government resources.
- *Opportunity:* disparity in potential to benefit from privileges; some people benefit less than others when equally qualified.

Displacement through Membership

Gender, race and ethnicity, and age are major contributors to income and wealth. Gender as a basis for inequality results from differential treatment of women and men in division of labor, assignment of roles and responsibilities, and allocation of rewards.[8] Racial and ethnic inequality is the result of social distinctions between racial and ethnic groups based on physical characteristics and place of origin or culture.[9] Some racial groups are more privileged, given more opportunity in the labor market, and better compensated than others. Age inequality is a function of unfair treatment of people with regard to resources, labor market opportunities, and privileges because of their age. Also known as ageism, it is a set of beliefs, attitudes, and values used to justify age-based prejudice, discrimination, and subordination.[10]

Gender inequality has been a topic of extensive discussion not only in academic, professional, and activist communities but also in governmental agencies and international bodies. Although women have made strides in work and society, they are not treated equally with men nor are they accorded the resources and access to benefits accorded to men. Some statistics:

- Women are underrepresented at the top and overrepresented at the bottom of the U.S. wage ladder. Female-dominated occupations—such as child care and domestic service—occupy the lower rungs of the U.S. wage ladder. Women make up 63 percent of workers earning the federal minimum wage.[11]
- Throughout the U.S. workforce, women remain vastly underpaid. Among full-time workers, women earned less than 81 cents for every dollar a man earned in 2016.[12]

■ American women earn less than men, on average, in all industries. The largest pay gaps are in management positions where men made $88,000 on average in 2016, compared to $55,000 for women.[13]

■ When a lifetime of work is considered, women with a professional degree, while working the same job as a man with the same title and responsibility, will make $2 million less than a man.[14]

■ Women leave the workforce with lower post-retirement resources. American women in 2017 held $42,000 in median retirement savings, compared to $123,000 for men.[15] The $15,000 average annual Social Security benefit for women lagged behind the benefit for men by $4,000 in 2017.

■ Crushing student loan burdens drag young Americans into the negative side of the wealth line, with the heaviest debt load carried by female students. Women comprise 56 percent of college students but hold nearly two-thirds of student loan debt.[16]

■ The gender poverty gap has widened over the past 50 years. In 1968, 10.8 percent of women aged 18–64 and 7.2 percent of men in this age group lived below the poverty line. In 2016, 13.4 percent of women aged 18–64 were living in poverty compared to 9.7 percent of adult men.[17]

Women's participation in work has been increasing globally, but women continue to earn lower wages than men. Structural impediments to career mobility prevent women from rising to upper rungs of the corporate ladder regardless of qualifications and achievement.

Racial and ethnic inequality has contributed to the persistence of gaps that perpetuate cycles of poverty and economic marginalization. The Economic Institute, a progressive think tank, released a report in 2018 that examined what has changed and what has not in the income divide between black and white Americans over five decades.[18] Seven numbers reported by Dwyer Gunn based on 2018 data tell the story of racial inequality in America.[19]

■ **92.3 percent:** the percentage of black Americans who graduate from high school. This number is slightly lower than the number of white Americans who graduate from high school (95.6 percent). Significant gaps persist, however, in college graduation rates. In 2018, only 22.8 percent of black Americans aged 25–29 were college graduates, in comparison to 42.1 percent of white Americans.

■ **21.8 percent:** the poverty rate among black Americans. While the gap between black and white poverty rates has narrowed since the 1960s, the black poverty rate in 2018 was still appreciably higher than the poverty rate among white Americans which stood at 8.8 percent.

■ **$40,065:** the median household income among black Americans in 2018, which was significantly lower than the median household income of white Americans ($65,041).

■ **$171,000:** the median household wealth of white Americans in 2018—approximately 10 times that of black Americans.

■ **1,730:** the number of black Americans per 100,000 in the population incarcerated in 2018. By comparison, only 270 white Americans per 100,000 were incarcerated.

■ **11.4:** the infant mortality rate, per 1,000 live births, for black infants. This was more than double the infant mortality rate of 4.9 for white infants.

■ **75.5:** life expectancy for black Americans in 2018 which is almost four years shorter than that of white Americans (79 years).

Further evidence of racial inequality is present in data showing median Black family and median Latino family share of wealth at 2 percent and 4 percent, respectively, of White family median wealth.[20] Put differently, the median White family had 41 times more wealth in 2019 than the median Black family and 22 more times the wealth of the median Latino family.[21] As with total wealth, home ownership is heavily skewed toward white families. In 2019, 72 percent of White families owned their home compared to just 44 percent of Black families.[22] Between 1983 and 2016, Latino home ownership increased dramatically but at 45 percent remained far below the rate for White home ownership.[23]

The data are clear: racial groups in the United States differ dramatically in their life chances. Compared to White families, Black and Latino families are likely to have much lower family income and much higher rates of poverty; they are also much less likely to have a college degree and have accumulated markedly less wealth. Beyond wealth, racial discrimination in education and hiring and pay practices contribute to a persistent earnings gap. In 2019, the median White worker made 28 percent more than the median Black worker and 35 percent more than the median Latino worker according to Bureau of Labor Statistics data.[24] Although the U.S. unemployment rate dropped considerably following the Great Repression and skyrocketed during the pandemic, prior to the pandemic, the 5.9 percent unemployment rate for Black job seekers was nearly twice as high as for white job seekers (3.2 percent).[25]

If current trends continue, by the middle of the 21st century, the United States will be a "majority minority" nation. If policy makers want to ensure a strong middle class, historically the backbone of the national economy, closing the "wealth divide" between white households and households of color will need to become a priority for economic policy and for business.

Age inequality is evidenced in beliefs, attitudes, and values used to justify age-based discrimination. In advanced societies such as the U.S., there is a tendency for the young and the old to be subordinated. Unequal access to wealth, assets, and rewarding jobs are the primary means by which the young and the elderly are subject to inequitable treatment. Young households today have not fared as well as young households of prior generations. Young families have fewer resources to invest in stocks or homes—the very assets whose value has risen steadily. Hence, they have not benefitted in the same way as higher-income families from asset gains tied to investment and home ownership.

Generational wealth differences are widening and the position of young adults is deteriorating according to data published by the United States Federal Reserve:

- Among households headed by people under 35 years of age, real median before-tax family income fell at an average of 0.1 percent per year between 1992 and 2016. In contrast, all other households except the 45–54 age group experienced gains in real median before-tax income during this period.[26]
- Households headed by people under 35 years of age were slower to recover from the Great Recession. Real median before-tax family income declined by 3.8 percent per year, on average, during 2007–2010—the sharpest among all age groups.[27]
- Young households were hit the hardest by the downturn in home equity during the Great Recession. Between 2007 and 2010, among all families that owned a primary residence, the real median value of residences fell the most for households headed by those under 35 years of age.[28]

Young households are much less likely to have business equity than were young households in earlier generations. In 1992, when about half of the baby boomers belonged to households headed by someone under the age of 35, 10.6 percent of under-35 households held some sort of business equity as an asset.[29] By 2016, however, the proportion of under-35 households that held business equity had fallen to 5.6 percent.[30] Given lower wealth and income levels, today's younger households are simply not as well-positioned to start their own business as were young households in the 1990s or early 2000s.

Older age groups are subject to cross-industry age bias resulting in differential access to jobs and job-related benefits. Twenty percent of all workers in the United States today are above the age of 55. In coming decades, the share of seniors age 65 and older in the U.S. working-age population is projected to rise sharply—from 19 percent currently to 29 percent in 2060—approaching equality with population groups aged 25–44 and 45–64.[31] Lower employment among those 65 and over will pose a fundamental public policy challenge as the "dependency ratio"—the ratio of nonworkers to workers—rises sharply and labor force growth slows. Policies have been introduced to increase the supply of older workers including reduction of Social Security benefits claimed at early eligibility age, elevation of the full retirement age, and reduction of taxation on earnings after Social Security benefits are claimed. These reforms, however, are easily thwarted when businesses do not respond to policy-induced efforts to boost labor supply by hiring older workers.

A report published in 2017 by the Federal Reserve Bank of San Francisco found systematic age discrimination in hiring workers nearing retirement age, particularly among women.[32] A university research team created fictitious resumes for young (aged 29–31), middle-aged (aged 49–51), and older (aged 64–66) job applicants and submitted these resumes to ads for 13,000 positions in 12 cities spread across 11 states. More than 40,000 applications were submitted for job categories employing large numbers of low- to moderate-skilled workers of all ages. The jobs included administrative assistants and secretaries (female applicants), janitors and security guards (male applicants), and retail sales (both genders). Callback data revealed age discrimination in hiring for both women and men. Across all job categories, the callback rate was higher for younger applicants and lower for older applicants.[33] Callback rates for female job applicants in administrative jobs and sales jobs were highest for young applicants, lower for middle-aged applicants, and lowest for older applicants. For male job applicants in sales, security, and janitor jobs, callback was lower for older men. The takeaway—women experience more age discrimination than men and age impacts opportunities in the job market more deeply for women than for men.[34]

Age discrimination will continue as the U.S. population grows older. By 2050, older workers are going to be in the workforce at record levels and each year until then, record levels are expected to be set. Until business addresses this problem and loopholes in legislation are resolved, ageism is going to be an ever-present threat and a significant human capital issue for society and for business

Economic Displacement

Economic displacement, commonly known as economic inequality, is a measure of the gap in income and wealth amassed by different groups in society.[35] Six data points about economic inequality in the U.S. published by FACTTANK illustrate the importance of the wealth divide in American public policy:[36]

- the highest-earning 20 percent of the U.S. households made more than half of all U.S. income in 2018
- the U.S. has the highest level of income inequality among G7 countries
- the black–white income gap in the U.S. has remained steady since 1970

- overall, 61 percent of Americans say there is too much income inequality in the country today, but views vary by political party and household income level
- the wealth gap between America's richest and poorest families more than doubled from 1989 to 2016
- middle-class incomes have grown at a slower rate than upper-tier incomes over the past five decades.

20 Facts About U.S. Inequality That Everyone Should Know published in 2011 by the Stanford Center on Poverty and Inequality depicts a steep and steady climb toward inequality in the U.S. that continues today.[37] Trendlines in this report use an array of indicators to gauge inequality: wage inequality, homelessness, gaps in education, child poverty, residential segregation, intergenerational income mobility, wealth inequality, and access to health care. The pattern of inequality profiled by these indicators is striking in terms of the disparity between societal groups living in dramatically different life circumstances. Perhaps most significant are trends in income and wealth inequality documented by the Pew Research Center in a 2019 report *Trends in Income and Wealth Inequality.*[38]

- *Wage inequality has increased substantially and uninterruptedly since 1980.* The overall level of inequality is approaching the extreme level that prevailed prior to the Great Depression. The rise in the U.S. income inequality is tied to several factors: technological change, globalization, the decline of unions, and eroding value of the minimum wage.
- *People on the lower rungs of the economic ladder are experiencing diminished economic opportunity and mobility.* In the face of rising inequality, a phenomenon referred to as The Great Gatsby Curve has evolved: the greater the income inequality in a country, the greater the relationship between the income of children and their parents.
- *Upper-income households have seen more rapid growth in income in recent decades.* Between 1971 and 2019, the share of American adults who live in middle-income households has decreased from 61 percent to 51 percent. From 1971 to 2019, the share of adults in the upper-income tier increased from 14 percent to 20 percent while the share in the lower-income tier increased from 25 percent to 29 percent. Overall, middle-tier incomes have not grown at the rate of upper-tier incomes. From 1970 to 2018, median middle-class income increased from $58,100 to $86,600, a gain of 49 percent. This was considerably less than the 64 percent increase for upper-income households. Reduction in share and tepid growth in the income of middle-class households led to a steep fall in the share of the U.S. aggregate income held by the middle class—62 percent in 1970 compared to 43 percent in 2018. Over the same period, the share held by upper-income households increased from 29 percent to 48 percent.
- *The wealth gap between upper-income families and middle- and lower-income families is sharp and rising.* The wealth gap between upper-income and middle- and lower-income families has grown wider this century. Upper-income families were the only income tier able to build on their wealth from 2001 to 2016, adding 33 percent to the median. Middle-income families saw their median net worth shrink by 20 percent and lower-income families experienced a loss of 45 percent. As of 2016, upper-income families had over 7 times as much wealth as middle-income families and 75 times as much wealth as lower-income families.
- *The rich are getting richer faster.* From 2007 to 2016, the median net worth of the richest 5 percent of the U.S. families increased by 4 percent to $4.8 million. In contrast, the net worth of families in lower tiers decreased by at least 20 percent from 2007 to 2016. As a

result, the wealth gap between America's richest and poorest families more than doubled from 1989 to 2016. In 1989, the richest 5 percent of families had 114 times as much wealth as families in the second quintile. By 2016, this ratio had increased to 248.

Countries in which there are greater social inequality bear consequences such as a decrease in life expectancy and higher incidence of disease and malnutrition because of diminished access to information, health services, and medicine. Susceptibility to mental health disorders and drug use is higher among low-income groups. And access to education and higher-paying jobs are limited for low-income groups resulting in diminished capacity to obtain goods and services.

The carefully chosen words of Winnie Byanyima, Executive Director of Oxfam International, to the World Economic Forum in 2020, put social inequality into contemporary perspective:[39]

Every January the world gets a glimpse of another world. A world of billionaires, of business and political elites, coming together for the annual meeting of the World Economic Forum in the Swiss mountain resort of Davos. Davos is an opportunity to take stock of the crisis of extreme inequality. Our inequality reports have charted the rise and fall of the lucky few over recent years. Our latest report, *Private Wealth or Public Goods*, shows that the wealth of the world's billionaires increased by 12 percent or $2.5 billion a day last year. A new billionaire was created every two days between 2017 and 2018. Meanwhile, the poorest half of humanity, 3.8 billion people, saw their wealth shrink by eleven percent. Just under half the world's population subsists on less than $5.50 a day—one school fee or medical bill away from falling into extreme poverty. . . . The extreme and growing gap between rich and poor is no accident. It is the result of policy decisions made by governments. Chief among them are decisions about how governments raise and spend our taxes. . . . Tax rates for wealthy individuals and corporations have been cut dramatically. Billionaires are paying lower rates of tax than their secretaries. In some countries, the poorest 10 percent of society are paying a higher proportion of their income in tax than the richest 10 percent. . . . At the same time, governments are allowing vital poverty-busting public services such as healthcare and education to crumble for want of funds, or outsourcing these services to private companies that exclude the poorest. These services serve as the foundations on which people can work their way out of poverty, and they're being ripped away from ordinary people. . . . Humanity can't live with this. And we don't have to. Government policies created this crisis—they can solve it by ensuring that corporations and wealthy individuals pay their fair share of tax and investing this money in free quality health care and education for all. . . . They are the basic rights of all people, and the foundation for stable societies and strong economies.

Forced Displacement

Forced displacement, commonly known as "forced migration," refers to the involuntary movement of refugees and internally displaced people from their country of origin.[40] *Conflict-induced displacement* occurs when people are forced to flee their homes as a result of armed conflict including civil war, violence, and persecution on the grounds of nationality, race, religion, political opinion, or social group.[41] *Disaster-induced displacement* occurs when people are displaced through natural phenomena (floods, volcanoes, landslides, earthquakes, and environmental change) and human-made phenomena (radioactivity).[42] *Development-induced displacement* occurs when people are compelled to move as a result of projects or policies implemented in support of development efforts.[43] Examples include infrastructure projects such as dams and airports, mining and deforestation, and conservation parks.

Conflict-induced displacement has a profound effect on inequality. The number of people forcibly displaced from their homes in 2017 occurred at a record rate of 44,000 per day.[44] This population swelled by a net 2.9 million in 2018, raising the cumulative total to 68.5 million people forcibly displaced by the close of 2018, further raising global levels of inequality.[45] The flow of forced migrants from countries such as Syria, Afghanistan, South Sudan, Myanmar, Honduras, Somalia, and Central and South American nations account for the majority of population displacement, as well as continuing conflict affecting religious and ethnic minorities. Recent efforts of the United States to limit immigration have further contributed to population displacement and increased levels of inequality.

Economic literature on migration as well as field experience of the World Bank and United Nations High Commissioner for Refugees (UNHCR) chronicle the impact of forced migration on receiving nations.[46]

- Forced migrants tend to arrive in localities where there are few job opportunities. In poor countries or regions receiving large numbers of migrants, the wages of native unskilled workers can be severely affected by refugees seeking work.
- When forced migrants arrive in large number in a poor region, they place enormous strain on public services, infrastructure, and the public purse—an occurrence that may severely fray the social and political fabric and weaken the investment climate.
- Concerns that accepting an increased number of forced migrants in advanced countries will place an undue burden on the public purse are largely unjustified. In most of the instances, the arrival of young people willing to work is likely to cause a proportionate expansion of investment and output and may also accelerate long-term economic growth.

Forced migration is a catastrophe affecting millions of families and endangering the stability of receiving nations. Because migrants do not have the option of returning to their homes, jobs from receiving nations are the only durable solution. Receiving nations will need to plan and prepare for an extended period of adjustment to large flows of refugees and will need to formulate a development plan capable of absorbing an expanded labor force. Countries that have a flexible labor market, sound macroeconomic essentials, and prosperous companies are well-positioned to absorb large numbers of refugees. Especially important are job training and employment programs sponsored by business which serve the dual purpose of stabilizing families and meeting emerging labor market needs.

Natural disasters displaced 4.5 million persons in the Americas in 2018; 1.2 million were U.S. citizens.[47] A United Nations report analyzing the human toll of natural disasters from 1998 to 2017 disclosed staggering numbers: 1.3 million killed and 4.4 billion injured, homeless, displaced, or in need of aid.[48] Worldwide reported economic losses from earthquakes, volcanic eruptions, floods, hurricanes, and other climate-related disasters totaled nearly $2.9 trillion over the past 20 years.[49] Climate-related disasters—primarily from floods, droughts, and heat waves—accounted for $2.25 trillion of the total.[50] The United States experienced more climate-related economic losses than any other country during the 20-year span—$944 billion, nearly twice the figure of China.[51]

Disasters induced by climate change are not just an ecological issue, they are also a human rights issue. Persons forcibly displaced by extreme meteorological conditions are not covered by refugee protection provisions of either their homeland or a receiving country. Climate "refugees" are difficult to count because climate change usually combines with other forces—for example, conflict, job opportunity, and quality of life—to force people from homes. Rough estimates, however, indicate that 16.1 million people were displaced worldwide by weather-related disasters in 2018, concentrated for the most part in East Asia, the Pacific, and South Asia.[52] Climate change will move disaster-induced displacement to the top of government policy agendas as rising temperatures heighten the incidence and severity of severe weather. The question is not one of "whether" this will happen but "how often" it will happen.

Development-induced displacement occurs when people are forced to leave their homes and/ or land as a result of development.[53] Historically, this occurrence has been associated with the construction of dams for hydroelectric power and irrigation, but it is also the result of projects such as mining and agriculture, the creation of military installations and airports, roadways, railways, urbanization, and industrial plants. Global estimates indicate that 15 million people each year are forced to leave their homes as a result of public and private development efforts and these numbers continue to increase as countries move from developing to developed nations.[54] Development has consequences beyond displacement. Loss of land and homes—principal assets for most of the families—is often accompanied by loss of livelihood and impoverishment. When assets are lost, the cost of recouping them is often beyond reach resulting in marginalization of socioeconomic status.

Consequences of Inequality

Even though social inequality has entered the mainstream of public consciousness, its consequences are poorly understood and subject to heated debate. Surprisingly, economists attribute negative and positive effects to social inequality. Separatist economists claim inequality is beneficial for stimulating growth through the trickle-down effect it generates.[55] Mainstream economists claim wealth concentrations create perpetually oppressed minorities, exploit disadvantaged populations, hinder economic growth, and lead to numerous social problems.[56]

Benefits of Inequality

Economists assigning an upside to social inequality argue that incentives for innovation and entrepreneurship are greater when inequality exists. Less wealthy members of society work harder, create new businesses, and invent new products to become part of higher-income groups. Kaldor maintains that long-term market patterns naturally evolve toward concentration of wealth.[57] When the gap between income levels is small, relatively low levels of investment result in lower profit margins, lower consumption levels, lower employment, and lower total income. Subsequently, markets demand higher levels of investment and innovation which require deep pools of capital to develop. The process of development and demand for investment leads to increasing concentration of capital which results in increasing division between lower classes and the wealthy investment class.[58]

Some economists argue that a society with pronounced inequality is ultimately fairer than a society with generally equal wealth distribution.[59] Unconstrained markets naturally develop pronounced economic inequalities which require redistributive policies such as progressive taxes to remediate. Taxes and redistributive policies that aim to reduce income inequality take assets from individuals without equivalent exchange. Such policies are said to benefit all segments of society, although the majority of costs are borne by the wealthy.

Harmful Effects of Inequality

Research indicates that social inequality has a significant impact on assets and opportunity in four areas: *economic growth, social cohesion, health,* and *political stability.*[60]

Economic Growth

A higher level of inequality means a higher level of poverty. As the income distribution of Americans becomes more polarized, interaction between groups on different sides of the income divide becomes more strained. Consumer spending accounts for 70 percent of all spending.[61] Because spending drives production, growth is helped or hindered by the spending habits of different income groups. Wealthy citizens save a larger fraction of their income than lower-income citizens.[62] When they receive and retain a larger share of national income in personal savings, total savings in the economy rise while spending falls. In this way, rising inequality reduces economic growth. Slower growth increases unemployment and unemployment reduces government tax revenues. Falling revenue places increasing pressure on governments to eliminate spending programs that benefit all income groups and to institute redistributive tax policies that discourage investors and slow economic growth.[63]

Social Cohesion

Social inequality is correlated with an array of social problems including higher rates of crime and addiction, poor school performance, and rising divorce rates. Correlation does not imply causation, but it is hard to dispute research evidence of an association between social inequality and a variety of social problems. Studies establish a positive relationship between income inequality and crime.[64] Disadvantaged members of society may be more likely to experience resentment and hostility as a result of their economic position resulting in a higher propensity for criminal behavior.[65] Fewer methods of lawfully obtaining resources are available for impoverished citizens in unequal societies. Even when the risk of punishment is taken into account, illegal methods of obtaining assets provide faster and better returns than legal means. Additionally, the gap between wealthy and poor may reduce enforcement spending in low-income areas and increase the crime rate. Wealthy citizens tend to cluster in secluded communities especially as the disparity between income groups widens. Affluent communities have more resources to police than poor communities resulting in less effective policing in low-income communities.

Beckman and Kawachi (2000) maintain that social inequality loosens the bonds of social solidarity and cohesion thereby dramatically altering life chances and decreasing life expectancy.[66] Access to education is limited for impoverished citizens, particularly among women. There is a higher rate of early pregnancy, increased susceptibility to mental health problems and drugs, alcoholism, and lack of access to information about healthy lifestyles. Access to health care becomes prohibitive for impoverished citizens as the cost of health care and a healthy lifestyle becomes more expensive.

Health

Impoverished citizens are subject to higher disease and mortality rates.[67] Lack of access to fresh foods is associated with obesity and higher incidence of diet-related disease among lower-income households. Poor diets are a cause of conditions such as diabetes, heart disease, osteoarthritis, and some cancers. Impoverished Americans are adversely affected by food deserts—places where residents do not have access to affordable nutritious foods such as fruits, vegetables, and whole grains. Instead of grocery stores or farmer's markets, food deserts are populated by convenience stores and gas stations which have limited shelf space for healthy options. Nutritious foods are virtually inaccessible for low-income families thereby incentivizing residents to purchase processed sugary and fatty items from convenience stores, gas stations, fast-food restaurants, and other sources of unhealthy food.[68] As a result, people living in food deserts are more prone to obesity and diet-related diseases.

Beyond the rising cost of health care associated with food deserts, poor health affects prosperity. It forces communities to cope with a marginal workforce, higher mortality rates, higher life insurance premiums, and economic decline. A weaker economy may diminish taxable resources and lead to higher overall tax rates or inferior public services. Low-income families are disproportionately burdened with higher tax rates, higher healthcare costs, limited opportunity for work, and a higher percentage of time spent on acquiring food.[69]

Political Stability

Inequality adversely impacts democracy. When wealth becomes concentrated in a small number of hands, political power tends to become skewed in favor of the wealthy few. Moneyed citizens have the capacity through connections, campaign contributions, and lobbying to influence policy in the direction of their interests. Political scientist Richard Bartel found that politicians tend to vote for the interests of their wealthy contributors rather than the constituents who elect them and whom they are supposed to represent.[70] Impoverished and working-class groups lack the connections, education, and resources to participate in the political process on equal footing with wealthy citizens. This is a cause and effect of tax reform that benefits large corporations and the wealthy, and why government does not pass legislation that would benefit the general public.

Political interest and involvement of low-income groups are substantially depressed in economically unequal societies. Survey research conducted by Frederick Solt revealed that individuals living in the most economically equal societies are four times more likely to be actively involved in politics and 2.7 times more likely to vote compared to individuals living in economically unequal societies.[71] Low-income groups are politically disadvantaged by inability to dedicate time for political activities. As families spend more time at work or securing basic needs, they are less able to invest time or resources to obtain political knowledge or participate in the political process. With decreasing participation comes political estrangement—an occurrence that further decreases participation by limiting influence that can be brought to bear on policy outcomes

Inequality, Human Rights, and Business

When one puts the "benefits" of inequality side-by-side with its negative consequences, a clear picture emerges of its appalling toll. Not only is it intolerable for ethical reasons—reduction of inequality and advocacy of human rights are also in the best interest of business. Extreme inequality is a root cause of economic inefficiency. In order to grow economically, a society must have robust rates of consumption. If most of the wealth of a country is owned by a small percentage of its population, that wealth is not spent—it is saved and invested by individuals. When consumption rates drop because of excess savings, banks may move to lower interest rates to increase the availability of credit which can further fuel speculative investment. If investment growth is not carefully monitored, asset price collapses can flatten growth such as the subprime lending crisis that occurred during the 2008 Great Recession.

When wealth is more evenly distributed among lower-income groups who spend more of their income on goods and services, consumption goes up. Lower-income families empowered through greater income equality drive consumption, new markets, and economic growth. On the surface, this line of reasoning would seem obvious even to the most casual observer, but will it hold water with business organizations and leaders? For the sake of argument, let's say that reduction of inequality and advocacy of human rights are good for business. Your shareholders concur and have expressed deep interest in furthering your company's commitment to human rights. They are looking for results and your company will need to change how it does business to deliver results. How will you do it? What would your company look like with a full commitment to human rights?

Companies of Principle

Companies with a full commitment to human rights—"companies of principle"—understand the distinction between expression and action on inequality. While both are important, recognizing the distinction is the first step in mobilizing to eradicate inequality. For decades, companies have given lip service to human rights but have failed to leverage discourse into action. Moving from discourse to action requires an understanding of the harmful consequences of inequality, an unwavering commitment to human rights, and a willingness to allocate resources to change. Companies of principle use assessment to shape their approach to inequality and their advocacy of human rights. They do so by asking fundamental questions about company culture, engagement with social issues, and business practices.[72]

Company Culture

- Is our workforce representative of wider society?
- Are our employees aware of, and responsive to, the needs of broad segments of society?
- Does our culture encourage outreach to communities? What are we doing to reach out to impoverished populations?
- As a company, what is our perspective on inequality and human rights?
- Is this perspective demonstrated in the actions and behavior of management and employees?
- Do our policies, practices, and communications accurately and consistently represent this perspective?
- What are our employees saying about inequality and human rights in internal communication and on social media?

Engagement with Social Issues

- What is the outlook of our employees on minimum wage? Do we support legislation increasing the minimum wage?
- As a company, do we support policy initiatives providing equal rights to economic resources, property, and goods and services?

- What is our position on immigration? Are we willing to apply company resources to aid migrants in our community?
- Do we support universal access to health care and universal health coverage?
- As a company, are we willing to invest in treatment and prevention programs for populations experiencing high rates of chronic health disorders?
- Do we support policy and programs providing access to quality preprimary education?
- Are we committed to eliminating gender, racial, and ethnic disparities in education?
- As a company, do we support programs to reduce public school dropout rates?
- Are we delivering, or willing to deliver, programs to low-income families for acquisition of knowledge and skills necessary for meaningful employment?
- Have we developed and implemented programs for job creation, entrepreneurship, and access to financial services for low-income families?
- Have we created, or are we willing to create, programs for reduction of youth disengaged from education, employment, and training?
- Are we committed to protecting labor rights and providing a secure work environment for all workers including migrants?
- Do we offer apprenticeship programs and on-the-job skill training for women, youth and minorities, and low-income families?
- Do we support and promote equal opportunity by working toward the elimination of discriminatory employment policies and practices?

Business Practices

- Do our company's mission and marketing statements clearly communicate our position on human rights?
- Have we developed and publicly shared a commitment to human rights through policy or written declaration?
- Do we employ regulatory and reporting mechanisms to protect human rights?
- Have we established company-wide standards and performance metrics that reward best practices toward equality and human rights?
- What changes have we made in our business practices to improve working conditions in global supply chains?
- To what extent have we integrated human rights principles into strategy to attract and retain investors, consumers, and employee talent for protection of human rights?
- Are our business practices built around awareness of human rights risks and impacts? Do they reflect awareness of our scope of responsibility?
- Have we established an education program for employees to ensure they are aware of basic human rights principles and can integrate them into business operations?
- Does our company report publicly on challenges and progress with human rights?
- Has our company embedded human rights principles in existing systems and processes?
- Has our company developed mechanisms for remedying problems when human rights principles have been violated?

Companies of principle engage in a variety of human rights practices including providing their human rights policy to suppliers and vendors and committing to quantifiable targets and goals.[73] They embed human rights responsibilities in their purpose statements and charters and their commitment is institutionalized—it is not a stand-alone program. Their strategy and business models clearly articulate the connection between long-term prosperity and human rights, and they are able to communicate how their commitment to human rights creates resources and opportunity, mitigates risk, and attracts talented employees.[74] These companies see the world beyond their company-owned assets. They take a long-term view of company viability and recognize that corporate citizenship means growing human capital and contribution to the well-being of the communities in which they operate. There is an awareness that the company's impact on people and communities lives far beyond the current tenure of executives. Their commitment to human rights is articulated in terms that are compelling for future generations.

Making a Difference

Companies have choices. They can stand pat or they can get into motion. They can build an equity agenda around promises and declarations, policies backed by action, or actions backed by resources. They can work to alleviate poverty by lobbying for legislation to increase the minimum wage, helping low-income families gain access to education and health care, and developing job skills through sponsored programs. Ethical and economic realities confront companies large and small. They must commit to equity or face the prospect of damaging brand reputation, and they must choose carefully among alternatives based on resources, culture, and scale. There is a big difference between commitment to human rights and action to eradicate inequality. Equity is resource intensive and beyond the scale and capability of any one company. It involves development of sustained economic growth policies and programs in health and education; creating and improving access to jobs and income; removing barriers to equal access to resources and services; and providing access to technology and innovation.

Corporate and company leaders are well aware of the importance of human rights in a rapidly changing business environment. They know what they need to do and their involvement extends beyond profitability. For many companies, human rights commitment begins with an element of serendipity.[75] An employee or investor recognizes a human rights need in the community that a company can help with and gets the company involved. Sometimes it is something that a leader may be personally passionate about that, over time, becomes a cause the company supports. Regardless of the genesis of effort, for most of the companies, the rationale for commitment to human rights is clear: *It is the right thing to do.*

Business has not always been at the table for policy discussion about social issues. Much has changed as a result of growing recognition that government is not in a position to address and tackle social issues alone. More can be achieved with government, business, and social services working together. Business has experience that has value in addressing social issues—taking solutions to scale, creating self-funded models, and ensuring success by finding out what works and then making it standard procedure.[76] The challenge facing business is not one of whether or not to engage in issues of inequality and human rights. It is one of determining how to participate in developing solutions within the limits of current resources, how to do so in ways that are compatible with stakeholder interests, and how to work in partnership with government and not-for-profit partners.

Beyond the Horizon

Inequality and human rights are now a central focus of public policy and a rising force in business strategy. In this environment, it is hard to imagine a company without a human rights agenda. Companies will manifest their human rights commitment or face the challenge of being called out for failing to do so. The challenge moving forward will be to extend commitment into action on social inequality as part of a three-fold agenda: inequality is ethically and socially intolerable, it is economically inefficient and counterproductive for business, and it is central to business strategy.

Deepening interest and involvement with social inequality will accelerate change in the conceptualization of business purpose. Leaders seeking to position their company at the vanguard of change will incorporate profit and social purpose into strategy in ways that distinguish brand identity from that of their competitors. Tomorrow's competitive arena will be dramatically different. Social inequality will move to the center of business strategy and in so doing create an environment in which social purpose and profit are inextricably linked.

Notes

1 United Nations Department of Economic and Social Affairs. *World Social Report 2020*, January 21, 2020.

2 United Nations Department of Economic and Social Affairs. *World Social Report 2020: Executive Summary*. ST/ESA/372, January 21, 2020.

3 Milanovic, B., "Global Income Inequality: The Past Two Centuries and Implications for 21st Century." *The World Bank*, 2011. Retrieved: February 15, 2020.

4 Wilkinson, R., Kawachi, L., and Kennedy, B., "Mortality, the Social Environment, Crime and Violence." *Sociology of Health and Illness*, 20(5) (1998): 578–597.

5 Wilkinson, R. and Pickett, K., *The Spirit Level: Why More Equal Societies Almost Always Do Better*. London: Allen Kane, 2009.

6 Ibid.

7 Retrieved from https://en.wikipedia.org/w/index.php?title=Social_inequality&oldid=903233923

8 Ibid.

9 Ibid.

10 Ibid.

11 Institute for Policy Studies, "Economic Inequality Across Gender Diversity." *Inequality.org*. Retrieved: January 22, 2020.

12 Hegewisch, A., "2018: Earnings Differences by Gender, Race and Ethnicity." *Institute for Women's Policy Research*. Report C473, September 13, 2018.

13 U.S. Bureau of Labor Statistics, "Highlights of Women's Earnings in 2018." *BLS Reports*. Report 1083, November, 2019.

14 Gaille, B., "37 Gender Inequality in the Workplace Statistics." *Brandon Gaille Blog*, March 24, 2017. Retrieved: January 18, 2020.

15 Kapadia, R., "Women's Retirement Savings Are Way Behind Men's: Here's Why That Gender Gap Persists." *Barron's*, November 18, 2019. Retrieved: January 15, 2020.

16 American Association of University Women, *Deeper in Debt: Women and Student Loans*. Report 126–17, May 2017.

17 Institute for Policy Studies, "Economic Inequality Across Gender Diversity." *Inequality.org*. Retrieved: January 15, 2020.

18 Gould, E., "State of Working Wages America 2018." *Economics Policy Institute*, February 20, 2019.

19 Gunn, D., "Four Figures That Explain Racial Inequality in America." *Pacific Standard*. February 27, 2018. Retrieved: January 25, 2020.

20 Collins, C., Asante-Muhammed, D., Hoxie, J., and Terry, S., "Dreams Deferred: How Enriching the 1% Widens the Racial Wealth Divide." *Inequality.org*, Institute for Policy Studies, 2019.

21 Institute for Policy Studies, "Racial Economic Inequality." *Inequality.org*. Retrieved: January 23, 2020.

22 Collins, Asante-Muhammed, Hoxie, and Terry, "Dreams Deferred: How Enriching the 1% Widens the Racial Wealth Divide."

23 Ibid.

24 Ibid.

25 U.S. Bureau of Labor Statistics, "Civilian Unemployment, Seasonally Adjusted." December, 2019. Retrieved: February 9, 2020.

26 United States Federal Reserve, "Changes in Family Finances from 2013 to 2016: Evidence from the Survey of Consumer Finances." *Federal Reserve Bulletin*, 103(3) (September 2017).

27 Ibid.

28 Ibid.

29 Ibid.

30 Ibid.

31 Best Companies AZ, "Revealing Age Discrimination Statistics [2019]." October 2019. Retrieved: January 12, 2020.

32 Neumark, D., Burn, I., and Button, P., "Age Discrimination and Hiring of Older Workers." *Federal Reserve Bank of San Francisco*. Report 2017–06, February 27, 2017.

33 Ibid.

34 Ibid.

35 Ventura, L., "Wealth Distribution and Income Inequality by Country 2018." *Global Finance Magazine*, November 26, 2018. Retrieved: March 1, 2020.

36 Schaeffer, K., "6 Facts About Economic Inequality in the U.S." *FACTANK: News in the Numbers*, February 7, 2020. Retrieved: February 22, 2020.

37 Stanford Center on Poverty and Inequality, *20 Facts About U.S. Inequality That Everyone Should Know*, 2011. Retrieved: March 3, 2020.

38 Horowitz, J., Igielnik, R., and Kochhar, R., "Trends in Income and Wealth Inequality." *Pew Research Center*, January 9, 2020. Retrieved: February 22, 2020.

39 Byanyima, W., "The Shocking Truth About Inequality Today." *World Economic Forum*, January 21, 2019. Retrieved: February 5, 2020.

40 The Harriet and Robert Heilbrunn Department of Population and Family Health, "Forced Migration Learning Module." *Columbia University Mailman School of Public Health*. www.columbia.edu/itc.hs/pubhealth/modules/forcedMigration/definitions.html. Retrieved: 2018.

41 Ibid.

42 Ibid.

43 Ibid.

44 UNHCR United Nations High Commission for Refugees, "GLOBAL TRENDS: Forced Displacement in 2017." 2020. Retrieved: April 5, 2020.

45 Ibid.

46 Dadush, U and Niebuhr, M., "The Economic Impact of Forced Migration." *OCP Policy Center*. Carnegie Endowment for International Peace, April 22, 2016. Retrieved: April 2, 2019.

47 Internal Displacement Monitoring Center. *Global Report on Internal Displacement*, 2018. Retrieved: April 30, 2020.

48 UNISDR, *Economic Losses, Poverty and Disasters 1998–2017*, 2018. Retrieved: April 30, 2020.

49 Ibid.

50 Ibid.

51 Ibid.

52 Hackbarth, A., "16.1 People Displaced by Weather Disasters, More than by Conflict." *American Security Project*, October 1, 2019. Retrieved: April 30, 2020.

53 https://en.wikipedia.org/w/index.php?title=Development-induced_displacementg&oldid=9344498643. Retrieved: April 30, 2020.

54 Cernea, M., "Development-Induced and Conflict-Induced IDPs: Bridging the Research Divide." *Forced Migration Review* (Special Issue) (2006): 25–27.

55 Birdsong, N., "The Consequences of Economic Inequality." *Seven Pillars Institute*, February 5, 2015. Retrieved: March 12, 2020.

56 Ibid.

57 Kaldor, N., "A Model of Economic Growth." *The Economic Journal*, 67(268) (December 1957): 591–624.

58 Ibid.

59 Birdsong, "The Consequences of Economic Inequality."

60 Ibid.

61 Conan, P., "Consumer Spending Is Keeping the Economy From Shrinking—But a New Survey of 10,000 Americans Says that Might End in 2020." *Inc.*, December 4, 2019. Retrieved: April 10, 2020.

62 Marion, D., "Why Inequality Is Bad for Business." *The Borgen Project*, July 24, 2015. Retrieved: April 22, 2020.

63 Ibid.

64 Stolzenberg, L. Eitle, D., and D'Alessio, S., "Race, Economic Inequality, and Violent Crime." *Journal of Criminal Justice*, 34(303) (2006): 303–316.

65 Ibid.

66 Kawachi, I. and Berkman, L. (2000) "Social Cohesion, Social Capital, and Health." In L. Berkman and I. Kawachi (eds.), *Social Epidemiology*. New York: Oxford University Press, pp. 174–190.

67 Birdsong, "The Consequences of Economic Inequality."

68 Ibid.

69 Ibid.

70 Pressman, S., "Consequences of Inequality Will Strike Everyone Indiscriminately." *The Globe Post*, March 19, 2019. Retrieved: April 22, 2020.

71 Solt, F., "Economic Inequality and Democratic Political Engagement." *American Journal of Political Science*, 52(1) (2008): 48–60.

72 The questions clustered under headings of company culture, engagement with social issues, and business practices were adopted from three sources:

Mcintire, L., "Ten Characteristics of the World's Best Sustainability Programs." *CSRwire Talkback*.

Powell, J., "Six Policies to Reduce Economic Inequality." *Othering and Belonging Institute*.

Olinsky, B., "6 Policies to Combat Inequality." *Center for American Progress*.

Newman Stewart Company. *Behaviors That Support Equality, Diversity and Inclusion Work*.

73 Maranjian, S., "5 Leading Companies in Human Rights." *The Motley Fool*, April 17, 2013. Retrieved: April 25, 2020.

74 Ibid.

75 New Zealand Business Council for Sustainable Development, *The Social Role of Business*. Executive Summary, December 2010. Retrieved: April 22, 2020.

76 Ibid.

Chapter 6

Polarization: Factions, Filters, and Antipathy

Our collective imagination puts us in one place or another, home turf or hostile territory. What happens if polarization and ideological diffusion have turned the center into no man's land?

Beverly Gage
Professor of History and American Studies, Yale University, 2019

Picture yourself at a crowded airport departure gate. Your flight is delayed and you are surrounded by a cacophony of contradictory opinions from fellow passengers, political commentators on the television monitor, and headlines staring at you from newspapers. The man on your left is engaged in a heated argument about climate change with another passenger. The overhead TV is tuned to CNN news—a relentless stream of information about distribution of the COVID-19 vaccine, stimulus checks to help working families, severe weather in the Southeast, details about the impeachment trial in the Senate, plus diatribes favoring and opposing impeachment from representatives of a divided government. The woman to your right is braying into her telephone about the need to crack down on far-right protesters, and the traveler three seats away is commenting about the inalienable right to protest. And not to be outdone, the traveler sitting across from you is listening volume-up on his cell phone to a scientist describing the causes and consequences of climate change and what must be done to save the planet.

Unless you have endless patience or are unconscious, many perhaps most of the elements of this cacophony will disturb you. Rarely does a news cycle pass without stories of political dysfunction or conflict between groups holding divergent views. Continuing reports of government stalemates, hostile rhetoric between groups, and failed negotiations have eroded public confidence in the integrity of American institutions. Public trust in government remains at or near historic lows. Research conducted by the Pew Foundation in 2019 marked a historic low of 17 percent of Americans believing they can trust the federal government to do what is right.[1] Worse yet, trust in government remains at or near historic lows across generational lines, political parties, and racial and ethnic lines.[2]

Fueling the divide is the emergence of excessive partisanship and deep ideological divisions among officeholders, citizen coalitions, and the population as a whole. In other words, polarization—a condition in which growing numbers of people are distributed at the extremes of thought and behavior while those in the center diminish in number.[3] Polarization is a growing challenge for business. It is also a factor in risk. Four questions depict its relationship to risk:

■ How will a divided nation respond to the threat of catastrophic risk?
■ Can elected officials put aside their differences and commit to a timely course of action to address risk?
■ Can organizations and leaders work collaboratively to harness discord and galvanize public opinion around risk?
■ Can citizens come together and collectively mobilize in response to risk?

Why is polarization a challenge for business? Think about partisan rancor among employees which diminishes productivity. Think about political ideology among customers which pits them against one another and against companies viewed as embracing a different ideology. Think about communities in chaos because of partisan antipathy which makes consensus impossible to achieve. Unrestrained polarization is costly in terms of efficiency, productivity, and profit. Understanding its root causes, how it evolves and the forms it can take, and what can be done to channel or restrain its negative effects is important for business. The road to business success runs, in part, through polarization and its antithesis—consensus and collective pursuit of change.

Root Causes of Polarization

The term "polarization" can be considered to be both process and product. As process, to "polarize" means to cause division of opinion: to make differences between groups or ideas clear-cut and extreme, hardening the opposition between them. As product, "polarization" describes the tension between antagonistic groups, forces, or interests around contrasting positions which defy reconciliation. Plausible determinants of polarization include *exogenous* and *endogenous* factors.[4] Exogenous factors are externally driven and include historical circumstances and the role of media and technology, while endogenous factors are internal in origin and include determinants such as changing norms and government discord. The description of determining factors that follow is extensively drawn from a Brookings Institution report, *Thinking About Political Polarization*, issued in 2003.[5]

Exogenous Factors

Historical Circumstances

The apprehension surrounding polarization conveyed by media, pundits, and social commentators is not new. Today's social conflicts and partisan strife pale in comparison with much of the nation's past. Recall the racial apartheid that scarred America for a century after the end of slavery, and the urban riots and anti-war protests that inflamed the country during the 1960s.[6] Epic struggles raged between advocates of slavery and abolitionists, between agrarian populists and urban manufacturing interests at the end of the 19th century, and between industrial workers and owners of capital early in the 20th century. Present-day observers consider intervals of stability such as the immediate post-World War II period to be a baseline for public accord. Our past, however, says something else. Polarization has been part of America for two centuries and it will continue to rear its discordant head in the future.

Role of the Media and Technology

Some critics argue that the "culture war" in American society is an artifact of extensive non-systematic coverage by the media including flawed coverage by respected news outlets.[7] News stories exaggerate the intensity of conflict because acrimony and strident rhetoric make good copy, whereas footage of people working collaboratively doesn't sell. The proliferation of news outlets has enabled growing segments of the public to select their sources of information on the basis of partisan proclivity. Republican-leaning viewers and listeners choose talk radio, the Fox News Channel, and *the Wall Street Journal* editorial page. Democratic leaners prefer National Public Radio, long-running television broadcast networks, and the *New York Times*. Technology is a fundamental force shaping public opinion. The revolution in communications—the Internet, direct mail, and cable TV—has enabled ideological like-types to seek out and find one another, form chat groups, and proselytize.[8]

Endogenous Factors

Factors internal to institutions and government are a second force of polarization. Elected officials, politicians, the party faithful, issue advocates, and talking heads—as distinct from the electorate at large—foment discord through speech and behavior.[9] Norms related to civility and collegial deference that used to be recognized and respected have changed. Adversarial behavior is more often on display and slash-and-burn tactics are used even when they appear to offer few advantages. Running herd on the voting patterns and proclivities of party members, for example, is now a common part of political processes such as confirmation proceedings and referenda on key legislation. Further evidence of polarization is present in government discord resulting from party control of different branches of government—as in the latter days of the Trump presidency. Republican control of the Senate and Democratic control of the House of Representatives permitted partisans to move their political agenda further to the left or right than would otherwise have been possible. With the opposition marginalized to a greater extent than customary in the American system of separated powers, grievances were more loudly voiced and relations with the ruling majority became more rancorous.[10]

The Dynamic of Polarization

Polarization unfolds as differences between groups on opposite ends of an issue intensify and dwindling numbers remain neutral in the middle. As the gap between attitudes and values widens, groups may begin to harbor a belief that disagreement represents a flaw in the moral character of members in an opposing group or represents a basic shortcoming in their ability to see reality for what it really is. Common ground begins to collapse and the motivation to separate and segregate grows.[11] In-group solidarity builds among group members through distancing from a common foe. On a larger scale, as society becomes more polarized, different groups no longer see each other as adversaries coexisting in a healthy civitas but as "misguided enemies to be vanquished," resulting in a breakdown of communication.[12]

Polarization is a group phenomenon. Commonly appearing words such as "in-group," "subculture," and "tribalism" describe patterns of behavior in which loyalty to a social group supersedes other loyalties or, derogatorily, to antipathy based on group differences.[13] People routinely harbor personal opinions about issues, but personal opinions harden in a group setting and may become more extreme.[14] This phenomenon is referred to as "the risky shift" by James Stoner.[15] According to Stoner, decisions made as part of a group are more risky than decisions made individually outside of group interaction.[16] When left to their own devices, individuals tend to hold moderate views, whereas, in the context of a group, these same individuals may adopt more extreme views to fit in. Group norms drive discussion which can become heated and energized when focused on social issues. This can move ideas faster and further than individuals originally intended and propel group views toward extremes in the absence of opposing views.

A pair of theories contribute to our understanding of group polarization. *Social comparison* theory, also known as normative influence, holds that people change their opinions when in a group to fit in or be looked upon more favorably.[17] An individual new to a group may express a more moderate or extreme view of an issue than the rest of the group. That can push the group to reject the views of the new member, move toward a more extreme or moderate view, or affirm the stance that best correlates with the views of the group leader. *Informational influence* theory states that people tend to enter a discussion with favorable information on both sides of an issue and then change their opinion favoring the side that provides more or better information in support of its viewpoint.[18] This occurs most often when an individual is uncertain about what he or she believes.

Climate change offers a ready example of informational influence and social comparison in group polarization. People are less likely to be antagonistic to scientific evidence about climate change when weighing and sifting information in private space. But in a social gathering of friends who are climate change naysayers or advocates, they might be inclined to suppress opinion or express strong feelings about climate change to maintain harmonious relations. Beyond the group, the effect of polarization is readily apparent in public discourse about scientific evidence and public policy related to climate change. Individuals holding moderate views may become less prejudicial in a group setting with members holding similar views, whereas individuals who are highly prejudiced may inflate their views in a supportive group environment. The effect of polarization does not depend on the location or proximity of a support group. Media platforms such as Facebook and Twitter transcend face-to-face contact as a medium for polarization as opinionated people come together and form chat groups that solidify opinion.

Dimensions of Polarization

Polarization can be profiled on dimensions of form, intensity, and leader disposition. *Form* is a function of group identity (left versus right, liberal versus conservative, change resistors versus change adopters) which binds individuals to a unique set of group norms. *Intensity* is a measure of how vigorously a position or point of view is held. *Leader disposition* refers to the inherent qualities of mind, character, and behavior of a leader which have an effect on polarization. Leader disposition can influence polarization by moderating, reinforcing, or exacerbating existing tensions between groups. These dimensions work individually or in combination to shape the course of interaction between social groups.

Form

America is divided and the divide is palpable. Bitter debates that were once confined to Congressional hearings and cable TV have found their way into every part of our lives—Facebook feeds, dinner conversations, and neighborhood encounters. Government and politics are the most obvious and visible example of polarization as evidenced in a front-page article in the January 16, 2020, edition of the *New York Times* titled "Its Reputation Tattered, Polarized Senate Faces a Steep Impeachment Test":[19]

> It is finally the Senate's turn. And if recent history is any guide, President Trump's impeachment trial will be an intensely partisan display that will make polarization of the Clinton era look like a bygone period of political harmony. While Democrats and Republicans managed to unanimously come to terms on how to start President Bill Clinton's trial in 1999, the two parties—and their two leaders—are today irreconcilably divided on how to proceed and whether the trial is even legitimate. Hanging over the showdown is a decade of intensifying conflict exemplified by ruthless party-line rule changes, constant filibusters, poisonous confirmation fights, and a dearth of legislative action as Senate leaders shy from votes that could threaten incumbents up for re-election.

Politics and polarization go hand in hand, but the practice of clustering people on the basis of group membership—age, gender, race and ethnicity, political affiliation, etc.—can gloss over nuances of thought and behavior that provide important insights into polarization. Recent research has concluded that America has become a nation of tribes with different codes, values, and facts.[20] Findings published in *The Hidden Tribes of America* describe a populace that no longer just disagrees but rejects one another's premises and doubts the motives of others.[21] We question each other's character and block out diverse perspectives. In the media, pundits score points, mock opponents, and talk over each other. On the Internet, social media has become a hotbed of outrage, takedowns, and cruelty—often targeting total strangers. In the words of the authors of *The Hidden Tribes of America*:[22]

> Many Americans wonder who and what they can still trust. The institutions that once bound us are disappearing, and we no longer have each other's backs. Everyone appears to have a varying version of world events and it appears harder than ever to separate fact from fiction. Our news feeds seem to just echo our own views and when people post alternative opinions they are often attacked by angry mobs. We don't seem to disagree anymore without perceiving another person's views as stupid, wrong, or even evil. We're being played off each other, and told to see each other as threats and enemies, not Americans just like us but with separate experiences and views. The loudest and most extreme voices get heard, and others just feel like tuning out altogether.

America is not split into two tribes—"left and right" and "us and them"—as we have been led to believe. *The Hidden Tribes of America* study identified seven distinct groups of Americans distinguished not by who they are and what they look like, but what they believe.[23]

Progressive Activists are deeply concerned with issues concerning equity, fairness, and America's direction today. They tend to be more secular, cosmopolitan, and highly engaged with social media.

Traditional Liberals tend to be cautious, rational, and idealistic. They value tolerance and compromise. They place great faith in institutions.

Passive Liberals tend to feel isolated from their communities. They are insecure in belief and try to avoid political conversations. They have a fatalistic view of politics and feel that the circumstances of their lives are beyond their control.

The Politically Disengaged are untrusting, suspicious about external threats, conspiratorially minded, and pessimistic about progress. They tend to be patriotic yet detached from politics.

Moderates are engaged in their communities, well-informed, and civic-minded. Their faith is often an important part of their lives. They shy away from extremism of any sort.

Traditional Conservatives tend to be religious, patriotic, and highly moralistic. They believe deeply in personal responsibility and self-reliance.

Devoted Conservatives are deeply engaged with politics and hold strident, uncompromising views. They feel that America is embattled, and they perceive themselves as the last defenders of traditional values that are under threat.

These tribes were identified through survey data collected from more than 8,000 citizens statistically representative of the U.S. population based on census data.[24] Survey participants answered hundreds of questions about many of today's most important issues and their hopes, fears, and concerns about the future. Survey research was designed to understand why people held the positions they did through a series of questions that helped to identify their core beliefs about the world.[25] A statistical process of clustering was used to identify people with similar core beliefs. This process revealed *hidden tribes*—groups with distinctive views and values tied to how they express core beliefs which are not necessarily aligned with conventional demographic measures such as age, gender, level of education, race and ethnicity, or political affiliation.[26]

While the depiction of tribes reveals the extent of division between Americans, of signal importance was a finding that opened a portal to group cohesion. The largest group uncovered through Hidden Tribes research was a group of Americans called the *Exhausted Majority*—a term describing four of seven tribes detached from extreme views.[27] These groups constituted a middle ground with members neither centrist nor moderate but holding a variety of views. What distinguished the Exhausted Majority was unity of perspective in important ways: they are fed up with the polarization plaguing American government and society; are often forgotten or overlooked in public discourse because their voices are seldom heard; are flexible in their views and willing to endorse different policies according to a specific situation rather than sticking ideologically to a single set of beliefs; and they believe we can find common ground.[28]

While partisans argue and rail against one another, those who are part of the Exhausted Majority are so frustrated with the bitter polarization of politics and society, that many have checked out, ceding the floor to more strident voices.[29] Members of the Exhausted Majority aren't ideologues who dismiss as evil or ignorant people who don't share their political views. They want to talk and find a path forward.

Intensity

Polarization is not new but its intensity and expression have changed in ways that make consensus more difficult to achieve. Americans are deeply divided on climate change, inequality, gun control, same-sex marriage, abortion, immigration policy, access to health care, poverty, and a host of issues which push emotional buttons. Alignment on these issues has become increasingly tied to partisan identity—an occurrence that not only impedes compromise in social policy but also has far-reaching consequences for mobilization in periods of crisis.

Echo Chambers and Filter Bubbles

Our cavernous partisan divides are increasingly attributed to "echo chambers" and "filter bubbles"—insular patterns of information access and consumption that reinforce preexisting beliefs and limit exposure to opposing views.[30] The vast majority of Americans now visit a social media site at least once each day and a rapidly growing number list social media as their primary source of news.[31] Despite initial optimism that social media might enable individuals to access and consume a greater variety of information about current events, there is growing concern that social media has exacerbated polarization because of the tendency of people to form network ties with those who are perceived to be similar.

Complicating the relationship between social media and polarization are research findings that challenge extant literature about stereotyping and intergroup relations. A vast literature posits that interpersonal contact between opposing groups can counteract stereotypes that develop in the absence of interaction.[32] The literature further posits that intergroup contact increases the likelihood of deliberation and compromise.[33] Face-to-face and virtual contact, however, are entirely different modes of interaction and prompt questions as to whether virtual contact creates the same type of mutual understanding as face-to-face contact or whether the anonymity of social media forums emboldens people to act in an uncivil manner. Recent studies, for example, suggest that exposure to individuals with opposing views may create "backfire effects" that exacerbate polarization.[34] People who are exposed to messages on social media that conflict with their own attitudes are prone to counterargue them using emotionally motivated reasoning, which accentuates perceived differences between groups and increases commitment to preexisting beliefs.[35] This tendency suggests that polarization could be driven and reinforced by exposure to views that people disagree with, rather than being separated from them by filter bubbles.

Motivated Reasoning

Social media has turned the web into a platform for discussion and debate over polemic issues, especially when evidence supporting one side of a polemic emerges such as scientific evidence of climate change. Motivated reasoning is part of a human tendency to give credence to conclusions that are desired rather than those that are logical.[36] It can lead to false beliefs or irrational conclusions despite substantial evidence to the contrary with the desired outcome acting as a filter affecting the evaluation of events, people, and groups.[37]

Motivated reasoning begins with an impetus to arrive at a desired conclusion which generates a quest for information that is consistent with the conclusion. If there are strong feelings attached to the conclusion, an emotional stake is established. New information bearing on the conclusion elevates emotion—a circumstance that can unleash strong feelings when information contradicts personal belief. Feelings and emotions "color" how facts are received and reasoning contradictions away is psychologically easier than revising feelings.[38] Feelings come first and evidence is used in service of feelings. Evidence that supports what is already believed is accepted; that which contradicts existing beliefs is not. If this pattern continues over an extended period of time, individuals become entrenched in their beliefs and the stage is set for polarization.

Political messages on Twitter offer a good example of the effect of reasoning on thought and behavior. Online social networks have become a platform for political elites to communicate directly with the public. Little is known, however, about processes that render some political elites more influential than others when it comes to online communication. Brady et al. gauged the influence of political elites on social media by examining how message factors (characteristics of the communication) interact with source factors (characteristics of the sender) to impact messages diffused through Twitter.[39] More than a quarter-million messages sent from federal politicians (presidential candidates and members of the Senate and House of Representatives) in the year leading up to the 2016 presidential election were analyzed. Across all types of elites, a "moral contagion" effect was found—the use of moral-emotional language was definitively associated with increases in message diffusion.[40] Ideological asymmetry was also discovered—conservative elites gained greater diffusion when using moral-emotional language compared to liberal elites using rational language.[41] Emotional expressions related to moral outrage—particularly anger and disgust—yielded greater impact for elites across the political spectrum.

These findings inform our understanding of the effect of motivated reasoning in the digital age. If people want to maximize their impact on media platforms, they need to resort to moral and emotive vocabulary. Language itself becomes news as reporters turn tweets into evocative headlines that generate anxiety between groups. The news cycle shifts toward polarizing and emotionally laden content that heightens the divide between groups and creates an irreconcilable polemic.

Leader Disposition

Do leaders have an effect on polarization through words and behavior? Do opinions remain static with deeply rooted beliefs guiding people toward consistent positions on issues? Or are personal beliefs malleable with people altering their position on issues when they learn about the opinion of leaders? Are leaders holding radical positions on issues capable of intensifying polarization between groups?

Consider the following events and forge your own opinion about the contribution of leaders to polarization:

- Ten Democratic presidential candidates talking back-to-back about climate change on a nationally televised CNN forum in June 2019 against a backdrop of towns along the Mississippi River experiencing the longest stretch of major flooding in nearly a century.
- A proposal by the Trump Administration in 2019 to revise the 50-year-old National Environmental Policy Act by exempting major infrastructure projects from environmental review—the capstone of a three-year effort to roll back clean air and water protections.
- An effort by Donald Trump to overturn the results of the 2020 presidential election by refusing to concede, challenging the results in courts throughout the nation, and rallying his supporters to storm the Capitol building as Congress was in session.

Polls show that a growing number of Americans express concern about the threat of climate change, but the concern is not uniform in direction; a deep ideological and party divide exists with an overwhelming majority of Democrats seeing a dangerous ecological crisis but only a fraction of Republicans agreeing with them.[42] And it's not just about science. Climate change has become a signature issue in the culture wars, with skeptics seeing efforts to curtail environmental damage as a ploy to destroy the American way of life, whether that means packaging take-out food in styrofoam containers or using plastic bags and straws. On the other side, are a growing number of Americans who believe that climate change is a burgeoning threat. A Pew Research Center poll released in August 2019 found that the number of Americans who view climate change as a "major threat" to the well-being of America grew from 40 percent in 2013 to 57 percent in 2019.[43] But when broken down by party lines, concern about climate change resided primarily with Democrats. Among Democrats and Democratic-leaning independents, 84 percent viewed climate change as a major threat to the country's well-being, up from 58 percent in a March 2013 Pew poll.[44] Views among Republicans and Republican-leaners barely moved between 2013 and 2019 with 27 percent viewing climate change as a threat in 2019 compared to 22 percent in 2013.[45]

Voters do not form views of issues in isolation—they listen and respond to the views of political leaders.[46] When leaders diverge, voter polarization increases and when leaders converge, polarization decreases.[47] To explore the influence of leaders on mass opinion, survey experiments were conducted in Australia on political party member views of climate policy.[48] Emissions trading plans and renewable energy targets have been central issues in Australian politics over the last decade, with members of the major political parties holding divergent positions on these issues. Survey research findings revealed that party members took different positions on climate change policy upon learning what positions party leaders held.[49] When party members learned that leaders maintained divergent positions on addressing climate change, polarization increased along party lines.[50] But when party leaders converged on a policy proposal, they brought those following them into alignment—evidence that partisan bias can be overcome when leaders come together on environmental policies.[51]

Closer to home, Democrats and Republicans taking cues from party leaders are becoming more polarized. The ten Democratic contenders participating in the CNN forum referenced earlier were largely in agreement on climate change. All wanted to reach net-zero carbon emissions by 2050 and to rejoin the Paris climate agreement—a position reflected in 2019 Pew poll data revealing an overwhelming majority of Democrats and Democratic-leaning independents concerned about the threat of climate change.[52] On the Republican side, Donald Trump repeatedly mocked Democratic environmental proposals as plots to take away Americans' gas guzzling cars, burgers, and low-efficiency light bulbs. When it came to policy, Trump took an in-your-face approach. During the week that Hurricane Dorian devastated the Bahamas and moved toward the East Coast, the Trump Administration announced plans to weaken rules requiring the use of energy-efficient light bulbs and to roll back Obama-era regulations requiring oil and gas companies to control methane leaks. The combination of Trump's position on environmental regulations and Democratic candidates' position on climate change accentuated the public divide on climate change. Diverging leader positions became a nexus for resistance to change in the American "way of life" among climate change naysayers and a rallying cry for opposition to weakened regulations among environmental advocates and climate change believers.

Where Is the Center?

Risk that was once on the horizon is now on our doorstep. The effects and consequences of climate change are more pronounced; the global recovery in the aftermath of the Great Recession has given way to a synchronized slowdown driven by rising trade barriers and growing geopolitical tensions; and technology cyberattacks and artificial intelligence pose questions to leaders about surveillance, weapons systems, and video authenticity.[53] Environmental, economic, and technological risks lend new urgency to the need for action. Although the window for mitigation is still open, we live in an era of turmoil so severe that the clock cannot be turned back to the milieu of moderation and progress that was part of post-war reconstruction. Conventional wisdom would say that progress on climate change, the economy, and technology will only be possible if we find a new middle—an ideological "center" for multilateral action in the face of unilateral headwinds. But conventional wisdom is yesterday and this is today. Questions loom: Where is the "center?" What happens if a "center" no longer exists or a fraction of the population lays claim to being "centrist?" What if the "center" has become something other than a static location between opposing factions—a constantly shifting position as new ideas move from the fringe to the center transforming what was once thought to be unthinkable into conventional wisdom?[54]

The shifting basis of the center can readily be seen in the attitudes and voting behavior of Americans. In a 2012 analysis of American National Election Studies data, Abramowitz found that the share of all voters placing themselves in the center of the ideological scale—or unable to place themselves—fell from 49 percent in 1972 to 35 percent in 2012.[55] Pew Foundation survey data reinforced this finding: the share of Americans taking mixed ideological positions, rather than consistently conservative or liberal positions, stood at 39 percent in 2014, down 10 points from its level in 2004.[56] Beyond politics, the center punches below its weight societally, on issues that galvanize the public. When discourse turns to climate change, deeply held partisan identities are capable of neutralizing ideological centrism and the expertise of scientists.[57] In a political spectrum that is no longer a continuum with opinionated Americans distributed along its length, there is an unseemly ease with which politicized statements can undermine scientific consensus. Yale historian Beverly Gage has described the political spectrum in America as one with a fluid center:[58]

> Has American politics—polarized, dysfunctional and averse to compromise—lost its 'center'? Or is this just what it looks like when the center is up for debate?. . . . Our collective imagination puts us in one place or another: Trump country or Obamaland, home turf or hostile territory. A more subtle metaphor is the "political spectrum," a straight line with opinionated Americans distributed along its length. This, too, has its distorting qualities. It presupposes that there are only two fundamental worldviews, left and right, and that peoples' preferences will align, neatly and self-evidently, somewhere between them. But what happens if the center ceases to exist—or if few people want to stand on it? This supposedly is our current situation, in which polarization and ideological diffusion have turned the center into no man's land.

Media articles have predicted dire consequences of the shrinking middle. As the left and right gain strength, initiatives become increasingly difficult to mount and finish. This has fueled longing for a more orderly political sphere in which answers to pressing questions like "What are the consequences if global warming is not limited to 2°C this century?" can be assumed and consistently delivered. According to Gage, "to yearn for the center is to imagine politics without conflict in which people of good will mostly agree on basic principles and deliberate calmly about everything else."[59]

Is the center an ideal or does it have limits? Is it possible that advantages that make the center so appealing are also its greatest weakness? It can be hard to rally people around a message of pragmatism and compromise.[60] It can also be difficult to stake out and hold a centrist position in an age of multiple clashing agendas. Centrism occupies space that changes with the political tide with much depending on what happens at the extremes. As extremes change becoming more or less vitriolic, the center shifts. Ideas that once may have been on the fringe move from impossible to inevitable, from unthinkable into conventional wisdom.[61] In a fast-moving world, the center cannot occupy a fixed position or it ceases to be the center. It must continue to adapt to new challenges—the issues that appear to be insoluble but are desperately in need of solutions. Climate change is part of the evolving center—a once unthinkable occurrence that has moved from impossibility to inevitability. As its consequences become clear, the center will shift as well as the dynamic of polarization.

Transcending Polarization

Polarization is a reflection of our society: divided politically, manipulated by technology, and rife with anger and hostility. We react rather than respond, talking over one another to have the satisfaction of expressing and hearing our own opinions. It is difficult to get things done when opposing factions cannot work together to address and resolve insoluble issues. Resolution depends on greater understanding of the forces driving polarization and acting on them. Here, however, we arrive at a perplexing question. What if the increase in partisanship is not about anything of substance? What if tribalism, not ideological disagreement, is behind much or even most of the rise of polarization.[62] What if emotional identification with a partisan group is driving ideology, more than the other way around? If there is merit in this approach to analysis, we'll need to look to social and cognitive psychology for answers.

Social psychologists would focus on societal forces driving polarization: economic insecurity, growing inequality, cultural change, and the weakening of communities.[63] They would argue that a sense of belonging is lost when communities are weakened—a circumstance that leaves people vulnerable to populists who fuel the us-versus-them narrative that is characteristic of polarization. If we follow this path, it would seem that early research on polarization may have been incomplete. *Feelings* and *ideology* drive polarization. Feelings take us to the domain of affective polarization—a domain in which partisan differences are a function of the sentiment people hold toward one another, not differences in what they believe.[64] Affective and ideological polarization work hand in hand. Feelings of isolation and estrangement drive individuals to emotional identification with groups holding partisan views; group ideology is reinforced through member interaction; and partisan feelings intensify through opposition to groups holding different views.[65] Over time, negative partisanship can develop and antipathy toward an opposing group may exceed one's identification with a primary group.[66]

This does not mean that ideology plays a limited role in partisanship; the power of ideology and affect have both increased and they are hard to disentangle. Nor does it mean that reason is inconsequential and that we are prisoners of emotion. What it does mean, however, is that a purely affective or ideological account of polarization is incomplete. It means, as well, that to transcend polarization, we will need to pursue answers in the domains of affect and ideology.

Affect

Affect is the psychological basis of mood. To a considerable extent, it is conditioned by group experience. People take meaning and identity from groups that help them define who they are, their perception of others, and their position and behavior in different social contexts. "Us" versus "them" sentiment is a natural extension of group membership. When taken to extreme, it is a pivotal element of polarization and a force driving affect into partisanship.

Tajfel and Turner (1979) identify three mental processes involved in "us" versus "them" behavior which explain the role affect plays in polarization.[67]

Social categorization. People perceive themselves and others in terms of social categories—that is, as a member of a group instead of as a unique individual. The process of assigning people to categories reveals something about them—something liked or disliked, accepted or rejected, favorable or unfavorable. Appropriate behavior is defined by group norms which become a basis for acceptance or rejection of people in other groups.

Social identification. People do not participate in social situations as detached observers. Their sense of identity and how they relate to others is tied to group norms. There is an emotional significance to identification with a group that serves as a basis for expression of affect (positive or negative) toward members of other groups.

Social comparison. People determine the relative value or social standing of a rival group and its members through comparison to their own group. Self-esteem is maintained or enhanced, when one's own group compares favorably to other groups. This is critical to understanding partisanship and polarization, because groups holding different values and beliefs will clash to maintain or enhance group standing.

Affect is difficult to redirect in terms of intergroup relations without altering the basis of group membership, values, and beliefs. Steps might include:

- Encouraging leaders and influential citizens to broaden their message to include values and beliefs of groups holding different perspectives.
- Urging elected officials and political candidates to speak to values that unify the nation instead of mobilizing their base toward affirmation of partisan beliefs.
- Persuading creative artists and media to highlight the extraordinary ways in which Americans in local communities build bridges, not walls.
- Convincing technology companies to turn their resources and analytical tools toward developing platforms that help do the toil of bringing people together, rather than the lucrative work of magnifying outrage in echo chambers and filter bubbles.

Will this be enough to stem the negative tide of polarization? Perhaps not. It may take something in the order of a disaster for people to pull together. If this is so, the pandemic should have mobilized people to collective action, but it didn't happen. People did not surrender their differences about social distancing and mask wearing and work collectively toward a solution. Nations and states individually pursued containment strategies and sought vaccine supplies instead of working as a world community.

Research on intergroup conflict supports the idea that group thinking may unite entities toward a common aim.[68] The United States and Russia, for example, joined forces in World War II toward the goal of defeating Axis powers. Despite geopolitical tension and rocky diplomatic relations, both nations decided that their differences were less important than the goal of defeating the Axis coalition. Will a threat such as climate change unite nations and world communities in pursuit of survival? The answer lies in the frequency and extent of trauma induced through heat waves, wildfires and drought, sea-level rise and rampant flooding, increasingly violent weather, and damage to infrastructure. How much will it take for a critical mass to accept the reality and gravity of a threat and mobilize before it is too late?

Ideology

Ideology has long been considered a driving force in polarization. Conventionally, it has been portrayed as representing positions on issues along a continuum—liberal to conservative or left to right.[69] Recent research, however, suggests that this conception is inadequate.[70] Issue positions can cluster along multiple dimensions making ideology more complex than a one-dimensional continuum. The labels "liberal" and "conservative" confer a general sense of group identity loosely connected to issue positions that may or may not promote partisan behavior. For this reason, ideology must be recognized as both a system of beliefs and a sense of connection to like-minded others who share the same belief or opinion.[69]

Mason argues that three conceptions of ideology—issue-based ideology, identity-based ideology, and issue-based identity—are powerful forces in polarization.[71] *Issue-based ideology* is one-dimensional—polarization associated with it tends to fall into the political divide of

Democratic-Republican and left–right. *Identity-based ideology* is characterized by a psychological attachment to groups holding labels such as "liberals" and "conservatives." The third form of ideology, *issue-based identity*, is defined by social attachment to people who agree with an individual on a particular issue. Merely holding the same opinion as others, however, is not sufficient in and of itself for a group to exist. Shared opinion needs to become part of one's social identity for polarization to obtain.

Polarization is generally characterized by increasing distance between partisan groups on ideology—a negative outcome and for many the only interpretation of polarization. Iyengar, Gaurav, and Yphtach (2012) advance an alternative view of polarization labeled "affective polarization."[72] In this view, partisans increasingly dislike one another, are biased against one another, are out to vanquish one another, and feel angry at one another, without direct connection to an ideological disagreement. Affective polarization provides insight into the partisan behavior that has gripped the nation. Social attachment to an ideological group generates bias against opposing groups that is not grounded in reason. This view of polarization is contradictory to the pedestrian analysis that populates the media. It is the juncture of ideology and group loyalty that drives polarization, not orientation to an issue position.

The takeaway is that so much of what contributes to polarization is identity-based rather than issue-based. In Mason's words:[73]

> When we are discussing ideology—a presumably issue-based concept—we are not entirely discussing issues. And when we wish to know how ideological our increasing polarization truly is, the answer is that the ideological roots of polarization are largely based in our social attachments to ideological labels, not to thoughtful collections of opinion.

The sense of personhood embodied in identity-based polarization makes polarization difficult to moderate or assuage. There are methods, but they come with limitations—in particular, the challenge of altering human thought and behavior honed through years of socialization experience. Palliative methods involving modification and redirection of deeply ingrained habits and behavior—changing how people see and relate to one another on issues, watch news and browse media, and engage in politics—have drawn attention but with limited evidence of effect. Similarly, the influence of peers on individual decision-making about group membership and acceptance or rejection of partisan views holds promise for new thinking about the relationship between ideology and polarization, but this is a road less traveled and research is in a formative stage of development.

Institutions

There is a third domain for research and action on polarization—social institutions. The public's loss of confidence in them has left a void in everyday life that makes discourse onerous and problems difficult to solve. What is missing according to political analyst Yuval Levin is a structure of social life to give shape, meaning, and identity, to what we do together.[74] Institutions embody rules that transcend individuals and govern social behavior. They discourage behavior in pursuit of self-interest, and they provide stability and resources to buffer economic and social disruption. By organizing collective effort, they focus people on the common good which reinforces a sense of purpose. There is a downside. Institutions can themselves be captured by tribalism. In the words of Jonathan Rauch:[75]

> When we begin to treat institutions as obstacles to personal fulfillment and sweep them aside in an excess of democratic zeal, they are replaced by atomization and vulnerability—which in turn breed fear and vulnerability. . . . So where does that leave us? In a swamp, but with a path out. We cannot change human nature. We are stuck with our Serengeti-evolved selves. But we are rational creatures, capable of analyzing and understanding the forces that beset us, and then capable of responding. Getting traction against affective polarization and tribalism will require some direct measures, such as civic bridge-building. Even more, it will require indirect measures, such as strengthening institutions like unions, civic clubs, political-party organizations, civics education, and others. Above all, it will require re-norming: rediscovering and recommitting to virtues like lawfulness and truthfulness and forbearance and compromise.

An important first step toward combatting partisanship through institutions is understanding and awareness. When common knowledge about the importance of institutions is shared by a critical mass, a threshold will be in place on which to build personal and community connections. Ironically, the sheer crudity and sociopathy of partisans who challenge and attack the power of institutions may become a lightning rod for strengthening institutions by mobilizing people into defending them.

A Challenge

Let's put polarization into action in the business of business. You are part of the executive team of a progressive mid-Atlantic company that has just completed a vulnerability assessment. Climate change has surfaced as a preeminent threat to the company's long-term viability, and the leadership team has determined that a climate action plan is necessary. Increasingly severe coastal weather and extensive inland flooding are threatening supply chains and company assets. Worse yet, insurance costs are blowing through the roof. This is taking place against the backdrop of a community that has yet to develop a climate action plan. Your company is the largest employer in the area and community leaders rely on it for leadership in times of crisis. The need for a climate action plan is urgent not simply for your company but for the community as well. Your company has little time to waste and there is no way out. It must have a climate action plan—pronto!

Developing a plan will not be a linear process. Your company has long been recognized as a quality place to work. Its culture has been employee-centered, and communication has been fluid among and between organizational units. Times have changed, however, and internal polarization has become a force to be reckoned with. Outside company walls, you are witnessing phenomena that you never expected to see—partisan acrimony playing between Democrats and Republicans, liberals and conservatives, climate change protagonists and naysayers, and much more. Inside your company, polarization has begun to rear its ugly head among employees divided along political party and issue lines. Coworkers who were once cordial to one another speak guardedly or limit discussion to "safe" topics and "safe" people. Information specific to issue positions—once safe turf in a culture that was tolerant of diverse opinions—is withheld out of fear of reprisal from peers. It has become increasingly difficult to get things done. Employees with partisan beliefs resist collaboration with coworkers perceived as holding different beliefs. This does not bode well for company efforts to develop a climate action plan.

Standing in the way of plan development is the uncomfortable reality of employee groups that see climate change differently. Naysayers are in denial, doubters embrace alternative explanations, and believers express a growing sense of urgency. A perfect storm is brewing—mounting evidence of climate change, increasing pressure to develop a company action plan, tension between employee groups, and a community looking for leadership. You have been asked to take the point in bringing people together and developing a climate action plan. Partisan drift among employees is a mounting concern. You've done your homework and learned that polarization is as much a matter of affect as it is ideology. People take meaning and identity from groups and partisan "us" versus "them" sentiment is an extension of group membership. There is a plan to develop. How will you approach the task? Where will you start? How will you turn employee groups from partisanship to partnership?

Notes

1 Pew Research Center, "Public Trust in Government: 1958–2019." *Pew Reports*, April 11, 2019.
2 Ibid.
3 Caves, R.W., *Encyclopedia of the City*. London: Routledge, 2004, 616pp.
4 Nivola, P.S., "Thinking About Political Polarization." Brookings Foundation. *Policy Brief #139*, January 1, 2005.
5 Ibid.
6 Ibid.
7 Ibid.
8 Ibid.
9 Ibid.
10 Ibid.
11 Maiese, M. and Tova, N., "Polarization." In Guy Burgess and Heidi Burgess (eds.), *Beyond Intractability*. Boulder: Conflict Information Consortium, University of Colorado, October 2003.
12 Ibid.
13 Abrams, D., Wetherell, M., Cochrane, S., Hogg, M., and Turner, J. "Knowing What to Think by Knowing Who You Are: Self-Categorization and the Nature of Norm Formation, Conformity, and Group Polarization." *British Journal of Social Psychology*, 29(2) (1990): 97–119.
14 Myers, D. and Lamm, H. "The Group Polarization Phenomenon." *Psychological Bulletin*, 83(4) (1976): 602–627.
15 Stoner, J., "Risky and Cautious Shifts in Group Decisions: The Influence of Widely Held Values." *Journal of Experimental Psychology*, 4(4) (1968): 442–459.
16 Ibid.
17 Festinger, L., "A Theory of Social Comparison Processes." *Human Relations*, 7(2) (1954): 117–140.
18 Turner, J. "Toward a Cognitive Redefinition of the Social Group." In: H. Tajfel (ed.), *Social Identity and Intergroup Relations*. Cambridge: Cambridge University Press, 1982, pp. 15–40.
19 Hulse, C., "Its Reputation Tattered, Polarized Senate Faces Steep Impeachment Trial." *New York Times*, January 16, 2020.
20 Hawkins, S., Yudkin, D., Juan-Torres, M., and Dixon, T., "The Hidden Tribes of America." *More in Common*, October 2018.
21 Ibid.
22 Ibid.
23 Ibid.
24 Ibid.
25 Ibid.

26 Ibid.

27 Ibid.

28 Ibid.

29 Ibid.

30 Bakshy, E., Messing, S., and Adamic, L., "Exposure to Ideological Diverse News and Opinion of Facebook." *Science* (June 5, 2015): 1130–1132.

31 Shearer, E., "Social Media Outpaces Print Newspapers in the U.S. as a News Source." *Pew Research Center*, December 10, 2018.

32 Pettigrew, T. and Tropp, L., "A Meta-Analytic Test of Intergroup Contact Theory." *Journal of Personality and Social Psychology*, 90(5) (2006): 751–783.

33 Pettigrew, T., "Intergroup Contact Theory." *Annual Review of Psychology*, 49(1) (1998): 65–85.

34 Silverman, C., "The Backfire Effect." *Columbia Journalism Review*, June 17, 2011.

35 Ibid.

36 Kunda, Z., "The Caser for Motivated Reasoning." *Psychological Bulletin*, 108(3) (1990): 480–498.

37 O'Leary, A., "Teaching Tip Sheet: Motivated Reasoning." *American Psychological Association*.

38 Sanitioso, R., Kunda, Z., and Fong, G., "Motivated Person Perception: Justifying Desired Conclusions." *Journal of Personality and Social Psychology*, 59 (1990): 229–241.

39 Brady, W., Van Bavel, J., Jost, J., and Wills, J., "An Ideological Asymmetry in the Diffusion Moralized Content Among Political Elites." *OSFHOME*, September 28, 2018.

40 Ibid.

41 Ibid.

42 Dunlap, R., McCright, A., and Yarosh, J., "The Political Divide on Climate Change: Partisan Polarization Widens in the U.S." *Environment*, 58(5) (2016).

43 Kennedy, B. and Hefferon, M., "U.S. Concern About Climate Change Is Rising, but Mainly Among Democrats." *Pew Research Center*, August 28, 2019.

44 Ibid.

45 Ibid.

46 Kousser, T. and Tranter, B., "The Influence of Political Leaders on Climate Change Attitudes." *Global Environmental Change*, 50 (May 2018): 100–109.

47 Ibid.

48 Ibid.

49 Ibid.

50 Ibid.

51 Ibid.

52 Kennedy and Hefferon, "U.S. Concern About Climate Change is Rising, but Mainly Among Democrats."

53 Brende, B., "The World Is Becoming Less Stable. To Fix It, We Must Learn How to Work Together Again." *Time*, January 15, 2020.

54 Gage, B., "The Political Center Isn't Gone—Just Disputed." *The New York Times Magazine*, February 7, 2019.

55 Rauch, J., "Rethinking Polarization." *National Affairs*, No. 42, Winter 2020.

56 Ibid.

57 Ibid.

58 Gage, B., "The Political Center Isn't Gone—Just Disputed." *The New York Times Magazine*, February 7, 2019.

59 Ibid.

60 Ibid.

61 Ibid.

62 Rauch, "Rethinking Polarization."

63 Ibid.

64 Ibid.

65 Ibid.

66 Groenendyk, E., "Competing Motives in a Polarized Electorate: Political Responsiveness, Identity Defensiveness, and the Rise of Partisan Antipathy." *Political Psychology*, February 13, 2018.

67 Tajfel, H. and Turner, J., "An Integrative Theory of Intergroup Conflict." In W. Austin and S. Worchel (eds.), *The Social Psychology of Intergroup Relations*. Monterey, CA: Brooks/Cole, 1979, pp. 33–37.

68 Sidanius, J. and Pratto, F., *Social Dominance: An Intergroup Theory of Social Hierarchy and Oppression*. Cambridge, UK: Cambridge University Press, 1999.

69 Zaller, J., *The Nature and Origins of Mass Opinion*. Cambridge, UK: Cambridge University Press, 1992.

70 Devine, C., "Ideological Social Identity: Psychological Attachment to Ideological In-Groups as a Political Phenomenon and a Behavioral Influence." *Political Behavior*, 37(3) (2014): 1–27.

71 Mason, L., "Distinguishing the Polarizing Effects of Ideology as Identity, Issue Positions, and Issue-Based Identity." *National Science Foundation*. Grant No. SES-1065054, 2015.

72 Iyengar, S., Gaurav, S., and Yphtach, L. "Affect, Not Ideology: A Social Identity Perspective on Polarization." *Public Opinion Quarterly*, 76(3) (2012): 405–431.

73 Mason, L., "Distinguishing the Polarizing Effects of Ideology as Identity, Issue Positions, and Issue-Based Identity." 2015.

74 Levin, Y., "Yuval Levin on Institutions, Congress, and the Conservative Intellectual Movement." *The Federalist*, January 31, 2020.

75 Rauch, "Rethinking Polarization."

Chapter 7

Changing Social Norms

Truth is something that can't be thought about in a linear, binary true-false, facts-non-facts sense—you can't do that anymore. It's just not the way it works.

Jacob Wohl
Fraudster and Internet troll, 2019

Norms are changing in American society, and we have reached a tipping point where progressive ideas customarily spurned have become part of mainstream discourse and practices previously deemed unacceptable have become part of a "new normal." Examples of progressive change are well-documented—the Me Too Movement, gun control reform, and greenhouse gas reduction. At the same time, behavior contrary to established norms is everywhere to be seen—falsehoods peddled as truths, politicians buffeted by scandals in an era of hyper-polarization, offensive language finding acceptance in public discourse, recurring episodes of uncivil behavior, and unorthodox ideas receiving air time in mainstream circles. Numerous factors are cited for shifting norms, most often permissive standards that encourage partisan behavior in a loosely knit culture. Irrespective of cause, however, one universal stands out: change is unsettling. It signals a loss of the known and familiar in favor of the new and unknown.

The aim of this chapter is to address questions that make normative change important for society, organizations, and business:

- Do changing norms constitute a "new normal"?
- What is the process of normalization and how does it work??
- Where do "truth" and "common knowledge" fit in the "new normal"?
- What are the implications of normative transition for organizations and leaders?

The chapter opens with a focus on divergent patterns of thought and behavior that have made their way into everyday life. Unorthodoxy changes rules of the game in social discourse and business strategy. Companies that understand their purpose and move with change will flourish in times of normative transition. Those that do not will wither away in a rear-view mirror of the past.

Changing Norms: A New Normal?

The "new normal" is a term used to describe a previously atypical situation that has become standard, usual, or expected following a period of change. In business and economics, it is used to describe extraordinary periods in which financial conditions are anything but normal—for instance, the 2008–2012 global recession.[1] In climate science, it describes a condition of accelerated global warming generating a slew of undesirable effects—melting glaciers, rising oceans, and destabilizing atmospheric conditions.[2] And in the media, it manifests itself in the form of recurring episodes of aberrant behavior falling outside of social norms. As described by Ted Anthony:[3]

> Anyone hungry for a pinpoint glimpse of early 21st-century America—a slice to slide under a microscope and reveal things that hide in plain sight—need only consider the first week of February 2019. As always, there were politics—bleeding over into most everything and pushing us down uncertain roads. But here's what you got, too: race and racism, sex and sexual assault, polarization and dark technology and climate change, capitalism and socialism, and—perhaps most American of all—tabloid sensationalism. . . . It is easier than ever for Americans to participate in the maelstrom that surrounds them. Yet it is also easier than ever to feel knocked around in the storm, buffeted by events like a weather reporter hoping for a wind-whipped shot on the beach as a hurricane rolls in. But what happens when this batch of upended orthodoxies, of revelations that release the same fleeting dopamine bursts as Instagram likes, never quite abates? How do we begin to navigate where we're going if we can't take a breath to take stock of where we are right now?

In our shifting landscape, episodes of what was once irregular behavior have become usual. What was once an obscure idea has gained relevance. Policies once dismissed as out of hand—Medicare for all, a 70 percent top tax rate, sweeping action on climate change, and abolishing immigration—are being discussed in mainstream circles. In politics, the unorthodox actions of a president linking international military aid to investigation of a political rival, abruptly purging military aides who testified in impeachment hearings, and exerting influence to reduce the sentencing recommendation of Justice Department prosecutors for a convicted felon defy long-established norms and constitutional law.

The Overton Window

The Overton Window (Figure 7.1) is a useful way to understand the movement of unorthodox behavior and ideas to acceptability. Named after Joseph Overton, the "window" depicts the range of ideas and behavior the public is willing to consider and accept at a given time.[4] According to Overton, the viability of ideas and behavior depends mainly on whether they fall into an acceptable range rather than on individual preference.[5] The window shifts over time in accord with trends in social thought. Reform movements such as Me Too and equal pay for women are examples of issues that have shifted the window into a range of acceptability. Each represents a position that was once unthinkably radical become prevailing wisdom. The opposite can also occur: ideas that were once considered mainstream can move outside the window and become unacceptable.

Overton introduced the concept in the 1990s while serving as an executive at the Mackinac Center for Public Policy, a conservative think tank in Michigan.[6] To explain to potential donors what a think tank was he created a brochure with a cardboard slider. The brochure listed the range of possible policies on a single issue from least to most government intervention. On education, for example, the window might run from zero public investment in education to compulsory indoctrination in government schools. Neither of these extremes would happen—only part of the range would be achievable. When the slider was moved, different policies fell into the range of political possibility. Grass roots mobilization could shift the window. So could repetition of ideas and behavior which become normalized over time. The key is that shifts move with and through the public via gradual acceptance of ideas and behavior that used to be outside the window.

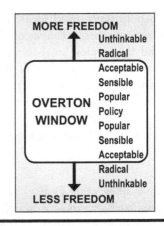

Figure 7.1 The Overton Window.

An apt description of how the Overton window works was provided by Maggie Astor in the February 25, 2019, issue of the *New York Times*:[7]

> The current shift toward progressive economic policies is clear and quantifiable. Take some of the legislation introduced by Senator Bernie Sanders, whose 2016 presidential campaign helped popularize these ideas. In 2015, his bills to make public colleges free and expand Social Security had no co-sponsors in the Senate. Two years later they had seven and 17, respectively, in addition to 50 and 133 co-sponsors in the House. His signature measure, the Medicare for All Act, had no Senate co-sponsors in 2013, but four years later it had 16, along with 125 in the House . . . His support for these policies set him apart in the 2016 Democratic field, but they are mainstream positions among the 2020 candidates—because, increasingly, they are mainstream positions among the voters those candidates are courting.

Generally speaking, policy change follows political change which follows social change. The most durable policy changes are those undergirded by strong social movements. When social forces bring about change, the window of possibility shifts up and down the spectrum and can also shift to include more options or shrink to include fewer. The window presents a menu of choices for politicians and leaders—relatively safe choices are inside the window and riskier choices are outside. The Overton Window doesn't explain everything, but it explains one important construct: in the face of resistance, politicians and leaders will be reluctant to push a policy of personal preference. Rather, they will do what is expedient to avoid defeat given prevailing societal conditions.[8] Applied to the world of behavior, people pattern thought and behavior in accord with prevailing norms. As social conditions change, norms will change and so, too, will behavior within a broadened window of acceptability.

Collapse of the Overton Window

Donald Trump instinctively challenged and defied the Overton Window with tweets, reprehensible comments, and directives that undercut government protocol. According to Window theory, only a narrow range of policies can be considered in a political arena at any given time, so politicians avoid ideas that might be considered radical by the public and pursue ideas that have a better chance of succeeding. From time to time, however, politicians attempt to expand the window so that what once was considered radical acquires daylight and edges toward the "acceptable" part of the window.[9] A policy emerges that tests the border of the Overton window. A policy initiative, for example, such as Trump's proposal for mass deportation of 11 million undocumented immigrants—something regarded as technically impossible, if not unthinkable.[10]

David French of *National Review* captured the essence of Trump's assault on convention and norms:[11]

> Then along came Donald Trump. On key issues he didn't just move the Overton Window he smashed it, scattered the shards, and rolled them with a steamroller. On issues like immigration, national security, and even the manner of political debate itself, there's no window left. Registration of Muslims? On the table. Bans on Muslims entering the country? On the table. Mass deportation? On the table. Walling off our southern border at Mexico's expense? On the table. The current GOP front-runner is advocating policies that represent mirror-image extremism to the Left's race and identity-soaked politics.

Collapse of the window marked the beginning of a voyage into discord, incivility, and heightened polarization. Ideas considered irregular became commonplace through a public all too willing to put emotion ahead of reason. An unending stream of scandals from Washington to state capitals to corporate offices gripped the nation prompting media pundits to ask whether a scandal overload had been reached—a cascade of aberrant behavior that had become part of the American way of life.

Power, Authority, and Impression

People form impressions of others on the basis of legitimacy they assign to behavior and ideas. Three decades ago, Fiske (1993) advanced the notion that power over the thought and behavior of others may be linked to processes of categorization and individuation.[12] Categorization is an effortless process employed to simplify perception. It is one of two complementary processes in a person's cognitive arsenal, the other being individuation. Categorization focuses on group membership as the basis for impression formation, whereas individuation focuses on individual characteristics as the basis for impression formation.[13] People who lack motivation to look beyond the surface to form an accurate impression of a person will use group membership to categorize the person. When people are more highly motivated, they will use their cognitive resources to form an individual-centered impression of the person.

Processes of categorization and individuation are mobilized, in part, by the behavior and ideas of people who occupy positions of power. If someone in a powerful position acts in a certain way or expresses a particular view, those actions and views may be associated with power and worthy of emulation.[14] Questionable behavior and ideas embraced by powerful people can shift norms at the speed of social life. When this happens, norms shift from the top and are reinforced by persuasive and constantly repeated media messages. This becomes the voice of authority and heretofore unacceptable behavior and ideas find a road to normalcy.

Authority figures have a strong effect on norms because they change individual assumptions about what others think. In the October 11, 2017, issue of *The New Yorker* magazine, Maria Konnikova described the process in terms of Supreme Court decisions which have shaped public impression:

> In a study in the September, 2017, issue of *Psychological Science*, Paluck and Tankard of the RAND Corporation, looked at the change in American attitudes toward same-sex marriage before and after the Supreme Court decision that established it as a constitutional right in June, 2015. In the months before the decision, Paluck and Tankard surveyed people in cities all over the country; they then repeated the survey after the decision was announced. They found that, while personal opinions on same-sex marriage hadn't shifted in the wake of the ruling, peoples' impressions of others' feelings had changed almost immediately. Americans, whether liberal or conservative, thought that their fellow-citizens now supported same-sex marriage more than before, even though, in reality, the only thing that had changed was the ruling of a public institution. The impression created by the ruling was that more Americans currently support same-sex marriage, and that even more will support it in the future.[15]

Our tendency to form impressions about people, issues, and ideas based on the opinions of authority figures helps to explain the cult-like devotion of a segment of the population to a polarizing political figure. The psychology of norms suggests that a populace holding extreme partisan views is not sufficient in and of itself to enable the use of partisanship as a social weapon. An authority figure could make the expression of partisan views—previously subtle and imperceptible—appear to be an acceptable way of showing feelings and beliefs. In the words of Betsy Paluck, Professor of Psychology and Public Affairs at Princeton University: "A leader could whip up everyone's frustration and channel it to scapegoats and make it normative to use partisan language. . . . Such an authority figure can create the impression of a social consensus where none exists."[16]

Normalization

The relationship between authority and impression offers an excellent example of the phenomenon of normalization—the process through which people no longer view irregular modes of behavior as inappropriate and accept them as normal and reasonable. For some, the process may touch off internal conflict because personal standards must be adjusted to the standards of another entity. Sociologist Diane Vaughan described the conflict between personal and extra-personal standards in a theory of normalization based on deviance from established norms.[17] Her work focused on organizations—a milieu in which deviation from established norms occurs when people become so accustomed to irregular behavior that they don't consider it irregular anymore, despite the fact that such behavior may exceed organizational norms.[18] The process is insidious. Ideas and behavior contrary to established norms are tested in low-risk situations. In the absence of rebuttal, they are repeated and reinforced, risk lessens, and ideas and behavior once considered deviant become a "new normal." The process moves through several stages:

- *Attraction:* A number of theories offer insight into why people become attracted to behavior and ideas diverging from norms. *Learning theorists* believe that people embrace divergent behavior by observing other people and witnessing the rewards or consequences their behavior receives.[19] For example, an individual watching a valued friend join a partisan interest group and adopting discriminatory beliefs of the group may be encouraged to adopt those beliefs to maintain the reward of kinship even if it is contrary to personal beliefs. *Structural strain* theorists trace attraction to a gap between cultural goals and the means available to achieve those goals.[20] When goals and means are in balance, people adhere to established norms. When they are out of balance, people are more easily attracted to ideas and behavior contrary to established norms. *Labeling* theorists argue that ideas and behavior falling outside of prevailing norms are not inherently abnormal.[21] Norms are established and enforced by people in power. By defining what is normal and abnormal and applying labels to people who adhere to or challenge prevailing norms, those in power reinforce the power structure. Subscribers to *social control theory* believe that people care about what others think of them and conform to norms because of their attachment to others.[22] Attraction to divergent behavior and ideas occurs when a person's or group's attachment to social bonds is weakened.

■ **Rationalization:** In psychology, rationalization is a defense mechanism used to justify questionable behavior in a rational or logical manner made tolerable by plausible means.[23] In the world of social norms, people facing intolerable conditions may reason that it is acceptable to embrace divergent behavior and ideas as a means for leveling an unlevel playing field.

■ **Reward:** When behavior and ideas contrary to norms are condoned or reinforced, people are rewarded for the behavior. Every positive experience with divergent behavior strengthens the reward for the behavior which, in turn, strengthens the allure of divergent norms.

■ **Normalization:** When reinforced with positive outcomes, divergent behavior evolves into a new "normal." Once this happens on a large scale, behavior and ideas previously falling outside of social norms come to be seen as a new standard for behavior.

The process of normalization, sustained over time, can lead to approach-avoidance conflict caused by simultaneous negative and positive effects of divergent behavior. People engaging in divergent behavior know that such behavior departs from prevailing norms but are motivated to do so because of the promise of a desired reward. As the reward comes into reach, awareness of negative consequences associated with norm departure may lead to indecision. If there are competing emotions attached to reward and negative consequences, the stronger of the two will prevail. For instance, a person might be motivated to join a group with extreme partisan views to experience the reward of group membership. On the other hand, he or she might avoid group membership because of the stigma associated with advocacy of extreme beliefs.

Truth and Common Knowledge

Where does truth fit in a world of partisan belief, facts that cannot be distinguished from falsehoods, authority creating the illusion of consensus, and aberration serving as a new standard for behavior? In this world, is there such a thing as "common knowledge"—knowledge that is shared, known, and accepted by a critical mass? What happens when falsehood overcomes fact, fallacy triumphs over truth, and unorthodoxy becomes the new normal? What are the implications of changing norms for a nation and world on the threshold of catastrophic risk? What are the implications for business of changing norms for thought and behavior?

The War on Truth

Almost a century ago, Walter Lippman published *Public Opinion*, an influential and disturbing critique of democracy and its future.[24] The mood in the U.S. was anxious—about immigration, about race, about civil liberties, about religion and science, and about the nation's role in the world. More Americans lived in cities than on farms, and the introduction of commercial radio was reshaping the nation's landscape. It was, in short, a time with many parallels to the time we are living in.

In *Public Opinion*, Lippman argued that the complexity of a changing world made true perception almost impossible. His mantra, "we do not first see, and then define, we define first and then see," epitomizes the condition of normative change in America today.[25] Audiences looking to affirm their own views see information more in terms of its value as a buttress for belief than a purveyor of reasoned and reliable intelligence. Recent Pew survey data found that more than half of Americans acquire their news from social media.[26] Primary among media conduits are Facebook and Twitter feeds full of articles posted by friends hailing from similar backgrounds who share similar opinions. Social media works off an algorithm that reinforces beliefs by learning what people like and feeding it back to them. Continuous repetition increases the perceived accuracy of information even if it is false and has been publicly debunked. When false information is given more weight than factual evidence, the result is a war on truth—a circumstance put into words by Peter Wehner, Senior Fellow at the Ethics and Public Policy Center:[27]

> We're in a dangerous moment. The danger is that people come to believe that nobody is giving them the facts and reality and everybody can make up their own script and their own narrative. In such a situation, truth as a concept gets obliterated because peoples' investment in certain narratives is so deep that facts simply won't get in the way.

Truth has become a diminishing commodity in American life. Recent surveys reveal a growing concern among Americans about their ability to distinguish fact from fiction. In a poll released in November 2019 by the *Associated Press-NORC Center for Public Affairs Research* and USA Facts, nearly two-thirds of Americans indicated that they often come across one-sided information and 47 percent indicated that they have difficulty in discerning if information is true.[28] False information has become a contagion-like phenomenon—a viral spread of ideas seeding in one mind and moving from mind to mind through the Internet.

Contagion is a suitable descriptor of how false beliefs propagate on the Internet. In 2011, when Donald Trump was vocally mulling over a presidential run, he publicly questioned Barack Obama's birthplace and launched a public pursuit of his birth certificate. Even though Trump did not end up running in 2012, the question of birthplace passed rapidly from person to person. The question's veracity was quickly evaluated and debunked. But as with long-standing memes, efforts to disseminate truth did not change how the rumor spread. As more individuals glommed on to the question, their misguided belief influenced friends who viewed Trump's statement and, in turn, passed the belief on to friends who simply trusted the information rather than checking its accuracy on their own. Making facts available does not help if no one bothers to check their accuracy. Closer scrutiny does not fully address and resolve the problem. False beliefs persist and spread even in communities where people are well-educated, vigilant, and persistent in gathering and sharing evidence.[29] Root cause and solution go deeper than education and cognition.

In Search of Truth

How, then, can we avoid the pitfalls of falsehood and form accurate opinions about information and events beyond our experience? Researchers have used studies in decision-making and network science to build understanding of how people process information in the face of uncertainty and incomplete knowledge. Ground-breaking research by Baruch Fischhoff at Carnegie Mellon University and Cailin O'Connor and James Weatherall at the University of California, Irvine offers insight into strategies that can be used to differentiate truth from falsehood.[30]

Clarity of Communication

Fischhoff has used climate science—a field in which scientific understanding is growing rapidly but is still incomplete—to illustrate behavioral dynamics associated with information processing and comprehension.[31] Information about climate change is heavily dependent on expert knowledge driven by evidence. It is problematic, however, for a public struggling to understand phenomena beyond personal experience and for scientists struggling to find ways to communicate with the public. In Fischhoff's words:

> The facts of climate science will not speak for themselves. The science needs to be translated into terms that are relevant to peoples' decisions about their lives, their communities, and their society. While most scientists are experienced communicators in a classroom, out in the world they may not get feedback on how clear and relevant their messages are. . . . Addressing this feedback problem is straight-forward: test messages before sending them by asking people to read and paraphrase a message. When communication researchers have asked for rephrasing about weather forecasts, for example, they have found that some are confused by the statement that there is a "70 percent chance of rain." The problems is with the words, not the number. Does the forecast mean it will rain 70 percent of the time? Over 70 percent of the area? Or there is a 70 percent chance of at least 0.01 inch of rain at the weather station?. . . . Sometimes people want to know more than the probability of rain when they make decisions. They want to understand the processes that lead to probabilities: how things work.[32]

Studies have found that climate change information is not intuitive for many people. The individual on the street does not understand why carbon dioxide is different from other pollutants or why clearing forest land increases CO_2 in the atmosphere. Lacking clarity, people more readily accept false information unless scientists can provide climate change explanations that are relevant to everyday life.

Two-Way Communication

Fischhoff has drawn on research in decision studies and climate science to illustrate the importance of two-way communication as a check on the veracity of information.[33] There is an important difference between comprehension and action when it comes to information. People can agree on facts but not necessarily on what to do with them. For instance, people who understand and accept the importance of carbon capture and sequestration may disagree on the means used to capture carbon. Cap and trade schemes are likely to be supported by some because they give companies a strong incentive to save money by cutting emissions. Others who understand how cap and trade works are just as likely to oppose them because they believe this method will benefit banks more than the environment. Two-way dialogue between parties is essential for resolution of communication gaps that, if allowed to stand, could lead to false perceptions of where people stand on issues. In Fischhoff's words:

> We need to learn what is on others' minds and make them partners in decision-making. . . . When laypeople make mistakes, it often reflects their reliance on mental models that have served them well in other situations, but that are not accurate in current circumstances. When people disagree about what decisions to make, it is often because they have different goals, not different facts. . . . Research points to ways to help people better understand one another and themselves. By reducing miscommunication and focusing on legitimate disagreements, decision researchers can help society have fewer conflicts and make dealing with the ones that remain easier for us all.[34]

Referent Influence is a strategy for mitigation of misinformation based on social network modeling. In *The Misinformation Age: How False Beliefs Spread*, O'Connor and Weatherall describe social networks as having two ingredients central to information processing: social trust and conformism.[35] Social trust shapes information processing when individuals treat some sources of information as more reliable than others. This is what happens when people trust information shared by members of their group more than evidence produced by experts. The net effect is a failure to learn from people who have access to accurate information on a subject. Communities polarize and those with misinformation squander opportunities to act on the basis of expert knowledge.

Conformism—a preference to act in the same way as others in one's group—explains the power of group membership as a conduit to misinformation. The urge to conform can lead individuals to accept misinformation as gospel.[36] Individuals subscribing to falsehoods consistent with group values may resist information provided by experts that equates with truth. Providing accurate information to naysayers will not help because of trust issues. And convincing experts or trusted community leaders to deliver important information could be counterproductive because of group loyalty. The most viable approach may be to identify individuals—"referents"—who share enough in common with a membership group to establish trust. A rabbi, for instance, may be an effective ambassador in Brooklyn, whereas in the southside of Chicago it might be an African-American community leader.

Implications for Organizations and Leaders

Changing norms are reinforced by social media that put the validity of established norms into question by exposing people to information that was limited or unavailable in the past. The ability to interact, debate, and express freely online has emboldened interest groups to challenge prevailing norms. Take for instance, the rise of climate change as an issue led by scientists and social activists. A growing volume of online scientific evidence with a borderless audience has led to worldwide awareness through repetition on media platforms. This has contributed to the normalization of discourse on climate change, pushing people and institutions to action, and putting pressure on organizations to recognize and factor climate change into their business models. The result is the evolution of a new norm—climate action—which organizations must address to maintain relevance.

All of this is well and good, but what do changing norms mean for business? Unquestionably, there is impact and it works through a company's response to change. Companies navigating uncharted waters cannot rely on legislation and regulations to do the heavy lifting of change. Regulations, if they exist, may not enforce desirable outcomes or may be at odds with changing norms. When this happens, cycles of socially damaging behavior and socially progressive behavior take on added importance. A critical mass of people adopting a new cause can rapidly spread that cause through a social network.[37] This is evidenced in the tendency of partisan groups to push unwonted ideas in public discourse and the behavior of influence groups in championing progressive norms.

Changing norms for discourse impact companies primarily through the attitudes and behavior of employees. Turning a deaf ear to uncivil behavior on the part of a small group of employees can have a groundswell impact on company culture as fellow employees observe the absence of consequences for unruly behavior. Aggressive and impudent employees are highly visible, their behavior is easy to copy, and emulation can lead to behavioral spread.[38] When a tipping point is reached, mirroring by fellow employees can lead to acceptance of unruly behavior and ultimately to normalization.

There is a virtuous side to changing norms realized in the efforts of progressive companies to incorporate new norms into culture. Initiatives such as the Me Too Movement, California legislation to increase the number of women on boards, and the Weinstein Clause offer an excellent illustration of business response to changing norms. Companies committed to gender equality have taken a hard look at their culture and values to determine whether or not their commitment to gender equality is manifested in their statements and day-to-day operations. They have done so in recognition of the value of engagement in social change and the importance of getting in front of changing norms, rather than lagging behind them.

Patsy Doerr, a leading expert in corporate social responsibility, has pinpointed three trends in corporate behavior in response to changing norms:[39]

- **Companies will embrace social impact—or fall behind.** Investing in social impact is no longer an option; it is a must for business. Until recently, companies were slow to integrate social impact into their day-to-day operations and long-term strategy. Evidence of company commitment to social responsibility is sought by talented workers weighing employment options. Companies will need to invest in social change to attract and retain the best talent as well as to engage customers and investors who care deeply about social issues.
- **Social pressure will encourage companies to use their voice.** Increasingly, companies and business leaders will take a public stand when it comes to political and social issues and in so doing utilize a powerful tool for inspiring brand loyalty. Marketing campaigns will focus more heavily on social issues and companies with a long-standing commitment to environmental issues, like Patagonia, will lean further into their brand values. Leaders will be expected to take a stance on social and political issues in response to stakeholders and consumers demanding attention to the changing sociopolitical environment.
- **Social impact driven by business investment will increase exponentially.** With the evolution of new norms, companies will move to alter business plans to accommodate social change. As social impact goals are set, strategies for achieving them will be put in place and companies will focus on long-term development in relationship to social norms instead of putting out fires for neglecting them.

Identifying and staying on top of social norms are a business essential. For leaders navigating uncharted normative waters, it will not be enough to trust trends or conventional wisdom.

Conventional wisdom can be quickly outmoded by social movements, and trends can disappear as rapidly as they appeared. A sensible path for leaders is to migrate toward norms that are evolving in a community of organizations.[40] When norms are stale, do not exist, or are changing rapidly, companies are faced with a choice of becoming a norm "taker" or "maker." There is safety in numbers for norm takers. Business communities are often bound by established norms that apply to companies that are part of the community.[41] The Forest Stewardship Council (FSC), a global body made up of timber companies, environmental NGOs, and forest certification organizations, has established a set of non-binding principles which have universal acceptance among timber companies. These principles give timber company managers assurance that by adhering to FSC certification standards, they can maintain legitimacy in periods of normative change.

In periods of turbulence norms are anything but static and sometimes they do not exist. When this happens companies are faced with the challenge of relying on norms fading into irrelevance or creating norms to fit new conditions—becoming a norm maker. Most often companies work together to create norms at the industry level or across industries through roundtables and associations. For example, facing pressure from media and stakeholders about supply chain practices and unsafe working conditions in Bangladesh factories, numerous U.S. textile brands responded with collaborative norm-making processes.[42] Twenty-eight U.S. firms formed the Alliance for Bangladesh Worker Safety—a binding five-year undertaking with the intent of improving safety in Bangladeshi ready-made garment factories. Companies can work individually as well as to create norms through strategic innovation and leading by example. This is what CVS did in 2014 when it became the first U.S. pharmacy retailer to pull cigarettes off its shelves.[43] The company's actions opened an industry-wide dialogue which led to the push for tobacco-free pharmacies in communities across the U.S.

Companies ignore norms at their own peril. At a minimum, leaders will need to stay on top of changing norms at the societal level and adjust company strategy and practices as necessary to maintain relevance. They also have a role to play in creating norms and leading by example at the industry level. Waiting is not an option. Norm taker or norm maker, normative change has become the business of business and an imperative for leaders in the changing world of risk.

Notes

1 El-Erian, M., "Navigating the New Normal in Industrial Countries." *International Monetary Fund*, December 15, 2010, p. 12.
2 Koop, F., "Extreme Weather Is the 'New Normal' (Among Other Depressing Climate Projections)." *ZME Science*, December 6, 2019.
3 Anthony, T., "Bezos, Virginia, SOTU: A Week of Telling American Glimpses." *AP News*, February 9, 2019.
4 "A Brief Explanation of the Overton Window." *Mackinac Center for Public Policy*. www.mackinac. org/12887. Retrieved: February 12, 2020.
5 Ibid.
6 Astor, M., "Once Radical, Now Mainstream: Explaining Shifts in Discourse." *New York Times*, February 25, 2019.
7 Ibid.
8 Lambert, B., "The Overton Window Collapse Theory: The Disturbing New Theory Behind Donald Trump's Political Rise." *FEELGuide*, February 21, 2016. Retrieved: February 14, 2020.
9 Shafer, J., "Donald Trump, American Demagogue." *POLITICO*, August 10, 2015. Retrieved: February 15, 2020.
10 Ibid.

11 French, D., "For Good and Ill, Donald Trump Has Brought Discussion of Political Impossibilities into the Open." *National Review*, October 8, 2015. Retrieved: February 15, 2020.

12 Fiske, S., "Controlling Other People: The Impact of Power on Stereotyping." *American Psychologist*, 48(6) (July 1993): 621–628.

13 Ibid.

14 Ibid.

15 Konnikova, M., "How Norms Change." *The New Yorker*, October 11, 2017.

16 Ibid.

17 Vaughan, D., *Controlling Unlawful Organizational Behavior: Social Structure and Corporate Misconduct*. Chicago: University of Chicago Press, 1986.

18 Ibid.

19 Ormrod, J., *Human Learning* (6th ed.). Boston, MA: Pearson, 2012.

20 Merton, R., "Social Structure and Anomie." *American Sociological Review*, 3(5) (1938), 672–682.

21 Blumer, H., *Symbolic Interactionism: Perspective and Method*. Hoboken, NJ: Prentice-Hall. Inc, 1969.

22 Gibbs, J., *Control: Sociology's Central Notion*. Urbana: University of Illinois Press, 1989.

23 Dowden, B., "Fallacy and Rationalization." *The Internet Encyclopedia of Philosophy*. www.iep.utm.edu. Retrieved: February 17, 2020.

24 Lippman, W., *Public Opinion*. New York: Harcourt Brace, and Company, 1922.

25 Ibid.

26 Geiger, A., "Key Findings About the Online News Landscape in America." *Pew Research Center*, September 11, 2019.

27 Baker, P., "In a Swelling Age of Tribalism. The Trust of a Country Teeters." *New York Times*, December 10, 2019.

28 Riccardi, N. and Fingerhut, H., "AP-NORC/USA Facts Poll: Facts Missing From American Democracy." *The Associated Press-NORC Center for Public Affairs Research*, November 20, 2019.

29 O'Connor, C. and Weatherall, J., "Why We Trust Lies." *Scientific American*, September 2019, pp. 54–61.

30 Fischhoff, B., "Tough Calls." *Scientific American*, September 2019, pp. 74–79.

31 Ibid.

32 Ibid.

33 Ibid.

34 Ibid.

35 O'Connor, C. and Weatherall, J., *The Misinformation Age*. New Haven, CT: Yale University Press, 2019.

36 Ibid.

37 Nyborg, K., Anderies, J. et al., "Social Norms as Solutions." *Science*, 354(6308) (October 7, 2016): 42–43.

38 Ibid.

39 Doerr, P., "Four Ways Social Impact Will Affect Businesses in 2019." *Forbes*, January 14, 2019. https://www.forbes.com/.../01/14/four-ways-social-impact-will-affect-businesses-in-2019. Retrieved: February 22, 2020.

40 Smith, N., "Identifying Social Norms Makes for Better Business." *INSEAD Knowledge*, June 12, 2017. Retrieved: January 29, 2021.

41 Ibid.

42 Ibid.

43 Ibid.

Chapter 8

Navigating and Falling Behind Change

Disparity is growing among countries, sectors, organizations, and individuals contributing to increasing political and social discontent with predictable results that have added to disruption.

Jacques Bughin and Jonathan Woetzel
McKinsey & Company, 2019

Powerful global forces are changing how we live and work. Prominent among them is a pandemic that has altered how we interact, where and how we work, how we travel, how we shop and dine, how we learn, and how we conduct everyday business. It has restructured the global economy and put organizations and people at risk. Whole industries have been recast, companies have shrunk or been shuttered, workers dislocated never to return to former jobs, and families thrust into financial hardship. Beyond the pandemic and its staggering impact are societies and economies roiled by the polarizing effect of inequality, the rapid spread of digital technologies, and occupational and skill shifts splintering long-held social contracts. Disruptive forces are a wellspring of opportunity for those who adapt to them successfully but a hazard for those who cannot. Worse yet, the gap between those who embrace change and those falling behind has grown disproportionately. For business leaders and policy makers, determining how to navigate change in these extraordinary times is not business as usual. It is a necessity and it requires radical rethinking.

There is a well-known quote attributed to Albert Einstein that surely guided his approach to science and thought: "The world as we have created it is a process of our thinking. . . . If we want to change the world, we have to change our thinking . . . no problem can be solved from the same consciousness that created it. We must learn to see the world anew."[1] This quote epitomizes the dynamic of change we are now experiencing because many of us know what change used to mean—a graduated process with time to catch up—and all of us know what it has come to mean today—pedal to the metal without let-up. In earlier decades, change happened through long-range planning, top–down initiation, and a stepwise approach to implementation. Words such as "early adopter" and "resister" were not part of our vocabulary. We could count on a flexible learning curve, extensive training, and tolerance for error that made change easier. This dynamic shaped our approach to life and work. Time was on our side—we could catch up if we fell behind.

All of this, of course, has changed. The fundamental notion of change—organizations and people moving from where they are to where they would like to be—has transitioned to organizations and people moving to where they must be as quickly as possible. This transition has made speed and elasticity key elements of success in an economy that has birthed entirely new industries and jobs and work settings that have been turned upside down by the pandemic. It has also brought us to a world in which more work is remote and processes and equipment require less human intervention. Imagine a "smart factory" with digital systems that monitor environmental conditions—humidity, temperature, lighting control—and make changes automatically based on occupancy or operational needs.[2] Imagine biotechnology innovations that start your day with a breakfast of synthetic eggs and lab-grown bacon tailored to your genetic requirements, outfit you with a biosynthetic suit made from fibers that can self-repair, transport you to work in a car using biofuels produced by microbes engineered through synthetic biology, and compute stress at work through a headset that measures brain waves and suggests ways to alleviate them in real time.[3] Imagine an "office" consisting of personnel working remotely from home, meeting and problem-solving through technology, and blending work and personal life to create business outcomes.

Forces Powering Change

The pandemic and technology breakthroughs have turned what until recently would have been a page out of a science fiction novel into a reality. Technology has changed the shape of occupations and jobs, and the pandemic has changed the nature of work. Discoveries have been made and new standards for the future of work have been set. Some are an improvement over the way we worked before, while others are a reflection of a new reality in which public health has taken center stage. The office that employees occupied prior to the pandemic might look the same, but it is markedly different.[4]

> The lobby at the entrance to the building has a "sanitation station" furnishing masks, neck gaiters, bottles of gel, hand wipes, and a receptacle labeled "If you touch it, wipe it." A staircase labeled for up and down traffic is used to ascend to upper-level offices rather than an elevator which can carry only two people at a time. Workers booting up a computer are greeted by a daily wellness check-in app confirming the presence or absence of symptoms. A "contact record" screen is then brought up for workers to record proximate interactions with coworkers during the work day. If someone needs help with a laptop, a technician will slip on a pair of gloves and receive the equipment through a plexiglass transfer window in the IT department. At lunch, employees put on a face covering to walk to a refrigerator and retrieve a bag brought from home. Anything left in the refrigerator is thrown away at the close of the day.

Among the impacts of the pandemic on work and workers have been the following:[5]

■ *More workers are working remotely.* The time it took to develop and administer a vaccine, the potential for additional virus surges, and financial incentives for companies to cut costs have swelled the ranks of workers working remotely.

- *Companies have turned to staggered schedules and closed floor plans for on-site workers.* Overcrowded workspaces became potential hotbeds of contamination. Staggered schedules spread workstations safely apart to reduce the number of on-site employees at any one time. They also produce savings by reducing overhead costs for employees.
- *Civic engagement and social responsibility have become more important.* Increasingly, companies have come to recognize the moral and ethical obligations they have not only to workers but to communities. The pandemic made clear the importance of awareness and responsibility for solving problems such as the adequacy of public health systems, disparities in access to health care, and educating people in life skills.
- *Work and life have been integrated.* The pandemic dismantled the notion of work–life balance. Work and life no longer exist at opposite ends of the same pole with little or no overlap. Workers have become not just employees but whole selves with family becoming part of work life.

In the domain of technology, digitization and automation have widened the gap between adopters and laggards in industries and companies and among workers. Companies investing in artificial intelligence and data analytic capabilities have distanced themselves from competitors. Automation has turned the workforce into a dichotomy of "haves" and "have nots." McKinsey & Company projections call for 15 percent of the global workforce—about 400 million workers—to be displaced by automation between 2016 and 2030.[6] Together, automation and artificial intelligence (AI) are powering four transitions that will reshape the workforce:[7]

- *Millions of workers will need to change occupations.* Occupations requiring physical activities in highly structured environments will decline, while those that are difficult to automate will grow.
- *Workers will need different skills to thrive in the workplace of the future.* Demand for digital skills will grow and automation will spur growth in the need for higher-level cognitive skills, particularly critical thinking, creativity, and complex information processing.
- *Workplaces and workflows will change as more people work alongside machines.* Workers and companies will be challenged by automation taking over more and more of basic operations. Workers will need to be retrained, and companies will need to become more adaptable.
- *Automation will put pressure on demand and average wages in advanced economies.* Worker demand and wages will decline in repetitive jobs dominated by automatable functions, while demand and wages will rise in jobs requiring advanced cognitive and analytical skills.

The forces fueling these transitions will widen the gap between haves and have nots. Companies will be pushed to rethink how they do business, and workers will be expected to adapt at a speed and intensity never before imagined. The mantra moving forward will be "change or perish."

Technology, Jobs, and Workers

In a March 2019 interview with James Manyika of *McKinsey*, Pulitzer Prize-winning author Tom Friedman described technology as moving in steps with each step creating new capabilities and setting up the next step.[8] The PC gave way to *connectivity* which included the iPhone and a suite of technologies including cloud, big data, and the beginnings of artificial intelligence. Connectivity became fast and deep, virtually free, easy to use, and invisible. It ushered in a world of commerce involving greater interconnection between systems, enhanced information accessibility and transparency, and automation. Beyond connectivity is a progression now underway toward a *psychic* stage of technology—accessing the entire psychograph of an individual through personal information on a cell phone.[9] And beyond that is *genomic* technology—a watch or smart clothes that read an individual's genome to determine the foods and medications one must acquire to stay healthy, one's need for exercise and intellectual stimulation, and so forth.[10]

What is remarkable about each of these steps is the rapid advance in capabilities they render to business and, simultaneously, the demand they place on workers to upgrade skills. We have reached a point where business success hinges more than ever on a company's ability to quickly adopt new technology but in a manner that does not completely outstrip worker capabilities. Many companies have built a strong technology foundation but encountered difficulty in upgrading current worker skills and locating skilled workers for new jobs. The intersection of advancing technology and worker skills is particularly acute in eight domains: artificial intelligence, big data analytics, the Internet of Things (IoT), sustainability, customer service, competition, workforce engagement, and skill shifts.

Artificial Intelligence

Artificial intelligence (AI) operates in three forms: (1) where machines perform tasks normally performed by humans; (2) machine learning where machines learn on their own; and (3) deep learning where machine learning chains together for rich learning.[11] AI functions today primarily in performance of repeatable tasks normally performed by humans. In the business world, it is an indispensable tool for predicting customer behavior, discerning customer needs, and directing customers to service. On the factory floor, it plays a critical role in anticipating machine failures, automating inventory, and working alongside humans to ease the burden of repetitive and physically demanding tasks. As machines learn on their own and perform an ever-larger share of tasks entrusted to humans, whole industries will be transformed:[12]

- *Transportation:* AI-guided autonomous cars will transport people to work and other destinations.
- *Health care:* AI will be used to diagnose disease and streamline drug recovery. Virtual nursing assistants will monitor patients and big data analytics will help to create a personalized patient experience.
- *Education:* Textbooks will be digitized through AI, virtual tutors will assist human instructors, and facial analysis will be used to gauge student emotions to tailor the learning experience to individual needs.
- *Customer service:* Context- and nuance-savvy AI assistants will place human-like calls to make appointments. AI will use highly customized content delivery automated to a customer's persona and lifestyle to ensure accuracy and relevance of communication.
- *Environment:* AI will have a major effect on sustainability, climate change, and environmental issues. Cities will be made more habitable through sensors that measure congestion and pollution and specify remedial action.

Is it realistic to expect that machines will displace lower-skilled workers performing repeatable tasks? It is already happening and the answer is "yes." Are machines likely to take over functions involving design and execution of processes and systems? It is underway and the answer is "yes." Will robotics and automation amplify the gap between haves and have nots in the world of work? The answer is "yes." Lower-skilled workers performing quantitative, repetitive, and scripted tasks—assembling parts, inspecting products, answering customer service calls—will be displaced in large numbers by AI. Investment in education to retrain individuals for new jobs will be essential to ensure worker success in an AI economy.[13]

Big Data Analytics

Big Data analytics is the often complex process of examining large and varied data sets to uncover information—hidden patterns, unknown correlations, market trends, and customer preferences—to make informed decisions.[14] Driven by specialized analytics and software, as well as high-powered computing systems, Big Data analytics power deep analysis of structured and unstructured data left untapped by conventional analytics programs. For example, web server logs, social media content, text from customer emails, survey responses, mobile phone records, and machine data captured by sensors that don't fit in traditional data warehouses.[15]

Big Data applications are now commonly used by retailers, financial services firms, insurers, healthcare organizations, manufacturers, and energy companies to generate information about consumer preferences that can be used to create market advantage. Their benefits include:[16]

- Provision of information about customer behavior, preferences, and consumption patterns that enable companies to develop new products and deliver better products and services.
- Optimization and improvement of operations including order fulfillment performance, inventory management, and distribution channels.
- Enhancement of the customer experience by applying analytics to design and control different facets of the exchange with customers.
- Improvement in the efficiency of company operations by optimizing the deployment of workers in accord with company needs and customer demands.

There are pitfalls in big data analytics. Workers have limited analytics skills, experienced data scientists and data engineers are costly, and the technology is expensive. Companies seeking to mine large volumes of data will need to invest in technology infrastructure comprised of large databases and processors with adequate computing power. Large companies have the resources to invest in sophisticated analytics but smaller counterparts do not. It's Lowe's and Home Depot versus the local hardware store and the result is predictable. The big guys win.

Internet of Things (IoT)

Internet of Things (IoT) is a rapidly evolving network of smart, connected devices, objects, and appliances that generate data touching every part of our lives.[17] Smart watches track each step we take and monitor heart rate. Smartphones in our pockets know our location at any moment, our hobbies, destinations to which we are traveling, and what we're considering buying. Smart thermostats monitor and regulate the temperature of our homes. We use smart speakers, smart light bulbs, smart home security systems—almost anything in a home can be made "smart" including appliances, toasters, toothbrushes, and toilets. IoT devices are constantly gathering and transmitting data via the internet and many are capable of carrying out tasks autonomously. Market forecasts from *Business Insider* predict that there will be more than 64 billion connected devices under the IoT umbrella by 2026—an increase of roughly 10 billion from the number of devices in 2018.[18]

IoT plays a key role in enabling digital transformation in business by:[19]

- *Improving business insights and customer experience.* Connected equipment in manufacturing, aviation, agriculture, health care, and other industries is creating data streams and analytics that provide companies with greater insight into business operations and how customers use their products and services. The link between IoT technology and improved customer experience is most apparent in the retail industry where success depends on connecting with the customer and reducing friction in the purchasing experience.
- *Reducing cost and downtime.* Operating costs and downtime caused by equipment failure can be eliminated by storing data in a digital twin capable of delivering information to engineers of component failure weeks in advance as well as the location of the component and how to replace it.
- *Enhancing efficiency and productivity.* By applying IoT to key production processes, companies can boost efficiency and productivity. Ford's Valencia Engine Assembly Plant in Spain is using a special suit with body-tracking technology to design less physically stressful workstations for employees to enhance its manufacturing processes.
- *Reducing waste.* Elimination of waste and inefficiency in supply chains is a key determinant of business efficiency and productivity. Typically, the more components there are in a business operation, the more it stands to benefit from IoT implementation. IoT tracking technology is being used by global firms to track and monitor assets in supply chains making supply chains the most significant adopter of IoT technology to date.
- *Developing new business models.* Internet-connected smart devices can feed customer usage data back to manufacturers and operators. IoT technology enables companies to move away from conventional business models to new revenue streams through customer data that enables them to offer the same products at reduced cost through subscription-based services.

Internet of Things has generated a technology revolution through tiny devices connected to the internet that increase productivity, minimize expense, and enhance security. Its application in manufacturing, agriculture, and health has enabled businesses to unlock previously untapped revenue, produce higher-quality products and services, and develop new forms of competitive advantage.[20] IoT comes with a cost. More and more devices interconnected among themselves and to the internet reduce the need for manpower and eventually lead to a loss of jobs.[21] Customer support jobs, for example, are now automated with most of the work being performed by chatbots. Robotic machines operate automatically in grocery checkout lines and ATMs. Jobs performed by real estate agents, telemarketers, dental assistants, and chefs are projected to be among the top 15 positions most likely to be automated in the future.[22] And this is only the beginning as IoT continues to change the way people conduct their daily lives and the way businesses are run.

Sustainability

Once seen as "nice to have, but not essential" for business, sustainability has become a vital component of business strategy. Driven by environmentally conscious consumers, companies worldwide have modified their operations to embrace sustainability:[23]

- A fifth of executive cash compensation at *Alcoa* is tied to safety, diversity, and environmental stewardship which includes greenhouse gas emission reduction and energy efficiency.
- *General Electric* has integrated sustainability into its corporate culture ranging from hiring practices and training to employee well-being programs.

- *Coca Cola* has improved the efficiency of its water use by 20 percent and incorporated rigorous third-party evaluation into its water management approach.
- *Ford Motor Company* has established requirements for first-tier suppliers to drive environmental and social expectations, including greenhouse gas emission reduction, down the supply chain.
- *Adobe* is using renewable energy technologies, including hydrogen fuel cells and solar arrays, to reduce greenhouse gas emissions. It is also reducing energy needs by improving the cooling efficiency of its data centers and "virtualizing" its systems, platforms, and devices.
- A significant portion of *Proctor and Gamble's* profit is now achieved through "sustainable innovation products"—products that provide a greater than 10 percent reduction from previous or alternative versions through energy use, water use, transportation, material used in packaging, and use of renewable energy or materials.

Corporate sustainability initiatives must balance a triple bottom line: people, environment, and profit. People are the linchpin in this equation. If you were asked "What carbon reduction practices have the highest internal rate of return in global corporations—transportation use, energy efficiency, something else"—how would you answer? According to research, the answer would be in the domain of people—behavioral change through employee engagement.[24] Employees can make or break corporate sustainability initiatives. A growing number of companies are on board with sustainability, but some lag behind even in the face of growing evidence of return on investment. This begs the question: If ROI potential is high and employee engagement is crucial for transition to a sustainability business model, why aren't more companies doubling down on engaging employees and inspiring commitment?

Employee Engagement

Ask anyone who has tried to engage employees in change and they will tell you about failed efforts. How hard it was to develop and implement effective programs, how employees were reluctant to participate, how hard change initiatives were to roll out and scale, and how hard it was to measure the results and the return. For employees, change is an uncomfortable reality in a rapidly shifting workplace. Past research has shown high levels of employee dissatisfaction—notably a 2018 Gallup study revealing 53 percent of global employees feeling disengaged at work and functioning below their potential.[25] On the basis of research, one would expect employees to resist sustainability initiatives—particularly workers using a cost–benefit calculus (what's in it for me) to guide behavior in companies dominated by maximizing profit. In these companies, employees would naturally migrate to behavior corresponding to profit in contrast to the more obscure motive of sustainability. If this is so, what behavioral options would employees have in a company transitioning to a sustainability business model? Would they embrace change, resist it, straddle the fence—something else?

Employee Motivation

Current research on sustainability and corporate social responsibility indicates that company-level sustainability activities are beginning to have a positive impact on employee motivation.[26] This finding is reinforced through the experience of companies finding benefit in sustainability practices as a means to bridge the tension workers feel between their personal values and work by providing a higher purpose. Unilever, for example, with an employee rating of 87 percent, has found ways to personally engage employees—from top executives to assembly line workers—in day-to-day corporate sustainability efforts.[27] Starbucks engages employees in sustainability programs—climate change, recycling and waste reduction, water and energy conservation, and LEED certification—by enforcing personal standards for recycling, reusable cups, and waste reduction.[28] Patagonia, a world leader in sustainability, promotes employee engagement in sustainability by paying employees to work up to two months for a non-profit environmental organization of their choice.[29]

If this is a direction of the future for companies, what will it mean for employees working with a profit motive and unwilling to change? Will they be left behind? Will they move to the periphery of company culture? Will companies stretch to engage them? Perhaps the larger question is one of the lengths to which companies will go to engage valued but resistant employees in a market demanding greater commitment to sustainability.

Customer Service

Customer service expectations continue to rise and the quality of customer service can make or break a business. Service quality is the single most important factor for customers when deciding which companies to patronize. One bad experience can be enough to persuade customers to switch to other companies. Companies are acutely aware of this and are using technology to enhance service quality by increasing the speed and convenience of customer interactions and providing customers with choice in how they access service. Technology is unquestionably an asset in terms of speed and convenience, but it has consequences, not all of which are positive. It is expensive, it comes with a steep learning curve, and it is costly in terms of jobs. Among the advantages that service technology offers to customers are:[30]

- *Personalized real-time service.* Customers expect business to be 24/7/365 and most prefer interaction using chat rather than phone or email. Bots sensitive to customer nuances are now being used to deliver instant real-time customer service across multiple channels thereby reducing the number of support requests that need to be handled by personnel.
- *Omni-channel service.* Social media, e-commerce, and third-party review sites enable customers to engage companies through a variety of digital mediums. Omni-channel platforms synchronize communication channels so service personnel and customers can work seamlessly to resolve problems.
- *Self-service efficiency and expedience.* Businesses are providing multiple types of self-service tools to customers including FAQs, knowledge bases, IVR phone systems, online discussion forums, interactive diagnostics, and virtual assistants. Self-service tools lower costs, but in doing so, they also push the envelope on more sophisticated methods of customer interaction.

Imagine a world where you interact most frequently with chat and messenger bots or location-aware mobile apps. You would consider it odd if a business did not offer these service channels and forced you to use something like a phone or email. Imagine searching the web for a specific service and finding most of the companies offering documented evidence of customer success but some focusing exclusively on service delivery. Embedded in these scenarios are "haves" and "have nots" in the rapidly changing world of customer service. Bots and AI are becoming standard in customer service. They free personnel from answering repeatedly asked questions, reduce the number of personnel engaged in customer service, and change the focus of customer service to customer success. The technology needed to document success, however, will disadvantage small companies and new market entrants by increasing costs and reducing profit margins.

Competition

Technology has changed competition by using speed and efficiency to achieve advantage. Rivals can leapfrog over one another overnight through advances in business process, customer interface, and deployment of personnel. Companies with profound knowledge and awareness of technology potential reap benefits at the expense of slower-moving rivals. Digital leaders achieve faster revenue growth and higher productivity than their less-digitized peers. They improve profit margins more rapidly and are agile innovators in their markets. Technology does not wait for companies to catch up. It makes competition a zero-sum game with winners and unseen competitors gaining advantage through innovation at the expense of laggards.

Technology, however, is a double-edged sword. On the one hand, the explosion in algorithmic capabilities, computing capacity, and data brought about by advanced automation and AI is spawning a new generation of system-level innovation. Machines surpass human performance in areas like image recognition and object detection—capabilities that can be used to diagnose cancer more accurately than humans can.[31] AI is contributing to the resolution of pressing societal challenges from health care to climate change to humanitarian crises, yet technology is not a silver bullet. Significant bottlenecks—especially relating to ROI and talent—confront companies large and small. High-performing companies capture significantly more economic profit as a portion of the market today than they did 20 years ago.[32] By contrast, the economic losses of low-performing companies are significantly larger on average than those of their counterparts 20 years ago.

Skill shifts accompanying the advance of new technologies in the workplace have changed the basis of work. The need for technological, social, and emotional skills is on the rise as demand for others, particularly physical and manual skills, is falling.[33] Competition is intensifying as companies scramble to fill new jobs created by artificial intelligence and displaced workers jostle for employment. Projections by McKinsey & Company detailing the impact of automation on workers reveal dual paths of loss and gain. Roughly 15 percent of the global workforce could be displaced by automation between 2016 and 2030; simultaneously, 550 million to 890 million new jobs could be created from productivity gains, innovation, and new labor demand from investment in infrastructure, energy, and technology.[34]

A shortage of skilled workers for new jobs and a surplus of workers displaced by automation will change the basis of competition. Facing simultaneous challenges of recovery from the pandemic and a shortage of talent for new jobs, businesses will turn to collaboration to achieve stability and build capacity. Companies will join forces to acquire new technology and networks of connected manufacturers, suppliers and contractors will vie for advantage in volatile markets. Networks and collaboration will become an important part of business strategy for the advantages they offer in building capacity and the benefit they offer in minimizing exposure to risk.

The Pandemic and Work

COVID-19 has forced companies toward swift action to safeguard employees and adopt new ways of working that even the most aggressive of business contingency plans could not have envisioned. Employees have had to adjust to conditions sharply different from the pre-pandemic character of work, and managers have discovered that many aspects of leading and managing have changed. Before the pandemic, the conventional wisdom had been that buildings and offices were critical to productivity, company culture, and winning the war for talent.[35] Companies competed for prime office space in major urban centers and focused on design that reflected modernity and progressivism. Densification, open office designs, hoteling, and co-working were buzz concepts.[36]

The coronavirus changed the nature of work by inducing categorizations of "essential workers," shutting down companies and plants, and dispatching millions of workers from offices to homes. In April 2020, 62 percent of employed Americans worked at home during the crisis compared to 25 percent in 2018.[37] McKinsey research with 319 companies in 2020 revealed high levels of employee satisfaction with remote work.[38] Liberated from long commutes and travel, employees found more productive ways to spend time, experienced greater flexibility in balancing personal and work lives, and indicated a preference to work from home rather than an office. Companies, in turn, realized advantages of reduced cost for facilities and access to new pools of talent with fewer locational constraints.

Data collected by *CNBC Make It* analysts Connley, Hess, and Liu from employment experts, CEOs, and designers (2020) revealed permanent changes in the structure and conduct of work resulting from the pandemic.[39] The *logistics of work* are changing: standard 9–5 office hours are becoming a thing of the past, working in an office could become a status symbol, meetings are being replaced by interactive technology and instant messages, and office buildings are being considered for use beyond office space. *Public health* has become a business priority: mandatory on-the-job medical screening could become the norm for many companies and fashion-ready face masks could become a wardrobe staple. *Remote work* will become more commonplace as companies find compelling evidence of productivity. Home office stipends could become a common perk and work could become more equitable and attractive for women as locational constraints ease. Finally, the *deployment of workers* will change as automation accelerates and middle-management positions are cut from the workplace.

People working remotely and in offices can readily meet face-to-face via technology, but central office space may not be part of the equation.[40] Office buildings could be recast as gathering places, while focused work is done remotely. In buildings with open floor plans, public health will take primacy.[41] Office layouts will change with desks spaced apart and partitions separating workspace. Cleaning stations stocked with hand sanitizer, antibacterial wipes, and touchless fixtures such as door sensors, automatic sinks, and soap dispensers, and voice-activated elevator banks could become the norm in many buildings. On-the-job medical screening for office workers could become the rule rather than the exception, and workers may be expected to wear masks at work as a matter of company policy.

As working remotely becomes the norm, flexibility will become essential for attraction and retention of talent. Leading companies will question long-held assumptions about how work should be done and the role of the office. Answers will be determined by the talent that is needed and available, how much collaboration is necessary, where facilities are located, the availability of technology and cost. Tough choices will be necessary and the skill set of leaders will broaden to include a capacity for driving change across functions and business units.

Asymmetry

Asymmetry—a lack of equality or equivalence—captures the condition of imbalance among organizations and workers impacted differentially by change. The pandemic has changed the environment for work, and technology has changed the skills required of workers. These forces advantage companies and workers that navigate them successfully and handicap those who cannot keep up as illustrated in Table 8.1.

Table 8.1 Asymmetry of Change

Advantaged	*Disadvantaged*
Companies	
* essential businesses flourishing during the pandemic	* non-essential and minimally capitalized businesses restrained by the pandemic
* companies with resources to shift operations to alternative venues	* companies with fixed product/service lines and insufficient reserves
* companies capable of acquiring advanced technology	* companies lacking resources to acquire new technology
Workers	
* workers continuing to work/returning to work during the pandemic	* workers permanently displaced from work by company closures
* workers with digital, cognitive, and advanced technological skills	* workers with physical and manual skills in repetitive task jobs
* workers with resources and opportunity to reskill	* workers lacking resources and opportunity to learn new skills

Coronavirus and Asymmetry

At the peak of the pandemic in May 2020, thousands of non-essential businesses closed. Retail industry estimates of business closures stood at 190,000 stores closed—roughly 50 percent of U.S. retail square footage.[42] Growing numbers of consumers shopping online and a surplus of brick and mortar stores undercut profit margins and brought scores of retailers to the edge of bankruptcy. Businesses defined as essential retailers—mass merchandisers, grocery and drug stores, hardware stores, convenience stores, and e-commerce retailers—continued to operate during the crisis and emerged stronger than before. So, too, did retailers with sufficient capital to withstand crisis and companies able to alter production to meet emerging needs. Procter & Gamble, for example, determined that plastic in Gillette packaging could be used to make face shields for healthcare workers and perfume-making equipment in some of its plants could be repurposed for detergents and fabric softeners.[43] Lock-step companies lacking a capacity for repurposing were left behind as were non-essential brick and mortar retailers and companies weakened by debt.

Many workers had their feet cut out from under them by the pandemic. At the peak of the pandemic in 2020, more than 33 million workers filed for unemployment and one out of five workers was unemployed.[44] Maxed out credit cards and negligible savings left families with nothing to fall back on. American household debt climbed to $14.15 trillion in 2020—$1.5 trillion over its previous peak in 2008.[45] Family dynamics changed as spending narrowed to essentials and debt was restructured with creditors. Missing or late payments lowered credit scores and put unemployed job seekers at a potential disadvantage with employers. The gulf between employed and unemployed workers widened through the pandemic leaving millions of Americans with bleak prospects for the future.

Technology and Asymmetry

Automation and artificial intelligence have forced workers to deepen existing skills or acquire new ones and changed the character of workplaces and workflows by placing people alongside machines.[46] Advanced digital skills are an increasingly important part of the skill arsenal workers will need to bring to the workplace. Equally important are social and emotional skills and higher cognitive skills—creativity, critical thinking, and complex information processing. Workers with these skills advance while workers without them are at a disadvantage as machines increasingly take over basic tasks.

Companies have been forced to rethink how work is organized as a result of advanced technology and results are mixed. *Leading companies* are retooling their approach to work, redesigning their structure and business processes, and focusing on talent to ease the gap between demand and supply of skilled workers. These companies have invested in continuous learning and agile ways of working including cross-functional collaboration and team-based work. Work allocation has been unbundled and rebundled to create middle-skill jobs by shifting tasks performed by high-skill workers to lower-skill workers.[47] *Under-performing companies* have struggled with how to acquire, deploy, and integrate new technology to achieve strategic priorities.[48] Poor user engagement rooted in faulty technology application and insufficient training is part of the problem. Leaders lacking information about employee interactions with technology and moving quickly between technology platforms are another part of the problem. And employees themselves are part of the problem. Lacking advanced digital and information processing skills and reluctant to reskill, recalcitrant employees put companies at a disadvantage in competition with market leaders.

Dilemma of the Zero-Sum

It would be easy to envision companies and workers as part of a zero-sum game in which gains and losses add up to zero. Essential, highly capitalized companies thrive in turbulent times while non-essential, poorly capitalized companies struggle to stay afloat. Workers with advanced technological and cognitive skills thrive while workers with physical and manual skills grapple with unemployment. Zero-sum thinking is natural to most perhaps because our minds have evolved in a win–lose world with a shrinking middle ground. It may also be because for most day-to-day matters, zero-sum thinking is adequate. Everyone knows that jobs are not unlimited, there is only so much market space for companies in the same industry and only so many workers can be hired each year. There are "winners" and "losers." One company's gain is another company's loss. A worker with the right skills in a digital economy will advance; one without skills will fall behind.

Does zero-sum thinking have utility in a business world on the threshold of catastrophic risk? There are competing answers to this question. "Positive-sum" ideologues see commerce in terms of abundance—resources and opportunities can grow so there is enough for everyone. Zero-sum ideologues see commerce in terms of scarcity—resources are limited and people and organizations can only gain at the expense of others. Zero-sum and positive-sum are game theory terms that refer to resources and measurable rewards that different parties receive. In zero-sum, a "fixed pie" must be divided between parties. The more one gets, the less available to the other and the total is always zero. In positive-sum, the total of winnings and losses is greater than zero. This becomes possible when the size of the pie is enlarged and there are more resources to distribute between parties than were originally available. All parties get what they want or need.

Can positive-sum be brought to the world of work? The answer is a qualified "yes" but work as we know it will change dramatically. We'll need to rethink the purpose of business, the scope and organization of work, and what it means to be a worker.

Broadening the Conception of Work

When an economy is fully competitive—free of market constraints such as catastrophic events, monopolies, or power imbalances—companies are free to pursue what is in their best interest. The ultimate objective is to maximize profit as a means of increasing net worth and return to shareholders. In the words of economist Milton Friedman, "There is one and only one social responsibility of business—to use its resources and engage in activities designed to increase its profits so long as it stays within the rules of the game, which is to say, engages in open and free competition without deception or fraud."[49]

The profit motive comes into question when forces intervene that run counter to a fully competitive economy. Critics and pundits contend that the pursuit of profit should not supersede the needs of people and the general welfare of society. Ideally, business should be an engine of social change and, ultimately, of societal well-being.[50] This evolving role has not gone unnoticed by business. The 2019 Business Roundtable statement on the Purpose of a Corporation clearly moved beyond shareholder primacy to a commitment to all stakeholders including people and communities.[51] In the words of Tricia Griffith, President and CEO of Progressive Corporation, "CEOs work to generate profits and return value to shareholders, but the best-run companies do more. They put customer first and invest in their employees and communities. In the end, it's the most promising way to build long-term value."[52] Under the banner of corporate social responsibility, the Roundtable statement is the first wave in a rising tide of business engagement in social and environmental issues.

Corporate social responsibility takes on new urgency in a world facing catastrophic risk. Consider the ongoing threat posed to families and communities of a cyclically repeating pandemic, a 100-year flood that occurs every year, increasingly violent weather events, an unending drought rendering farmland useless, and perpetual food and water shortages leaving millions vulnerable. Where can people and communities in harm's way turn for help in times of crisis? What entities have the talent and resources to lead in crisis? Business is in a unique position to mobilize communities in response to risk. For this to happen, the world of "work" as we know it will need to broaden to encompass social responsibility. Three dynamics will be at the center of this world:

- Social responsibility as a core function of business.
- Workers and managers engaged in systemic outreach with communities.
- Community outreach as a compensated component of work.

Connecting Work and Social Responsibility

The threat of catastrophic risk presents an opportunity for business to rethink the meaning of work and what it means to be a worker while also helping communities adapt to rapidly changing circumstances. With advances in technology, companies can reach a broad audience through the efforts of individual workers. By connecting workers to social responsibility and identifying employee potential for different types of outreach, companies can tailor actions that create benefits for people and communities. An agenda for action incorporating business process and social responsibility will be possible in companies that:[53]

- Invest in and maintain a purpose-driven culture keyed to people and issues in the community
- Connect workers to social issues beyond the job, train them, and help them contribute to the public good

- Use segmentation to parcel workers into social responsibility and community outreach roles
- Link community outreach to compensation and performance appraisal

Invest in a Purpose-Driven Culture

As pandemic-induced dimensions of risk have become clear and ways of working have shifted, business has become more attuned to the needs of people and communities. Experience with community involvement puts companies in a position to communicate the importance of social responsibility to workers and help them adapt to new roles and responsibilities working with communities. Companies with a purpose-driven culture:

- *Assess community needs and share information with workers.* Conditions and needs change quickly in a circumstance of risk. Purpose-driven companies stay current with change, make information available to workers, and encourage outreach in response to need.
- *Create and utilize a network of employee teams to identify actions and resources needed to address community needs.* Teams can quickly decipher the issues facing a community and resources necessary for resolution while also building understanding of community needs among workers.
- *Cultivate an appreciation of service for the public good and the importance of action.* Leaders and managers model behavior that values outreach to community, the importance of action beyond words, and commitment to outreach as a dimension of work.

Connect Workers to Social Issues Beyond the Job

A purpose-driven culture can build a sense of appreciation of social responsibility as a dimension of work. Workers who understand the nature and gravity of challenges facing communities and the urgency for action are more likely to engage with communities than those who do not. Companies that connect workers to issues in the larger community embed information about the challenges facing people and community in communication with workers. They also bring the impact of challenges to life at the individual level and maintain continuous dialogue about worker roles and responsibilities in relationship to community needs.

Segment Workers Into Social Responsibility and Community Outreach Roles

Worker experience with social issues and community outreach ranges from extensive to minimal. There are differences between employees working remotely and non-remotely relative to capacity for community outreach. There are also variations within worker groups. Some workers may exhibit a high level of interest in community engagement, while others are reluctant or disinterested. Companies tailoring worker outlook to community outreach use segmentation to determine worker readiness for outreach. They also use training models personalized to worker readiness to prepare them for outreach, assess worker performance in the early stages of outreach, and provide additional training as necessary.

Link Community Outreach to Compensation and Performance Appraisal

Corporate commitment to social responsibility and community outreach could be perceived as hollow if detached from compensation and performance appraisal. Workers expected to do more or to work differently may experience loss of morale if reward and compensation are not connected with responsibility. Similarly, what does not have teeth may not be perceived as important. Involvement in outreach must be of sufficient importance to become part of employee performance assessment. Companies budget and measure what they value. Proof of corporate commitment lies in the bottom line of the budget and annual performance review.

What It Will Mean to Be a Worker

The worker of tomorrow will not be the same as the worker of today. The pandemic and the advance of technology have made that a certainty. Tomorrow's workers will be part of a flexible work environment, they will communicate and collaborate using emerging technology, they will engage in continuous learning, and they will merge work, life, and social responsibility through community outreach.[54] As Tom Friedman has observed, "What's going on is that work is being disconnected from jobs and jobs are being disconnected from companies, which are increasingly becoming platforms."[55]

Not only will the environment for work be different, but also the social contract between employers and employees will be different. Employers will have an increasingly broad continuum of options for finding talent, from hiring traditional full-time employees to availing themselves of managed services and outsourcing, joint venture employees, independent contractors, gig workers, and crowdsourcing.[56] Orchestrating this complex of different workforce segments will require new models. The traditional employee life cycle model of attract, train and retain will change to a holistic model where the key question will be how to access, curate, and engage workforces of all types.[57] Companies will have the opportunity to optimize the benefits of different types of talent relationships. Making the most of this opportunity, however, will require a complete rethinking of talent models in ways that allow companies to match worker motivation and skills with organizational needs.

Changes in the environment for work and the employer–employee relationship cannot be understated. Just as important, however, will be the juncture of social responsibility and work in a world ever more at risk. When people and communities are threatened by catastrophe, work can no longer proceed with a singular focus. It must broaden to include involvement in societal issues and community. The role of workers must similarly broaden to include service to the public good. Whatever form it takes, service to community will, by necessity, become an institutionalized and compensated dimension of work in the environment of burgeoning risk that will be the future of business.

Notes

1 Top 25 Quotes by Albert Einstein, "A-Z Quotes." www.azquotes.com/author/4399-Albert_Einstein. Retrieved: May 14, 2020.
2 Summary, S., "Five Key Characteristics of a Smart Factory." *Welcome.AI*. www.welcome.ai/news_info/five-key-characteristics-of-a-smart-factory. Retrieved: May 15, 2020.
3 Chui, M., Evers, M., and Zheng, A., "The Disruption Ahead Extends Well Beyond Healthcare. Are You Prepared?" *McKinsey Quarterly*, McKinsey & Company, May 2020.
4 Excerpted from an article titled "Office Doors are Opening in Maine. . . . But Just a Crack" by Tux Turkel in the July 5, 2020 edition of the *Portland Press Herald*. Retrieved: July 6, 2020.
5 Multiple sources were consulted to identify impacts of the pandemic on work. See for example:

Connley, C., Hess, A., and Liu, J., "13 Ways the Coronavirus Pandemic Could Forever Change the Way We Work." *Make It*, April 29, 2020. Retrieved: May 15, 2020.

Meister, J., "The Impact of the Coronavirus on HR and the New Normal of Work." *Forbes*, March 31, 2020. Retrieved: April 18, 2020.

Cheremond, R., "9 Future of Work Trends Post-COVID-19." *Gartner*, June 8, 2020. Retrieved: June 15, 2020.

Boland, B., De Smet, A., Palter, R, and Sanghvi, A., "Reimagining the Office and Work Life after COVID-19." *McKinsey & Company*, June 2020. Retrieved: July 2, 2020.

6 Bughin, J. and Woetzel, J., "Navigating a World of Disruption." *McKinsey & Company*, Briefing Note Prepared for the World Economic Forum, January 2019. Retrieved: June 23, 2019.

7 Ibid.

8 Manyika, J. and Friedman, T., "The World's Gone From Flat, to Fast, to Deep." *McKinsey & Company*, March 1, 2019. Retrieved: August 9, 2019.

9 Ibid.

10 Ibid.

11 Joshi, N., "7 Types of Artificial Intelligence." *Forbes*, June 19, 2019. Retrieved: September 5, 2019.

12 Multiple sources were consulted to identify impacts of AI on industry. See for example:

Robotics and Automation News, "AI in Education: What the Future Holds." July 6, 2020. Retrieved: July 10, 2020.

Faggella, D., "The State of AI in Health Care: An Overview of Trends." *Emerj*, March 5, 2019. Retrieved: July 5, 2020.

Kerrigan, S., "The 25 Ways AI Can Revolutionize Transportation: From Driverless Trains to Smart Tracks." *Interesting Engineering*, April 22, 2018. Retrieved: July 9, 2019.

Walch, K., "AI's Increasing Role in Customer Service." *Forbes*, July 2, 2019. Retrieved: September 11, 2019.

Snow, J., "How Artificial Intelligence Can Tackle Climate Change." *National Geographic*, July 18, 2019. Retrieved: August 23, 2019.

13 Thomas, M., "The Future of Artificial Intelligence." *Builtin*, June 8, 2019. Retrieved: September 10, 2019.

14 Rouse, M., "Big Data Analytics." *TechTarget*, *WhatIs.com*. Retrieved: May 3, 2020.

15 Ibid.

16 Bonheur, K., "Advantages and Disadvantages of Big Data." *Profolus*, March 21, 2019. Retrieved: May 15, 2020.

17 Hobbs, A., "Five Ways the Internet of Things Is Transforming Businesses Today." *Opes Technologies*. Retrieved: May 22, 2020.

18 Meola, A., "A Look at Examples of IoT Devices and Their Business Applications in 2020." *Business Insider*, December 18, 2019. Retrieved: May 21, 2020.

19 Hobbs, "Five Ways the Internet of Things Is Transforming Businesses Today."

20 Ibid.

21 EDUCBA, "IoT Disadvantages." www.educba.com. Retrieved: June 2, 2020.

22 Ibid.

23 Confino, J., "Best Practices in Sustainability: Ford, Starbucks and More." *Guardian*, April 30, 2014. Retrieved: June 5, 2020.

24 IEDP Editorial, "Employee Engagement and Sustainability." *IEDP Viewpoint*, October 6, 2016. Retrieved: June 5, 2020.

25 Harter, J., "Employee Engagement on the Rise in the U.S." *Gallup*, August 26, 2018. Retrieved: June 30, 2020.

26 Polman, P. and Bhattacharya, C., "Engaging Employees to Create a Sustainable Business." *Stanford Social Innovation Review*, Fall 2016. Retrieved: June 6, 2020.

27 Ibid.

28 Warnick, J., "5 Things to Know About Starbucks New Environmental Sustainability Commitment." *Starbucks Stories and News*, January 21, 2020. Retrieved: June 7, 2020.

29 CSR Central, "Patagonia—The Clothing Company with a Revolutionary Approach to CSR & Sustainability." March 4, 2015. Retrieved: June 10, 2020.

30 Assurant, "4 Digital Trends Transforming Business As We Know It." August 26, 2019. Retrieved: June 25, 2020.

31 Renukasoni, "Image Detection, Recognition and Image Classification With Machine Learning." *AITS Journal*, July 26, 2019. Retrieved: June 28, 2020.

32 Bughin and Woetzel, "Navigating a World of Disruption: Briefing Note Prepared for the World Economic Forum."

33 Ibid.

34 Ibid.

35 Boland, B., De Smet, A., Palter, R., and Sanghvi, A., "Reimagining the Office and Work Life After COVID-19." *McKinsey & Company*, June 9, 2020. Retrieved: June 14, 2020.

36 Ibid.

37 Brenan, M., "U.S. Workers Discovering Affinity for Remote Work." *Gallup*, April 3, 2020. Retrieved: June 26, 2020.

38 Boland, B., De Smet, A., Palter, R., and Sanghvi, A., "Reimagining the Office and Work Life After COVID-19." June 9, 2020.

39 Connley, C., Hess, A., and Liu, J., "13 Ways the Coronavirus Pandemic Could Forever Change the Way We Work." May 4, 2020.

40 Ibid.

41 McConnell, L., "7 Ways COVID Has Already Changed the Future of Work, According to Experts." *Ladders*, May 6, 2020. Retrieved: June 14, 2020.

42 Danziger, P., "List of Retail Companies on Bankruptcy Watch Is Growing Fast Amid Coronavirus Crisis." *Forbes*, April 3, 2020. Retrieved: June 21, 2020.

43 Shapiro, E., "Procter & Gamble CEO David Taylor Talks Equality, the Economy, and Why Leaders Wear Masks." *TIME Leadership Brief*, June 14, 2020. Retrieved: June 22, 2020.

44 Bredemeier, K., "33.5 Million Workers Have Now Filed for Jobless Compensation." *VOA*, May 7, 2020. Retrieved: June 25, 2020.

45 Swaminathan, A., "U.S. Household Debt Hits Record High of $14.15 Trillion." *Yahoo Money*, February 15, 2020. Retrieved: June 12, 2020.

46 Bughin, J., Hazan, E., Lund, S., Dahlstrom, P. Wiesinger, A., and Subramaniam, A., "Skill Shift: Automation and the Future of the Workforce." *McKinsey & Company*, May 23, 2018. Retrieved: September 23, 2019.

47 Ibid.

48 Knight, R., "Convincing Skeptical Employees to Adopt New Technology." *Harvard Business Review*, March 19, 2015.

49 Friedman, J., "Milton Friedman Was Wrong About Corporate Social Responsibility." *Huffington Post*, August 12, 2013. Retrieved: June 4, 2020.

50 Baldor, L., "Occupy Wall Street Protests Give Voice to Anger Over Greed, Corporate Culture." *PBS Newshour* (Associated Press), October 5, 2011. Retrieved: June 30, 2020.

51 Business Roundtable Statement, "Business Roundtable Redefines the Purpose of a Corporation to Promote 'An Economy That Serves All Americans'." *Business Roundtable*, August 19, 2019. Retrieved: June 30, 2020.

52 Ibid.

53 Newlands, M., "How to Incorporate Social Responsibility Into Your Business." *American Express*. Retrieved: July 1, 2020.

54 Morgan, J., "The 7 Principles of the Future Employee." *Forbes*, November 11, 2014. Retrieved: July 5, 2020.

55 Engelbert, C. and Hagel, J., "Deloitte Interviews Thomas Friedman: The Future of Work." *Consultant's Mind*, July 31, 2017. Retrieved: July 5, 2020.

56 Schwartz, J., Jones, R., Hatfield, S., and Anderson, S., "What Is the Future of Work? Redefining Work, Workplaces, and Workforces." *Deloitte Insights*, April 1, 2019. Retrieved: July 8, 2019.

57 Ibid.

SHAPING THE FUTURE

Chapter 9

Rethinking Business Purpose and Strategy

Put people first, not make tons of money first.

Arthur Blank
Home Depot Founder and Atlanta Falcons Owner, 2019

If you think the coronavirus was bad, you haven't seen anything yet. Climate change is moving relentlessly forward—a calamity with the potential to radically reshape how we live. COVID-19 will recede in the wake of a vaccine that will provide immunity for many and some semblance of normalcy. Climate change will not recede. If we move decisively, its most harmful effects may be alleviated and we'll adapt to a new way of life. If we temporize and fail to achieve net-zero CO_2 emissions by 2050, our future will be compromised.

The 2015 Paris Climate Agreement called for greenhouse gas emissions to be limited to levels that would prevent global temperatures from increasing more than 2°C (3.6°F) above the temperature benchmark at the beginning of the Industrial Revolution.[1] If we fail to limit emissions, scientists foresee profound consequences, among them rising sea levels, exposure to extreme heat, greater incidence of drought and flooding, loss of arable land, water and food scarcity, and trillions in infrastructure and asset destruction. Scenarios for mitigation rely on "negative emissions" to achieve 1.5°C and 2°C temperature rise goals. This means removing CO_2 from the atmosphere using carbon capture and storage technologies, which to this point have only been used on a small scale with mixed results. It also means restoring forests over immense areas of the planet. Most importantly, it means emitting fewer greenhouse gases—an effort that will require substantial changes in how we live. Altogether this is a tall order, particularly given the global and national political landscape.

Evolving Business Scenario

A 2013 working paper on crisis by the Risk and Crisis Research Centre provides a helpful interpretation of the meaning of crisis by drawing a distinction between catastrophe and episodic events such as emergencies and disasters.[2] *Emergencies* are short term, reasonably predictable, and

159

capable of being handled by emergency response organizations.[3] They have a definitive beginning and end and life goes on as usual upon their conclusion A *disaster* may outstrip the capacity of a community to respond. Neighborhoods may be destroyed, infrastructure may suffer businesses may be closed, and highways and bridges may be impassable. Life as we know it ceases during a disaster, but recovery is imminent. *Catastrophe* is a state of extreme ruin and distress. It can take the form of an event, a change in circumstances, or a gradually unfolding set of conditions. Communities in catastrophe can be heavily impacted by infrastructure damage, loss of essential services, and multiple region impact that prevents help from neighboring communities.[4] Ongoing functions—work, education, recreation, and government—can be sharply interrupted and communication and transportation systems disabled. Recovery efforts are impeded by destruction vastly in excess of community resources and capability to resolve. Business and government take on important roles in catastrophe because of the leadership and resources they bring to response and recovery.

Climate Catastrophe

Climate change met by reticence is the exemplar of catastrophic risk. It touches everything and at its center is business—an institution with growing recognition as an engine of social change in advanced societies. Business is the nexus of a climate movement with pressure for action from multiple sources: investors and shareholders calling for reduction of CO_2 emissions, corporate leaders moving to address simultaneously occurring near- and long-term climate threats and growth opportunities, rating agencies exerting pressure through inclusion of climate risk in rating methodologies, suppliers striving to meet particle emission standards, government agencies establishing greenhouse gas regulations, and consumers making decisions based on carbon footprint.[5] What needs to happen is obvious, but CO_2 mitigation comes with a price. It is expensive and firms will understandably exercise caution in adopting and implementing carbon management practices—a tendency evidenced in research by Deloitte in 2019 revealing a proclivity toward temporization with company measures against climate change focused primarily on short-term cost savings.[6]

Given the urgency of climate change and growing awareness of its impact on the environment, one must ask: What if conditions worsen and stated carbon goals are not met? Consider the effects of a 2°C (3.6°F) global temperature rise by 2050:[7]

- billions in additional annual cost to the U.S. economy caused by infrastructure and asset destruction caused by droughts, extreme weather, and wildfires;
- forced migration of millions of people due to environmental changes;
- viral spread of infectious diseases caused by increasing heat, humidity, and precipitation;
- wildfires burning two to four times as much land for each Celsius degree of warming;
- water scarcity affecting whole communities and millions of people;
- increasingly powerful hurricanes and extreme weather events driving damage costs significantly beyond available resources;
- sea-level rise of 1.5 to 2.5 feet in coastal regions putting millions of people and trillions in assets at risk;
- food insecurity due to eradication of farmland through drought and flooding;
- rising numbers of malnourished children due to declining crop yields; and
- increase in mental illness, particularly depression and anxiety, caused by disasters.

Civilian Response

Climate change is met in the U.S. by a citizenry divided along lines of wealth, geography, political affiliation, and ideology. Ours is a nation of people clustered in like-minded communities some of which have morphed into superclusters of like-minded citizens.[8] Immense geographic regions share a common culture and political ethos, far-right and far-left protestors square off in street battles, and conservatives and liberals agree on one thing—they see the world differently. Climate change gives rise to enmity between groups holding irreconcilable beliefs. Extreme events in the form of intense hurricanes, wildfires burning millions of acres, and sea-level rise erasing coastal communities are not sufficient to dissuade naysayers from questioning the reality of climate change. Scientific evidence does not matter—climate is cyclical and things will eventually get better. On the other side, are climate activists who believe that climate change is a substantiated global threat. The evidence is compelling and it is manifested in increasingly harsh conditions—science must be followed.

Climate change is profiled primarily through its impact on the environment. There is a secondary impact, however, which exacerbates its effect—partisan behavior that deters response to risk. Look back to the climate effects earlier and pick one—perhaps extreme heat and prolonged drought occurring simultaneously. Consider their impact on communities. Huge swaths of arable land will be lost leaving water and food in short supply. To conserve water and ensure adequate food supplies, conservation mandates will be put into effect. Response to these mandates will be divided. Naysayers will disregard them on the belief that high temperatures and drought are temporary and will pass. Climate activists will adhere to the mandates believing that climate change is a clear and present danger. In the absence of intervention, opposing views will harden and the threat of climate change will be on its way to becoming a climate crisis.

The crisis has environmental and human impacts beyond the capacity of communities to resolve on their own. Put yourself in the position of CEO of a company that has been called upon to ease the crisis using its resources, expertise, and political leverage. For humanitarian reasons, "no" is not an option. You must act, but where will your company get the biggest bang for its buck? Shoring up food and water supplies? Helping to enforce water conservation mandates? Deploying employees to volunteer service in the community? Educating the community on water conservation techniques? Acquiring and making available water conservation technology? What does it tackle first—climate conditions causing the crisis or human behavior deepening the crisis? Your company has the wherewithal to address environmental conditions using technology, but it is not in the business of managing human behavior. The crisis has two dimensions—the physical character of climate change and the behavior of people. Neither will be solved without solving the other. What will you do?

Rethinking Business Purpose

Rethinking business purpose in a time of rapidly changing conditions and uncertain revenue streams? You've got to be kidding—it's not in the realm of possibility. Before you dismiss the idea and move on, however, step back and ponder a few questions:

- What are the consequences of a community coming apart during crisis?
- Can business stand apart from a community in tough times?
- What is the responsibility of business to the community in a time of crisis?

Think about your company and the risk landscape it is operating in. Think about climate change and changes your company will need to make to adapt to climate crisis. Should your business plan be broadened to include a commitment to action on climate change? Are senior managers fully aware of the dangers posed by climate change? Do they understand its potential for evolution into a crisis? Does your company have a crisis response plan? Is the community in which your company is located part of the plan? Is your company prepared to respond to rapidly shifting community needs? Does your company understand the human dimension of crisis? These are not academic questions. Get a pencil and rate your company.

Has your company's strategy and business plan been broadened to include a commitment to action on climate change?

No, remains the same   Under consideration   Yes, we have a stated commitment

Are senior managers fully aware of the threat posed by climate change?

No, not at this time   Don't know   Yes, they are aware

Do they understand the potential for climate change to evolve into crisis?

No, not to my knowledge   Don't know   Yes, definitely

Does your company have a crisis response plan?

Not at this time   Don't know   We have a plan

Is the community in which your company is located part of the plan?

No   Don't know   Yes

Is your company positioned to respond to rapidly shifting community needs if climate change escalates into crisis?

No, this is beyond our capacity   Don't know   Yes, we are ready

Do senior managers understand the human dimension of crisis?

No, not to my Knowledge   Don't know   Yes, definitely

These questions provide a simple but effective barometer of a company's outlook on risk and its preparedness for response. Their premise is simple: If your marks fall somewhere in the middle or to the left, the focus of your company may be inward, its outlook on risk myopic, and its preparedness for response insufficient.

A firm's strategy and business plan provide insight into its position on risk. They disclose its focus on conditions contributing to risk, the resources it allocates to risk, and its capacity to respond to risk. Conventional and catastrophic risks place different demands on business. Conventional risk can be assessed and managed through standard analytical techniques, probability calculations, and operational controls. Catastrophic risk is different—heretofore an occurrence so rare as to require minimal attention. COVID-19 abruptly changed this dynamic by bringing catastrophic risk into the mainstream of public consciousness and business operations. Companies had to shift gears to minimize loss. Business models were shifted to digital platforms, crisis response plans were created, cross-functional teams were tasked with identifying threats and company vulnerabilities, and communication plans were developed to convey up-to-date information to consumers. These actions disclosed two aspects of business that are fundamental to strategy during crisis:

■ The importance of scale and resources in minimizing loss. Companies are not equal in the resources they can deploy in crisis—large companies can more readily weather adverse conditions and more rapidly achieve stability than smaller companies.

■ The need not only to protect assets during crisis but also to direct resources to consumer needs. Businesses are thrust into the position of becoming dual-purpose organizations during crisis—a position juxtaposed to the singular goal of creating shareholder profit.

It takes courage and a willingness to stretch organizational boundaries and resources to pursue dual purpose in a period of crisis. The intellectual depth and business acumen of leaders is put to the test by tasks such as how to assess the effects and consequences of catastrophic risk, how to plan for and manage crisis, and how to balance competing aims of profit and commitment to the common good. The common good has become increasingly prominent on corporate radar screens. Business leaders understand its importance and possess the emotional intelligence to empathize with the needs of others. Empathy has always been an important dimension of leadership and it is critical in times of crisis when people are thrown off balance by changing conditions. Side-by-side with the need to help people, however, is the need to protect company assets and ensure continuity. The dual challenge of helping people and protecting company assets will be a major focus of business strategy moving forward in an environment of catastrophic risk.

Strategy Dynamics

The pandemic revealed a major gap in the approach to strategy employed by many businesses. The ongoing focus of strategy has been on growth, cost control, and quality—factors that sustain an organization and its services into the future. Conventional analytic tools are used to predict the future and become the basis for strategic direction. Many factors are involved, but absent is an estimation of uncertainty and an explicit accounting for risk—key elements in a vision of the future sufficiently precise to be crafted into strategy according to public policy expert Christine Springer.[9] In uncertain times, conventional strategy is at best marginally helpful and at worst potentially dangerous. Underestimating uncertainty and failing to account for risk can result in strategy that neither shields a company against risk nor takes advantage of opportunities that higher levels of uncertainty provide.[10] More importantly, it can lead to strategy which turns a company inward on itself and away from stakeholders in tough times—the very time at which help and support are most needed. Companies focusing strategy on business continuity leading up to the onset of COVID-19 lacked the analytical capacity to create a set of assumptions sufficient to anticipate the consequences of a fast-moving virus infecting millions of people. Companies building predictive strategy prior to onset through active discussion of unlikely events and their consequences were in a better position to gauge whether or not company strategy would be sufficiently robust to withstand the disruptions caused by catastrophe.[11]

Beyond business continuity, catastrophe planning lacks predictive value in determining the human effects of catastrophe—its impact on the common good. More is needed and the "more" is strategy to mitigate in advance the harmful effects on humans of catastrophe.[12] Global warming, for example, is projected to cause food and water shortages that will disrupt millions of people if CO_2 emissions are not capped. Scientists can chart the severity of conditions based on emissions and temperature rise, but they cannot predict if and when extreme conditions will be experienced because much depends on human behavior.[13] In business, firms cannot create strategy to ward off the harmful effects of climate change once a tipping point has been reached. They can, however, craft strategy to alleviate its most harmful effects by creating a blueprint for crisis response, formulating emergency and disaster relief plans, and purposing operations to support communities during crisis.

Creating a strategy that works to mitigate the harmful effects of catastrophe in advance requires an approach that avoids the trap of "frontloading"—building strategy exclusively on the basis of conditions that could obtain. Leaders do not have the knowledge and foresight to accurately gauge the array of forces that contribute to catastrophe; nor do they have the analytics to precisely estimate its consequences and probability of morphing into crisis.[14] An alternative to frontloading is to "backload" strategy—build strategy on the basis of human needs in crisis and act on those needs in a manner that enhances company assets. This is *relational strategy* and its goal is to bind consumers to business through products, services, and resources that deliver unparalleled value during crisis. What follows is a framework for relational strategy based on tailoring strategy to needs during crisis.

Relational Strategy

The success of every company is dependent on its ability to create products and services that meet customer needs. The primacy of needs in corporate strategy can be viewed as falling into three categories relative to their impact on company assets.[15] First, and of lesser impact, is commitment to serving stakeholder needs in statements of purpose. Second, and of greater impact, is purposing of products and services in response to changing customer needs. Third, and of greatest impact, is basic needs intervention through engagement with communities in times of crisis—for instance, partnering with local charities to provide essentials, opening disaster and relief centers, and repurposing company operations to provide essential goods for citizens. Business performance in the first and second categories is clearly evident. Corporate purpose statements—most recently a statement on the Purpose of the Corporation by the Business Roundtable in 2019—indicate an unwavering commitment to serving stakeholders beyond investors.[16] And beyond repute is the performance of businesses in repurposing products and services in response to consumer needs during the coronavirus pandemic.

Corporate Commitment

Shareholder profit has long stood as the highest priority of corporate America—a single-minded devotion superseding the interests of customers, employees, and communities. By 2018, the realization sunk in that the traditional language of business was out of step with the times.[17] Stakeholders began calling on companies to be more responsible. Pressure mounted to fight climate change, to reduce income inequality, and to improve public health. At gatherings like the World Economic Forum in Davos, Switzerland, discussions turned to how businesses could help solve thorny global problems. In August 2019, a statement released by the Business Roundtable, chief executives of 129 of the largest companies in the world, called for "businesses to commit to balancing the needs of shareholders with customers, employees, suppliers and local communities."[18] The Roundtable statement did not provide specifics on how to carry out its newly stated ideal, offering more of a mission statement than a plan of action. But corporate leaders vowed to "protect the environment by embracing sustainable practices across our businesses" and to "foster diversity and inclusion, dignity and respect."[19]

Business Purposing

When COVID-19 erupted, companies came face-to-face with the reality that business-as-usual approaches to meeting consumer needs, serving customers, and working with suppliers would no longer work. For many, the goal was survival and speed became paramount. From decision-making and productivity to utilizing technology in new ways, to accelerating innovation, COVID-19 demanded a moment of existential introspection. What defined company purpose—its reason for being? Was it shareholder profit, societal benefit, satisfaction of consumer needs? Companies faced the challenge of defining purpose through their response to COVID-19 or falling victim to it. Lip service to noble aims would not be sufficient—aims mean little unless backed by practical action. In the words of McKinsey & Company analysts:[20]

> In boardrooms real and virtual, frantic questions have the floor. How long will this last? How will we pay furloughed workers? What are our peers doing? What should we do first? Global corporations have never had as much power as they do right now to leverage their scale to benefit society in a time of global crisis. Executives have also never had a more intense spotlight trained on their behavior and actions. In moments of crisis, the default expectation is that businesses will hunker down and focus on bottom-line fundamentals. Indeed, many CEOs feel constrained to making defensive moves to protect their businesses. But in this crisis, stakeholder needs are already so acute that the opportunity for businesses to make an indelible mark with human support, empathy and purpose is greater than it has ever been.

Businesses shifted their focus, redirecting assets and capabilities to fill in gaps and support global response to the pandemic. Distilleries and breweries leveraged supply chains and equipment to produce hand sanitizers. Automakers manufactured ventilators and respirators. Hotels provided space for quarantining and rooms to those without homes. Company after company redeployed unique capabilities to meet immediate needs. Luxury goods giant LVMH switched production lines from making perfume to making hand sanitizer; Procter & Gamble started making face shields for health workers from plastic used in Gillette packaging; McDonald's employees in Germany helped retailer Aldi cope with customer rush; Johnson & Johnson donated a million surgical masks to Chinese health workers; and IKEA outfitted hospitals in affected areas.[21] At the heart of these examples was speed. Activities that would normally take months, were executed in weeks, even days. The pandemic forced businesses to remove boundaries and silos and streamline decisions and processes. If there was a silver lining to COVID-19, it was the realization that organizations could make massive and fundamental shifts when needed and did not have to return to old ways of operating.[22]

The many layers of the COVID-19 crisis changed the relationship of business to social institutions and to the public. As the limits of existing systems became clear, business had little choice but to join the coronavirus front line. Benefits and liabilities were part of this move. Cost was the liability—company assets would be used to repurpose products and services. The benefit was good will—consumers reward businesses that use their powers for good.[23] Companies that uphold clear values and pursue a larger societal mission have the capacity not only to shape consumer behavior but also to build good will among the wider public.[24] This is the essence of relational strategy— *building relationships through business purpose centered on a larger societal mission.* Savvy business leaders understand this ethic and take a longer view, offering people and communities security and stability in periods of great need.

Engagement

The highest priority of leaders during a crisis is keeping their company afloat and employees safe. At the same time, many look outside the organization for ways to help communities. A prime example is Zoom. At the height of the pandemic, Zoom offered free video conferencing accounts to any K-12 school that had to shutter due to COVID-19.[25] This in-kind contribution allowed students to keep up with their academics without further taxing school budgets. Zoom could have realized a huge profit through K-12 schools, yet the company made a choice for the public good.

Examples of business engagement with communities in periods of crisis range from contributions of cash and equipment to repurposing facilities and technology to enhancing logistics and supply lines. Community extends beyond the location of company facilities and the extent of contribution need not be prodigious. Consider Disney Plus's decision to start streaming *Frozen 2* three months ahead of schedule to help parents confined at home with their out-of-school children.[26] 3BI, Media—a fee-based newswire service specializing in social impact and sustainability issues—waived fees for nonprofits making public health announcements during the COVID-19 outbreak.[27] Great Western Bank—a regional bank serving small communities in the Midwest—awarded small grants to communities hit hard by historic floodwaters and bank employees helped load supplies at warehouses in flood ravaged communities.[28] 3D Wave Design—a Nova Scotia-based 3D animation and communications company—developed and deployed software simulating the effects of flooding and wildfires to help communities along the Atlantic coastal region prepare for catastrophic results of climate change.[29] 3D modeling, laser scanning, and environmental data were blended into an online application that enabled users to plan for the worst through simulation of storm surge, inland flooding, and wildfires over 3D representations of real communities.

The scale of business engagement with communities in crisis is perhaps best illustrated by company response to hurricanes Harvey and Irma in 2017. Billions were donated by companies at ground zero and throughout the nation in response to Hurricane Harvey. Companies also donated goods and their own employees and offices to help with disaster relief.[30] For example:

- Gallery Furniture in Houston opened up a chain of its stores as shelters for impacted families.
- Bass Pro Shops donated 100 boats to government agencies and rescue organizations for use in devastated areas and tons of supplies to the American Red Cross.
- Hubbell Power Systems sent hundreds of thousands of pounds of utility products to affected areas along with company teams of Storm Soldiers armed with emergency response kits to aid communities in distress.
- Home Depot pledged $1 million to organizations helping with relief efforts and dispatched Team Depot volunteers to communities to help with clean-up efforts.

A similar pattern of corporate support was evidenced in response to the devastation wrought by Hurricane Irma in 2017. Dick's Sporting Goods donated $3.5 million worth of clothing and footwear and $2 billion to rebuild and refurbish youth sports programs; FedEx contributed $1 million in transportation support to deliver critical medical aid and supplies; Lowe's contributed $1 million for Irma relief in product donations; and Goldman Sachs committed $500,000 to organizations involved in immediate search, cleanup and recovery efforts following Irma.[31] Big name and lesser known companies across multiple industries have an impressive legacy of benefaction to community in times of crisis—Walmart, UPS, FedEx, Cargill, Cisco, IBM, Google, Microsoft, Allstate, Proteus, Project Jomo, Caterpillar, Ceres Environmental, and many more.[32] They help by developing and deploying technologies that enable communities to withstand disasters. Insurance and reinsurance industries, for example, educate communities about the importance of disaster mitigation and preparedness.[33] Logistics companies such as FedEx and UPS help by transporting equipment and supplies. Companies such as Walmart and Cargill help by getting supply chains moving and needed goods and services back into circulation.[34] Oft-maligned retailers play an important role by bringing vital products to consumers through convenience stores and gas stations.

Competition to Collaboration

The restorative function of business with communities during crisis is beyond question. Most of the disasters, however, are *punctuated crises*—crises with a definitive beginning and end. But what about business strategy in a *sustained crisis*—a crisis without interruption such as that posed by climate change?

Climate Crisis

Let's return to the example in Chapter 1—a midwestern city besieged by climate conditions that have morphed into a catastrophe:

- searing temperatures—40 consecutive days of temperatures in excess of 100 degrees
- extended drought—two years of minimal rainfall
- extreme weather—two weeks of drenching rain and an extended forecast calling for more rain
- flooding—a river 15 feet above flood stage with no sign of abatement
- food and freshwater shortages—transportation arteries and depots are underwater and inaccessible
- economic strain due to farmland destruction and low crop yields
- a citizenry polarized along lines of political persuasion, wealth, and ideology
- citizens in denial when confronted with data and scientific evidence of climate change
- impatience edging toward civil disorder with government leaders perceived as incapable of addressing and solving problems
- growing despair among citizens feeling isolated and powerless in a community perceived to be operating outside of deeply rooted norms

Thousands of residents have been displaced from their homes; highways, bridges and water, and sewage treatment plants have been damaged beyond repair; and tens of thousands of acres of farmland are underwater. Worse yet, you are not alone—cities and towns in the entire western part of the state are facing the same or similar conditions. Add to this mix evidence that climate conditions will worsen and cannot be reversed by technology, infrastructure damage totaling billions, and citizens "climate challenged" and unwilling to heed public safety mandates. Total it up—the result is a crisis of extreme magnitude that will not go away.

Business Response

Three building supply companies are located in the region and are working vigorously to respond to the crisis. They have chosen different paths. Company A, a family-owned business with deep roots in the area, has jumped in and is providing full support—$10 million in building supplies, a 6-month renewable supply of bottled water, warehouse space to house citizens displaced from homes, and employee volunteers to help distribute food, water, and household supplies. It has maintained pricing at a pre-crisis level and regulated inventory to ensure continuing product supply. Company B, a long-standing regional competitor, has chosen a more modest approach—$2 million worth of building supplies and equipment and discounted prices. It is operating on a narrow profit margin and has opted to restrict employees to in-store work. Company C, a corporate franchise, is the newest of the three companies. It is bankrolled by a parent corporation and on an aggressive path to gain market share through deep cuts in product pricing and aggressive marketing. The crisis has not changed C's approach to business. It has opted not to go the donation route on the belief that deep discounting, continuing product availability, and desperate consumers will move inventory off the shelves.

Company C's competitive strategy could prove effective over the short term if saving money and product availability are a primary concern of consumers. Company A's strategy has good will going for it but with stable pricing, it may not sell enough product to cost-conscious consumers to remain viable. Company B is probably in the most vulnerable position. It has a history in the area, but its discount strategy is modest and may not be sufficient to maintain sales volume. Time may be the most important factor for the three companies. During a crisis, competitive strategy may lose its edge over time and give way to good will and customer loyalty. Companies that establish they are in business not only to sell but also to partner with the community build inestimable customer loyalty. Their connection with customers may transcend the boundaries of transaction as people associate good will with purchasing from a noble company rather than a money-minded competitor. This is the essence of *relational strategy*—strategy that enables "relational" companies operating on good will to counterbalance the market power of "transactional" companies operating on continuity and profit during crisis.

Benefit Through Collaboration

The distinction between *relation* and *transaction* is important, but it is not sufficient to deliver optimal value to communities in hard times. Companies engaged in competition fail to leverage the power of collaboration during crisis. Supply chains contribute to the problem. Under pressure to deliver inbound materials and outbound products during crisis, supply chains have little choice but to assign priority to big players. It's the business version of the Matthew effect: the strong get stronger. Large geographically distributed companies are perceived to have more liquidity than smaller companies and less likely to run aground. As smaller companies face growing financial stress and diminished access to supply chains, collaboration with a larger company becomes more attractive. The benefit is reciprocal—small regional companies have the leverage of customer loyalty to offer big companies while receiving the benefit of big company access to supply chains. Collaboration benefits all of the parties as the scale created through alliance increases leverage with suppliers.

Beyond the advantage of scale, other factors argue in support of collaboration. Conventional wisdom suggests that smaller companies benefit when economic activity shifts to the virtual world because they are more nimble with information technology. In reality, the effect may be the opposite—larger companies have the resources and expertise to use IT more efficiently. They also offer the advantage of security during crisis. Workers may be more comfortable accepting jobs at a larger firm, where employment is more secure and benefits are more readily available.[35] Similarly, customers may be more confident in products and services from larger companies whose name brands seem safer.

The Power of Collaboration

Collaboration is similar to but distinctly different from strategy antecedents of competitive collaboration and coopetition which embrace elements of competition. Competition is pursued to gain market share in a zero-sum game. Companies enter into collaboration to achieve common goals where collective well-being becomes more important than individual profit maximization.[36] These different logic structures assume that companies are comfortable operating in an either-or dichotomy—either share the pie through collaboration or capture a larger piece of the pie through competition.

Is zero-sum viable in a world coming out of pandemic and coming face-to-face with the growing threat of climate change? Climate change will place demands on business that will not be met purely through competition. It requires higher-order thinking and leaders who are able to devise strategies that change the rules of the game. If this is true, what is the future of competition and where does collaboration fit in? According to Hamel, Doz, and Prahalad (1989), it is *competitive collaboration*—joint ventures, outsourcing agreements, product licensings, and cooperative research which strengthen companies in alliance against outsiders while maintaining an ethos of competition.[37] Companies enter alliances with clear strategic objectives and awareness of how their partners' objectives will affect their success. Employees are cognizant of skills and technologies that are off-limits to partners and intelligence that partners receive is carefully monitored.[38] Essentially, competitive collaboration is collaboration with an underlying basis of competition for skills, new technologies, product competencies, and talent. The ultimate goal is advantage—and profit—through acquisition of learning from partners.

Collaboration took a step forward in 1996 with the publication of *Co-opetition: A Revolution Mindset that Combines Competition and Cooperation.*[39] Brandenburger and Nalebuff describe coopetition or "cooperative competition" as strategy using insights from game theory to understand when it is better for competitors to work together to increase benefits for all. Too often, business is characterized in terms of war when, in fact, most businesses succeed when other businesses succeed. The Microsoft/Intel relationship is a prime example of coopetition. "The demand for Intel chips increases when Microsoft creates more powerful software. Microsoft becomes more valuable when Intel produces faster chips."[40] This is a win–win proposition. It doesn't imply that businesses should not compete, but it does suggest that competitors can work together while tending to their self-interest.

The "Wintel" partnership, although no longer in place, is but one variation of coopetition. Other examples include Ford and Toyota teaming up in 2013 to design the Atlas Ford F-150 Hybrid concept. Over time, Ford has sold America's most popular truck, and Toyota has made the world's best-selling hybrids.[41] Mortal enemies Apple and Microsoft teamed up to license mobile operating system features and patents, and Google and Mozilla worked together to limit the influence of rival browsers. In today's world of business, companies, and organizations routinely collaborate as a means of amplifying service and cutting cost. USPS partners with direct competitors FedEx and USPS to lower operating costs and increase revenue. In the NGO sector, rival beverage companies collaborate to address global warming. Coca-Cola, Pepsi Co, Red Bull, Unilever, and others established Refrigerants Naturally, a non-profit global initiative, to jointly develop sustainable refrigeration technologies to combat climate change and ozone depletion by replacing fluorinated gases with natural refrigerants.

Collaboration to Alliance

Competitive collaboration and coopetition brought collaboration to business strategy but they did not anticipate its value for business in periods of extreme stress. The value of collaboration can best be understood through questions about business strategy in hard times. What conditions would impel business to shift from competition to collaboration? Are strategies marrying collaboration and competition sufficient to deliver optimal value to communities in times of crisis? Can organizations with competition embedded in their DNA align with one another to support and mobilize communities in response to threats?

A common denominator during catastrophe is collective action to help people and communities in crisis. Collective action can take many forms, but in crisis it is interdependent organizations working together in *alliance* toward community well-being. Alliances can take many forms—regional competitors working together toward a common goal, companies in different industries collaborating in response to community need, and private–public cooperation to support and mobilize communities. Common to all forms, however, is the multiplying effect of *synergy*. The reasoning behind synergy is simple: the output of multiple organizations working in combination will be greater than the sum of outputs created by organizations working individually.[42] In alliance, organizations create "operating synergy" by enabling individual companies to leverage their output. Communities benefit from alliance through economies of scale, favorable pricing, and sustained product availability resulting from greater influence over suppliers, lower cost through streamlined operations, and functional strength consolidation which improves output and operating efficiency.[43]

Business is a lifeline for communities in crisis. The reasons are self-evident: the financial costs of disasters cannot be handled by the public sector alone; key elements of infrastructure (electricity, telecommunications, and transportation) are owned and operated by private businesses; and business must return quickly to normal operations during recovery to meet subsistence needs.[44] Beyond the obvious, however, is an untapped role of business during crisis. Researchers have found that efforts to mobilize people and communities in disaster recovery are most effective when run through existing networks and organizations.[45] People are more readily motivated to participate in collective effort through groups and organizations in which they normally participate or routinely engage, rather than as isolated individuals. This is especially important in communities in which a major part of the workforce is engaged in the private sector. Employees are a conduit to community participation in crisis response and recovery. This is an extension of the employee role and it is a segue to a dimension of business yet to be fully realized—business as social purpose.

Business as Social Purpose

Businesses have typically helped communities in times of crisis through philanthropic largesse. They have also used leverage with partners to enhance citizen access to resources and developed technologies to help communities manage recovery more effectively. Business processes, for example, are driving risk management and being used to educate communities about the importance of disaster mitigation and preparedness. Helping communities through response and recovery, especially in circumstances of extreme distress, is not only ethically right, but it is also in companies' enlightened self-interest.[46] The smaller the number of companies that hit the wall during crisis, the better for the overall health of the economy.

Business tactics in response to crisis run on a continuum ranging from actions that are *business-focused* (essential for company survival) to actions that are *community-focused*, to actions that advance the common good—*societal well-being*.

Business-Focused

- *protecting employees and company assets*
- *creating and maintaining a crisis response plan*
- *establishing cross-functional crisis response teams*

- *communicating with customers*
- *insulating and stabilizing supply chains*

Community-Focused

- *providing emergency resources of food and water*
- *donating money, equipment, and supplies*
- *repurposing space for displaced citizens*
- *redeploying employees to volunteer service*
- *shifting production to meet critical needs*

Societal Well-Being

- *building social awareness and commitment to the common good*
- *enhancing relational skills of leaders and employees*
- *deploying employees to bring stability to communities in crisis*

Business Focus

Actions companies must take to ensure survival during crisis are self-explanatory. Companies pivoted at the height of the pandemic to business models conducive to short-term survival and long-term resilience. Company assets and employees were protected, customer communications were shifted from marketing to helping, and supply chains were insulated from market turbulence.[47] Small businesses severely impacted by broken supply chains pursued alternative customer markets. After seeing their sales to restaurants and specialty stores plummet during the lockdown, small-scale farms shifted their focus to homebound consumers.[48] Farmers and local stores moved products to Spotify, the Canadian e-commerce platform targeting sales at distances of less than 15 miles between sellers and buyers—a segment of the online market that behemoths like Amazon passed over.[49] Spotify's asset protecting pivot was to offer a comprehensive cloud-based bundle of services that helped vendors manage expenses, pay bills, anticipate cash-flow problems, and optimize deliveries.[50]

Name-brand manufacturers and retailers unable to stock shelves to keep up with customer demand, watched brand loyalty evaporate. Product availability and convenience became a driving force in consumer shopping behavior leaving companies little choice but to change or be left behind. Soaring demand for essential products prompted companies like Unilever to prioritize essential products—packaged food, surface cleaners, and personal hygiene product brands—over products where demand had fallen.[51] Ed tech companies threw out their roadmaps and changed course to remote and hybrid learning models to meet burgeoning demand during lockdown.[52] Manufacturers began selling directly to consumers to cut costs and improve efficiency. Businesses from motorcycles to restaurants scaled back variety to ensure product availability and profitability. For consumers, it was not only what to buy and how to buy but also where to buy. Considerations of safety, cleanliness and demonstrated care for employees drove where to buy decisions. Heightened awareness of consumer sensitivity to how businesses interact with communities in times of crisis pushed consumer sentiment to the top of the corporate strategy agenda.

Community Focus

Business has a long record of helping communities through financial support and volunteerism. But the pandemic ushered in new ways of helping. Practically overnight, big-name brands diverted resources and skills to helping communities and small businesses by adopting new practices to deliver goods and services to needy consumers. Businesses amplified their social media presence, FaceTimed customers for personal shopping and curbside pickup, and offered a delivery service to get items directly to customers without contact.[53] Big business moved to fill gaps in emergency response by altering production lines to produce critically needed supplies for first-line providers.

Among the more unusual practices in response to the pandemic was help offered by specialized service companies to critical populations. In the United Kingdom, companies from airlines to boat hires deployed idle fleets at their own expense to provide relief and supplies.[54] Tour operators mobilized minibuses to pick up food and prescriptions for people self-isolating. When bookings for canal boats vanished, Norbury Wharf in Staffordshire, UK offered its boats for free to first-line workers needing to self-isolate. When British footwear and accessories brand Kurt Geiger was forced to close its 70 UK stores, it asked 2,500 store staff to volunteer for community initiatives while they remained on payroll.[55] XITE Energy delivered no-cost crates of energy drinks to infirmaries and first-line workers across the UK. Parking companies pledged free parking to health workers and parking enforcement agents transitioned to managing queues at supermarkets and other essential outlets.

Societal Well-Being

Although "society" is commonly identified as a business stakeholder, the reality is that companies acting on their own cannot achieve broad societal goals. All companies, however, can make a meaningful difference in the communities in which they operate, particularly in troubled times. Societal well-being is a wide-ranging concept best understood in terms of sustainable development goals—ending poverty and hunger, promoting economic growth, ensuring healthy lives, assuring equitable access to quality education, promoting climate action, and ensuring justice and strong institutions. It begins with a broad corporate social responsibility mandate, extends to providing resources to communities in times good and bad, and plays out in employee engagement within communities. Volunteerism, the most common form of employee engagement, is a standard practice of business and for good reason. Studies have shown that volunteerism can positively impact employee engagement, particularly within the Generation Y demographic.[56] Employees care about how their employer is perceived in the communities in which they live and work. They also care about quality of life and forces within communities that contribute to and detract from quality of life. For example:

> Imagine that you are an executive overseeing a multinational consumer goods corporation headquartered in the Midwest. In addition to the normal challenges you face as one of the company's leaders, you are faced with a raft of new challenges. Your supply chain was disrupted by the pandemic and is not fully back on track. Your company is being challenged by upstart competitors muscling into your market with cut-rate prices and product availability. Brand loyalty has taken a hit, but retail store shelves are stocked fully with your product and you expect sales to improve. Market analysts see your company as overvalued and underperforming with static revenue growth and falling stock value. The year ahead could be rocky, but your company has a proven track record and will move past any downturn. It will be a player for years to come.
>
> There is something ominous, however, that is really disturbing—something you cannot stop thinking about. It has to do with the intersection of risk, a pandemically challenged and ideologically fractured nation, and citizens inured to the threat and consequences of risk. Your first inkling of trouble came several years ago when climate naysayers disputed growing

evidence of climate change. Civility gave way to partisan bias as naysayers and climate activists vilified one another. Further dividing the nation were events that took on a life of their own—systemic racism, the devaluation of science, and alarming citizen behavior. The Black Lives Matter movement took on new urgency with Americans reacting to protest in ways that threw communities into turmoil. The pandemic raged anew and science was put on hold by government leaders putting the economy ahead of human lives. COVID-19 brought many changes to life and with it an undeniable impact on mental health—rising levels of stress, anxiety and depression which impacted judgment and behavior. Most alarming was the behavior of citizens putting others at risk by flaunting public health guidelines. These events garnered your attention and gave rise to questions: Can people holding divergent views and beliefs come together in response to risk? Is there anything I can do as an individual to help? Is there something my company can do?

There are no simple answers to these questions, but doing nothing is not an option—not for you and not for your company. The communities in which your company operates and its employees reside are enmeshed in forces that significantly impact quality of life. They disrupt communities at a scale and speed that is unprecedented with people, organizations, and institutions hanging in the balance. No company or leader is exempt from or invulnerable to these forces. You have to respond. What are you going to do? What should your company do?

Business and Societal Well-Being

The effects and consequences of crisis and the extraordinary demands it can place on organizations and leaders were brought into full view by the pandemic. The massive scale of the outbreak and its overwhelming speed gave rise to questions about the capacity of businesses to adapt. Companies did, however, adapt and learned valuable lessons about what to do to survive a sudden onset crisis. Sudden onset crises, however, are an entirely different animal than a gradually developing crisis and they are easier to address and resolve.[57] Climate change, for example, has grown out of familiar circumstances which, until recently, masked its overall impact. A slow-developing crisis requires companies and leaders to overcome a normalcy bias which can cause them to underestimate its long-term impact and consequences. Companies cannot turn on a dime as they would for sudden onset events using plans drawn up in advance. Slow-developing crises require actions focused not only on company survival but also on stakeholder impact and the common good.[58] There is an existential element vastly beyond managerial action.

Business investment in societal well-being can best be understood through questions about business purpose and the work of leaders in a world edging toward catastrophic risk:

- Should business purpose be broadened beyond corporate social responsibility to include goals related to societal well-being?
- Should employee roles and responsibilities be augmented to include humanitarian work with communities?
- What skills will leaders and employees need to perform effectively in a business world purposed on societal well-being?

Societal well-being is a state of being in which basic needs are met including nutrition, shelter, safety, social stability, and a sense of belonging.[59] Given the enormity of intervention required to stabilize communities in times of crisis, government and non-profit organizations cannot ensure well-being on their own. Business will need to step up and fill critical gaps.

From Corporate Social Responsibility to Well-Being

Corporate social responsibility has evolved from a niche trend into the mainstream of business over the last decade. Businesses not donating a percentage of their profits, participating in volunteer work, or taking steps to better communities, face the prospect of falling behind.[60] Business practices that contribute to the common good are smart business and for good reason. Consumers can access information instantaneously on the Internet, search a company's record at any time they want, and talk about it using social media. Prospective employees indicate growing interest for work in companies that promote good in the world. A growing volume of research reveals a preference among young job seekers for employment in companies that have a strong CSR policy.[61] With the adoption of CSR, business has become a recognized change leader— a role historically performed by government and non-profit organizations and assumed more recently by business.

While CSR has been found to improve brand and ultimately increase profitability, exposure to risk has deepened and commitment to social responsibility may not be enough to help communities in crisis. What if risk is perpetual and becomes part of a new normal? What if worsening climate conditions lead to an uninterrupted sequence of extreme weather events, 100-year floods every year, drought that runs over years instead of months, and water and food shortages that drive entire populations from homes and jobs? What role beyond financial largesse would business play in stabilizing people and communities? Is there a humanitarian element of business yet to be fully realized that would accelerate return to normalcy?

Partisan Behavior and Collective Action

The call to action for business to play a humanitarian role in stabilizing people and communities in times of crisis will rise to a clarion level in the risk environment we are entering. Experience with social behavior during the pandemic and partisan behavior on the heels of the 2020 presidential election indicate that reasoned action in response to risk will be a tough slog. A record-breaking surge in coronavirus cases in the United States nine months into the pandemic was driven to a significant degree by the casual social behavior of a "pandemiced out" populace. Maskless close contact parties, game nights, sporting events, carpools, neighborhood gatherings, bar patronage—all were part of a transmission trend reflecting pandemic fatigue. As the U.S. moved deeper into the pandemic, people became inured to risk, let their guard down, and interacted in loose-knit webs of social contact. These webs or "bubbles" grew larger with minimal effort to trace people in one web to persons in other groups they were part of.[62] Contagion lines formed between groups and the virus surged to new heights.

Partisan resistance to the results of the 2020 presidential election proliferated after the election beginning with Donald Trump's refusal to concede and extending to Republican lawmakers and voters steadfastly refusing to accept the election's outcome. Divisions between red and blue rose to a level that made bipartisan effort toward goals almost impossible. In the words of a Texas voter, "This is contempt of half of the country to the other half of the country. If the conclusion was for Biden, I would look at it as illegitimate, and I and many others expect to be part of the so-called resistance."[63] The election took on an existential quality—a referendum on more than politics with views of the election wrapped up in a range of issues including systemic racism, COVID-19 response, and the economy. The battle for the "soul of the country" did not end with the election. It intensified into an ongoing war between partisan groups with different outlooks and beliefs.

Partisan behavior illuminates the effect that a divided citizenry can have on risk. The ongoing threat of pandemic will not be overcome without civilian adherence to public safety guidelines. The ability of government to create and execute legislation protecting national well-being will be severely tested by a divided citizenry. Efforts to mitigate the harmful effects of climate change will be compromised by clashing partisan ideology. Remediation is essential and entities beyond government will need to step up to ensure well-being. Business is one such entity.

Launching the Humanitarian Side of Business

The CEO faced a difficult decision. Community leaders were asking for assistance following a weather disaster which put most of the county under water. Businesses and schools were closed, families were displaced from homes, and stress levels were off the chart for citizens reeling from a wave of bad weather events. What the community leaders wanted, however, was decidedly different from past calls for help. They were not asking for donations—disaster relief funds and emergency supplies had been secured through federal and state agencies. Nor were they asking for help in finding shelter for displaced families—facilities had been made available through local school districts and non-profit organizations. Instead they were asking for help with citizens edging toward disorder. Certainly the area's largest employer—a respected company and a pillar in the community—would be able to bring calm to the community. Its leaders could appeal for patience and restraint and be heard.

The CEO had never considered the company to be a contributor to the community beyond material means. The company was a partner, but not a social service provider. There was, however, the matter of long-standing tradition and responsiveness to community needs. Ignoring the community was not an option. Locals bought company products, staffed its production line, and contributed to its bottom line. Something had to be done in response to the call for help. But what? The CEO did not have deep information about the mindset of regional citizens—their needs and interests, their motivation for change, and their willingness to listen. The company did not have personnel who could provide insight into the sociological and psychological makeup of the community. There was only one course of action that made sense, but it was long-term—bring in a community well-being officer and train and empower employees to contribute to the community in ways beyond their job description.

What Is a Community Well-Being Officer?

Healthy communities create value that drives growth and profit. Communities thrown into disarray by disruptive forces such as dislocation from jobs and income, business and school closures, and empty store shelves experience anxiety that interrupts consumption. We know from research that large-scale interventions undertaken by collaborating organizations can stabilize communities in times of crisis.[64] We also know that communities left to their own devices do not have the resources for effective response to crisis.[65] Help from multiple organizations is necessary and business is in a prime position to help. However, unless there is a commitment from the top, business engagement in community well-being will remain static. This is where a *community well-being officer* comes in.

In business parlance, a well-being officer (CWO) is responsible for improving the overall health and well-being of employees.[66] Deloitte and Kirkland & Ellis LLP are among the leading companies that have hired a well-being officer.[67] Although the work of this officer is internal to the organization, well-being is about more than employees. It is also about the community and what a company can do to contribute to the well-being of people outside of company walls. A community well-being officer is a strategist and a change agent driving company-wide attention to community needs. Individuals in this role:[68]

- raise awareness and provide intelligence to company leaders about community needs and the benefit of building resilience,
- provide strategic vision and direction for company initiatives in response to community needs,
- organize and coordinate information gathering from employees about community needs, interests, and preferences,
- monitor employee engagement in the community and measure return on investment,
- provide human relations skill training to employees in preparation for community outreach,
- collaborate with community organizations to deliver needed services and improve civilian access to resources, and
- relate community well-being to profit and the company's bottom line.

Ideally, a community well-being officer would have extensive knowledge of the community, its demographics and organizations, and the values and beliefs of its citizens. This officer would know what works and does not work in mobilizing citizens, how to bring employee skills to bear in times of need, and when to lead and follow working with community organizations. An effective well-being officer would be an exceptional people manager with superbly developed human relations skills—a mentor capable of instilling relational skills in employees and motivating them to engage with the community. The most important trait in this officer's arsenal would be an ability to communicate the value of community well-being to the board, executive managers, employees, investors, and stakeholders.[69] Community well-being is a profit generator. Healthy communities bring greater purchasing power to company products and services and greater purchasing power means profit.

Employees and Community Well-Being

Singularly important among the responsibilities of a community well-being officer is unleashing employee potential for community engagement in times of crisis. Employees are on the ground with neighbors and participate in community organizations. Recognition of the value they bring through community engagement acknowledges their importance not only as workers but also as consumers with deep knowledge of community and what people want. The message employees receive is that the company cares about them and what they bring to the organization beyond job skills. Everyone wins—employees feel valued, the company gets better employees, and the community gets a company more sensitive to its needs through information provided by employees.

Employees bring enormous potential to communities in times of crisis. People suffering from emotional distress need help as quickly as possible. Diffusion of emotion through assistance rendered by trained responders could limit the harmful effects of distress. Working under the supervision of a community well-being officer and in collaboration with community organizations, employees with proven relational skills could serve as volunteer responders—a novel extension of their role, but important when communities are crumbling under the weight of crisis.

People First

Extant knowledge that companies have about communities is not sufficient to make a substantive difference in times of crisis, even though deep knowledge could ultimately benefit the bottom line. Rethinking business strategy to deliver optimal value to communities facing risk is not only an important step toward stabilization but also a step toward building consumer loyalty and hiring and retaining top talent. When extreme risk morphs into crisis, life completely changes. Human behavior recedes to the bottom of the Maslow scale with physiological and safety needs foremost. Business as usual vanishes in the blink of an eye and a whole new world of enterprise opens up. In this world, business strategy is about people, not profit. In the words of Arthur Blank, "People first, not make tons of money first."[70]

Being part of a company with a stated mission of putting people ahead of profit is an opportunity. Being part of a company that actually acts on this promise is a privilege. In 2011, a multinational company launched an extraordinary effort to alleviate mass starvation in the Horn of Africa.[71] The worst drought in 60 years in sub-Saharan Africa, coupled with conflict in Somalia, left 13 million people at risk for starvation and malnutrition. In the face of this unprecedented disaster, the company donated 10,000 metric tons of rice to support the World Food Program. The rice was enough to feed nearly 1 million people for one month. In the words of a company executive:[72]

> The donation grew out of a conversation between an administrator of the United States Agency for International Development (USAID) and the company chairman and chief executive officer. The administrator described how thousands more children in the Horn might die without specific action to save their lives. The company's CEO decided that the company needed to respond in an unprecedented way given "its mission to nourish people, the desperate need, and its unique ability to source and move food to where it is needed." With financial support from its family shareholders, the company committed to a $5 million shipment of rice.

A company team was assembled to originate and source the rice and manage ocean transportation and logistics to deliver and donate the grain. This task required deep commitment and exceptional coordination both within the company and with the World Food Program. The company was Cargill Corporation based in Minnesota.

What is most important—generating profit or helping people and communities in need? In a world edging toward catastrophic risk, there is only one answer.

Notes

1 Broom, D. and Gray, A., "The U.S. Is Set to Rejoin the Paris Climate Agreement: Here's What You Need to Know." *World Economic Forum*, November 11, 2020. Retrieved: November 20, 2020.

2 Linnell, M., "Community Approaches Involving the Public in Crisis Management." *Risk and Crisis Research Centre*. RCR Working Paper Series (FP7/2007–2013), 2013.

3 Ibid.

4 Ibid.

5 Coppola, M., Krick, T., and Blohmke, J., "Feeling the Heat? Companies Are Under Pressure on Climate Change and Need to Do More." *Deloitte*, December 12, 2019. Retrieved: November 2, 2020.

6 Ibid.

7 Lindwall, C., "The IPCC Climate Change Report: Why It Matters to Everyone on the Planet." *NDRC*, November 21, 2018. Retrieved: October 9, 2020.

8 Cohen, J., "The Clustering of Like-Minded America." *Medium*, January 10, 2019. Retrieved: October 12, 2020.

9 Springer, C. "Strategic Management of Three Critical Levels of Risk." *PA Times*, 32(10) (2009), The American Society for Public Administration. Retrieved: October 11, 2020.

10 Ibid.

11 Ibid.

12 Ibid.

13 Wilkinson, C., "Catastrophe Modeling: A Vital Tool in the Risk Management Box." *Insurance Information Institute*, February 1, 2008. Retrieved: October 15, 2020.

14 Redman, T. and Davenport, T., "Getting Serious About Data and Data Science." *MIT Sloan Management Review*, September 28, 2020. Retrieved: October 12, 2020.

15 Williamson, S., "A Hierarchy of Stakeholder Needs." *Harvard Law School Forum on Corporate Governance*, June 22, 2020. Retrieved: October 17, 2020.

16 O'Brien, G., "What's the Purpose of a Corporation." *Business Ethics*, September 10, 2019. Retrieved: October 5, 2020.

17 Eccles, G. and Klimenko, S., "The Investor Revolution." *Harvard Business Review*, May–June, 2019.

18 O'Brien, "What's the Purpose of a Corporation."

19 Ibid.

20 Schaninger, B., Simpson, B., Zhang, H., and Zhu, C., "Demonstrating Corporate Purpose in the Time of Coronavirus." *McKinsey & Company*, March 31, 2020. Retrieved: September 5, 2020.

21 Betti, F. and Heinzman, T., "From Perfume to Hand Sanitizer, TVs to Face Masks: How Companies Are Changing Track to Fight COVID-19." *World Economic Forum*, April 13, 2020. Retrieved: September 4, 2020.

22 De Smet, A., Mygatt, E., Pacthod, D., Relyea, C., and Srernfels, B., "Unleashing Sustainable Speed in a Post-COVID World: Rethink Ways of Working." *McKinsey & Company*, September 8, 2020. Retrieved: September 12, 2020.

23 Polman, P., "How Responsible Businesses Can Step Forward to Fight Coronavirus." *World Economic Forum*, March 20, 2020. Retrieved: September 11. 2020.

24 Ibid.

25 Kashner, M., "What Your Business Can Do to Help the Community During the Coronavirus Crisis." *Kellogg Insight*, March 21, 2020. Retrieved: September 5, 2020.

26 Ibid.

27 Ibid.

28 Bass, D., "Midwest Floods Disaster Relief." *Great Western Bank*, April 17, 2020. Retrieved: September 2, 2020.

29 Meloney, N., "Mi'kmaq-Designed Software Helps Communities See How Climate Change Could Impact Them." *CBC News*, March 2, 2020. Retrieved: September 2, 2020.

30 Rampton, J., "25 Companies Helping With Hurricane Harvey Relief That You Should Support." *Inc.*, September 4, 2017. Retrieved: September 18, 2020.

31 Wattles, J., "Here's What Big Companies Are Giving for Irma Relief." *CNN Business*, September 15, 2017. Retrieved: September 21, 2010.

32 Jordan, S. and McSwiggan, G., "The Role of Business in Disaster Response." *U.S. Chamber of Commerce*, May 30, 2012. Retrieved: October 30, 2020.

33 Ibid.

34 Ibid.

35 Orszag, P., "The Pandemic Will Make Big Companies More Dominant Than Ever." *Yahoo Finance*, April 27, 2020. Retrieved: October 25, 2020.

36 Shah, S. and Jha, A., "Collaborating With Your Direct Business Competitors." *Mint*, April 19, 2017. Retrieved: October 21, 2020.

37 Hamel, G., Doz, Y., and Prahalad, C., "Collaborate With Your Competitors—and Win." *Harvard Business Review*, January–February 1989.

38 Ibid.

39 Nalebuff, B. and Brandenburger, A., *Co-opetition: A Revolution Mindset That Combines Competition and Cooperation*. New York: Crown Publishing Group, 1996.

40 Ibid.

41 Web.com Blog, "What Is Coopetition and How Are Smart Companies Using It to Grow Their Businesses?" Retrieved: October 25, 2020.

42 Hattangadi, V., "What Is the Meaning of Synergy in Business?" *Strategic Management*, June 15, 2017. Retrieved: October 28, 2020.

43 Ibid.

44 Cho, A., "Disaster Resilience: The Private Sector Has a Vital Role to Play." *The Guardian*, October 22, 2013. Retrieved: October 30, 2020.

45 Linnell, "Community Approaches to Involving the Public in Crisis Management."

46 Polman, P., "How Responsible Businesses Can Step Forward to Fight Coronavirus." *World Economic Forum*, March 20, 2020.

47 Farazi, S., Koss, S., and Johnson, N., "COVID-19: How Firms Can Protect Their Workforce, Operations and Values." *EY.com*, July 23, 2020. Retrieved: October 20, 2020.

48 Guillen, M., "How Businesses Have Successfully Pivoted During the Pandemic." *Harvard Business Review*, July 7, 2020.

49 Ibid.

50 Ibid.

51 Burstein, R., "When the Pandemic Hit, Ed Tech Companies Threw Out Their Roadmaps and Changed Course." *EdSurge*, October 2, 2020. Retrieved: October 30, 2020.

52 Marr, B., "How the COVID-19 Pandemic Is Fast-Tracking Digital Transformation in Companies." *Forbes*, March 17, 2020. Retrieved: September 5, 2020.

53 Meno, S. and Rogers, S., "10 Creative Ways Businesses Are Serving Customers During COVID-19." *University of New Hampshire Cooperative Extension*, April 3, 2020. Retrieved: October 20, 2020.

54 Tims, A., "The Firms That Have Turned COVID-19 Crisis Into a Chance to Serve." *The Guardian*, March 29, 2020. Retrieved: October 20, 2020.

55 Ibid.

56 Grensing-Pophal, L., "Pitfalls of Employee Volunteerism and How to Avoid Them." *SHRM*, September 13, 2013. Retrieved: October 31, 2020.

57 D'Auria, G. and De Smet, A., "Leadership in a Crisis: Responding to the Coronavirus Outbreak and Future Challenges." *McKinsey & Company*, March 16, 2020. Retrieved: October 12, 2020.

58 Ibid.

59 Davis, T., "What Is Well-Being: Definition, Types and Well-Being Skills." *Psychology Today*, January 2, 2019. Retrieved: October 29, 2020.

60 Young Upstarts, "Why Corporate Social Responsibility Is More Important Than Ever." November 11, 2020. Retrieved: November 22, 2020.

61 Beeler, C., "Young Job Seekers Value Corporate Social Responsibility." *Mower*, March 29, 2019. Retrieved: October 31, 2020.

62 Forster, V., "Why 'Bubble Dining Pods' Are a Terrible Idea During the COVID-19 Coronavirus Pandemic." *Forbes*, October 21, 2020. Retrieved: October 26, 2020.

63 Herndon, A., "Many on the Right Reject the Call for Healing." *New York Times*, November 15, 2020.

64 Clift, K. and Court, A, "How Are Companies Responding to the Coronavirus Crisis." *World Economic Forum*, March 23, 2020.

65 Barbas, S. and Smith, R., "To Help Communities Survive Crises, Trust and Invest in Their Leadership." *The Kresge Foundation*, September 9, 2020. Retrieved: November 10, 2020.

66 Panwar, P., "Deloitte Chief Well-Being Officer Jen Fisher: 5 Ways That Businesses Can Help Promote the Mental Wellness of Their Employees." *Authority Magazine*, October 16, 2020. Retrieved: October 25, 2020.

67 Reilly, C., "The Rise of the Chief Wellbeing Officer." *Forbes*, July 7, 2020.

68 Kishore, S., Ripp, J., Shanafelt, T., Melnyk, B., Rogers, D., Brigham, T., Busis, N., Charney, D., Cipriano, P., Minor, L., Rothman, P., Spisso, J., Kirch, D., Nasca, T., and Dzau, V., "Making the Case for the Chief Wellness Officer in America's Health Systems: A Call for Action." *Health Affairs*, October 26, 2018. Retrieved: November 10, 2020.

69 Ibid.

70 Chesto, J., "Home Depot Cofounder Arthur Blank Visits Babson, One of His Beneficiaries." *The Boston Globe*, October 18, 2020.

71 U.S. Chamber of Commerce, "The Role of Business in Disaster Response." *Business Civic Leadership Report*. Retrieved: October 12, 2020.

72 Ibid.

Chapter 10

Mobilizing

Our society is more separated than it has ever been. . . . Business has an incredible role in helping us as a republic stay together. Business leaders have to step up.

Kenneth Frazier
Chairman and CEO, Merck & Company, 2019

In 2020, business endured a global pandemic and a massive economic crisis layered on top of forces fundamentally reshaping society. The consequence is clear: business has entered a landscape in which catastrophic events will occur more frequently and priorities of continuity and crisis response will parallel those of profit and growth. Extreme risk is all encompassing and will touch every part of business from strategy to operations. No organization will be exempt and nearly all organizations will need to strengthen their approach to risk management to be prepared for change that comes quickly. With every downside, however, there is an upside. Although extreme risk is a threat, it is also an opportunity for growth and renewal as companies moving to digital technologies discovered during the pandemic.

Business learned a lot during the pandemic but its most important lesson was about humanity. Empathy and compassion can unleash the full potential of organizations and command the allegiance of customers. Companies focusing on employee health and making the buying experience easier for customers gain market share. Companies reaching out and helping communities in hard times establish good will and enhance their stature. Human-centered principles are gaining ground in business which bodes well for communities but it is only a beginning. Yet to be realized is the contribution of business to overall community well-being—a general sense of wellness based on balance among physiological, emotional, social, and economic conditions.[1] When these conditions are out of balance, as they were during the pandemic, wellness is at risk. At the height of the pandemic, the prevalence of depression among citizens tripled.[2] One in three workers reported problems with insomnia, alcohol and substance use, or diminished energy for nonwork activities.[3] Rank and file citizens suffering from pandemic fatigue endangered the health of others by ignoring health advisories concerning mask use and the importance of social distancing. Rates of infection surged and communities reeled under the weight of overburdened health systems, business closures, and families in financial ruin.

By the close of 2020, a specter of polarization and disinformation had cast a shadow over a nation looking for a fresh start. The result was a conundrum that stood as a stark reminder of where we had been:

the improbability turned to probability that partisan antipathy could divide the U.S. population and disinformation from the highest levels of government could confound public perception of events. In normal times this would be far-fetched, but 2020 was anything but normal. In retrospect, it was the launch pad for people and communities searching desperately for stability and a new sense of normalcy.

What If?

What are the implications for business of communities in search of stability? Look at the community in which your company is located. Look at the circumstances and events that command attention. Look at people and their behavior in response to adversity. Look at the resources available to the community in hard times. Look at the ease or difficulty community leaders experience in mobilizing people toward a common goal. Look ahead and ponder the ability of the community in which your company is located to develop and sustain a sense of well-being.

Now ask yourself: What is my feeling about helping communities in times of need? What kinds of assistance, if any, should my company provide? What would our objective be—helping the community get back on its feet, mobilizing citizens, contributing to long-term well-being, or something else? What would be the consequences of inaction? What is my company's role and responsibility in relationship to the community?

And finally, in a business environment in which successful companies are increasingly pursuing humanitarian objectives, what is the relationship between company vitality and community well-being; between protecting company assets and helping communities; and between vulnerability and opportunity? If you are stuck in neutral, consider the following dimensions of risk that could be at play in the community.

- *Pandemic fatigue* in combination with worsening climate conditions and intensifying societal forces have destabilized the community. People are restless, experiencing emotional highs and lows, and resorting to aggressive behavior to cope with change.
- *Sustained risk* has led to toxic stress—a condition of strong and prolonged adversity affecting the overall health of the community.[4] Citizens are at risk for mental and physiological disorders as well as impairment of cognitive functioning.
- *Aberrant behavior* is on the rise in response to stress—denial, loss of reasoning capability, incivility, and paralysis. Pressure on health systems and social services has risen to an intolerable level; they are close to a breaking point.
- *People with impaired judgment* are hampering the ability of the community to mobilize in response to risk. The harmful effects of risk are deepening, rendering recovery more difficult and thrusting the community into instability.

The economic cost of extreme risk can run into the millions for large businesses and put small companies out of business. More importantly, the human cost of extreme risk is forbidding—lives thrown into chaos by prolonged instability, economic deprivation, and declining health. What if the conditions fostering risk were to become so extreme as to render people and communities incapable of functioning? What would this mean for your company? How would you respond? What would you do?

Risk, Uncertainty, and Response

Extreme risk brings an element of uncertainty that makes comprehension and response difficult. We don't know in advance what its impact will be, how long it will last, or what it will take to mitigate its effects. Effective response depends, in large part, on getting people to understand the uncertainty that accompanies risk and to mobilize in response to it. This is a daunting task because grappling with uncertainty is contrary to our emotional makeup. As the gravity of risk increases, confusion and paralysis may set in and the desire to confront risk may diminish. In a best-case scenario, people may retreat from the totality of risk and focus on the parts they can understand. In a worst-case scenario, they may completely withdraw. Ritholtz describes it this way:[5]

> Most of the time, people exist in a happy little bubble of self-created delusion. We engage in selective perception, seeing only the things that agree with us. Our selective retention retains the good stuff and disregards most of the rest. . . . In short, we construct a reality that bears only a passing resemblance to the objective universe. During those brief instances when the façade fades, the curtain gets pulled back and the ugly reality becomes clear. We get a glimmer of understanding about our own lack of understanding. That is when the grim reality of the human condition is revealed—and it terrifies us.

Multiple factors are at work that impede response to risk. People disregard danger that contradicts personal beliefs, interferes with immediate pursuits, or becomes inconvenient.[6] Response is also inhibited by confusion and misunderstanding. Research has shown how seemingly benign ways of thinking can impair risk response even among people eager to learn the truth.[7] The concept of "probability," for example, can lead people to underestimate the possibility of risk when the likelihood of it happening is perceived to be low. For example, if residents of a town in central Florida hear a climate scientist say that there is a 10 percent chance that a climate catastrophe will strike the state in the year ahead, they may think, "We're not near the coast, so the likelihood is probably less than that." The problem is the 10 percent has already taken location into account so the full extent of risk is underestimated. Similarly, people miscalculate risk by failing to understand unfamiliar units of measurement and ambiguous language.[8] An increase from 1,000 ppm (parts per million) of CO_2 in the atmosphere to 5,000 ppm of CO_2 may be inconsequential to people who do not understand what parts per million means. In fact, this increase is hazardous—respiratory function can be affected and the central nervous system compromised.[9] In the domain of language, terms such as "improbable" and "unlikely" are so ambiguous they can mean almost anything. When asked to define an "unlikely" outcome, people tend to view "unlikely" as having little or no chance of occurring when in fact the probability of occurrence is higher.[10]

The bottom line is that communicating risk and getting people to understand and act on it is difficult. In an ideal world, people would recognize that they are dealing with a phenomenon involving uncertainty and seek more information. This involves effort, however, that many may not be willing to invest.

Perception and Risk Response

Uncertainty obfuscates response to risk and perception channels response into comfortable places that cushion its impact.

■ In 2011, the Fukushima Daiichi nuclear disaster in Japan caused by the Tohoku earthquake and tsunami released radioactive contamination into the atmosphere. This incident dominated news coverage for weeks and created widespread anxiety as people at great distance ignored scientific data disclosing negligible radiation exposure from the disaster. Thousands of miles away, pharmacy shelves in the U.S. were depleted of potassium iodide pills because people heard that the drug could help prevent radiation-induced thyroid cancer.[11] Fear shaped the perception of risk and fueled irrational behavior.

■ In 2017, Donald Trump labeled climate change a "hoax" in public statements and announced his intention to formally withdraw the United States from the Paris Climate Agreement. He publicly dismissed a landmark climate report by 13 federal agencies and more than 300 climate scientists in 2018 with the statement "I don't believe it."[12] These events affirmed the belief of naysayers that climate change is exaggerated and even fabricated by scientists. During Trump's term in office, monumental hurricanes lashed Houston and Puerto Rico, California forests burned out of control, and extreme weather events became more frequent and intense, yet scores of people continued to dismiss evidence of climate change. Among naysayers, scientific evidence elicited a host of reactions—frustration, denial, and a search for alternative explanations—all of which flew in the face of facts. Emotion and intuition shaped the perception of risk and nullified the capacity to factor scientific evidence into cognition.

Perception is rarely entirely rational. People assess risk using a mixture of cognitive skills (weighing the evidence, using reasoning and logic to reach a conclusion) and emotional appraisals (intuition and imagination).[13] For risk we routinely face, perception and response are fluid—part of a finely tuned system. Catastrophic risk, however, involves a level of uncertainty and complexity that is more readily met by emotion than reason—a circumstance that may flaw perception. Unlike a hurricane or forest fire with a definitive end, catastrophic risk is prolonged, life changing, and has the potential to extinguish human life. It is more likely to be resisted and elicit reactions that hamper response to risk. Among the possible reactions are:

■ *cognitive complexity*
■ *cognitive dissonance*
■ *intuitive thinking*
■ *satisfice*
■ *normalization*

These factors were examined in Chapter 2 and are restated here to illustrate the impact of perception on response to risk.

Cognitive Complexity

The capacity of people to comprehend complex circumstances and events.[14] People with highly developed cognitive skills employ multidimensional thinking—they have the capacity to analyze a situation, discern its constituent parts, and explore connections among the parts. In the domain of risk, multidimensional thinkers are able to comprehend the effects and consequences of catastrophe whereas others may be overwhelmed by it and cede response to people whose skills they cannot easily judge. This is known as *complexity mismatch* and it is a primary cause of reticence in response to risk.[15]

Cognitive Dissonance

A state of conflict induced by circumstances and events that are contrary to personal beliefs and assumptions.[16] The reaction of naysayers to scientific evidence of climate change is a good example of the tension that can result when facts contradict belief. People can reduce the tension by choosing to reject the evidence as part of a belief that climate change is natural and cyclical. They can demand more conclusive evidence or filter information by paying attention only to reports that confirm their beliefs. They can choose to avoid climate statistics altogether or seek out kindred souls to garner support. Taken as a whole, these reactions amount to sculpting perception to conform to belief—not the best strategy for tackling climate change.

Intuitive Thinking

Simple thought—a knee-jerk reaction to a complex condition or circumstance.[17] Intuition comes first and dominates reasoned judgment. Thought is effortless, based on gut feelings causing people to underestimate and underreact to the consequences of risk. It is effective in ordinary situations but problematic in high consequence situations where rational and deliberative thought is necessary. Intuitive thinkers evaluate risk based on the ease with which similar instances can be recalled. This is known as *availability bias* and it hampers response to risk.[18]

Satisfice

A union of "satisfy" and "suffice" to explain behavior when circumstances make it impossible to forge an optimal solution.[19] Decisions are made on the basis of convenience and acceptability because achieving an optimal solution would cost more in time and effort. People search for available alternatives until an acceptable threshold is met. In the domain of risk, optimal and acceptable are one and the same. Optimal is reduced to acceptable—a circumstance that could temper the response of communities to risk.

Normalization

The process through which ideas and behavior outside of established norms come to be regarded as acceptable.[20] Perceptions of "normal" change over time as people become accustomed to deviations from routine despite the fact that they exceed prevailing norms. In politics, leader behavior once considered to be outlandish comes to be seen not only as typical but also as admissible and less worthy of outrage. In the domain of risk, normalization occurs through an intuitive process of accommodation and adjustment to change. Extreme temperatures associated with climate change, for example, become part of an undifferentiated normality of "hot" or "cold" irrespective of how extreme they are. People do not inquire into the root cause of extreme temperatures—they adjust by wearing suitable clothing and adjusting their outlook to fit prevailing conditions.

Denial, intuitive thinking, sub-optimal decision-making, and normalization are behavioral manifestations that hamper response to risk. They intensify in periods of extreme stress when people and communities are confronted by rapidly changing conditions. People respond on the basis of experience, ideology, and outlook. Some alter behavior in an effort to understand and act on risk; others vary their orientation as necessary to adhere to avoid conflict; and others hold steadfastly to deeply embedded beliefs at odds with risk. Norms holding people together break down—a prominent feature of communities in crisis and a circumstance that predisposes them to mismanagement of risk. When disruptive cycles of collective behavior are of sufficient force to spawn inertia, response to risk is compromised.

What Leaders Must Know

Unquestionably, the gravity of risk in and of itself is important but just as important are people whose sociological and psychological characteristics make a community more or less vulnerable to risk. This perspective assumes that the threat of risk is greatest when met by a community lacking the capacity to anticipate, cope with, and recover from its impact. Consider the plight of a community divided against itself and incapable of managing risk.

The Community: Your company is located in a coastal community that has emerged from the pandemic experiencing the aftershock of business and school closures, massive unemployment, mental health issues, and households in disarray. People are under extreme stress and embroiled in partisan politics which have divided the community into factions with sharply different views on local issues and problems facing the nation. Of particular concern is climate change—an issue that has evoked a strong emotional reaction from people affiliated with different political parties. Conservative Republicans believe that scientists and the media exaggerate the threat of climate change while liberal Democrats believe climate change is a clear and present danger. Severe weather events have ravaged the community. In the past year, a massive hurricane eroded major portions of the coastline, severely damaged infrastructure, displaced families from homes, and sharply curtailed food and water supplies. Ten-year climate projections call for weather events to become more frequent and severe including the probability of a major hurricane yet many continue to reject the evidence of climate change. Exposure to scientific evidence and truth do not matter—personal beliefs and values are what matter most. Conflict between believers and naysayers has reached a boiling point and your company, a major employer in the community, is right in the middle.
The Challenge: In a community facing extreme risk and edging toward disorder:

- *What are the implications for your company?*
- *Can your company afford to stay on the sidelines?*
- *What are the risks of doing nothing?*
- *What role, beyond financial largesse, can your company play in helping the community?*
- *Are there untapped resources that your company can deploy with the community?*

Your company has endured the crisis of pandemic and is heading into a risk environment marked by climate change and the angst of a divided community. Standing on the sidelines is not an option nor is putting company assets at risk. Looming large in the space between protecting company assets and helping the community is the need to understand behavior and dynamics of the community in which risk plays out.

Understanding Behavior

The context described earlier, although extreme, is not far from reality in vulnerable communities facing the worst effects of climate change. In extreme circumstances, there are two dimensions of risk—the *actual risk itself* and the *attitudes and behavior of people* in response to risk.[21] People approach risk with interests that differ depending on where they sit and what they stand to gain or lose. The interests of a business executive, for example, have much to do with economics: What steps need to be taken to prepare for and counteract risk? What will be the cost? What do I need to do to protect company assets? What will be the short- and long-term impact on stakeholders? Interests of citizens vary according to personal beliefs but ultimately come down to protection of values and a way of life. Both sets of interests are important, but citizen beliefs and interests vary widely and are more difficult to quantify. This translates more often than not into inattention to the behavioral side of risk—an oversight that may not factor human behavior fully into a risk event or circumstance.[22]

To remedy this oversight, business leaders need to pay careful attention to the behavioral side of risk. What are the attitudes and beliefs of local citizens in relationship to risk? What forms of partisan bias are at work in the community that affects response? How have citizens responded in the past to circumstances requiring collective action? What works and does not work in mobilizing people to action? Answers to these questions provide valuable information about the capacity of a community to respond to risk through collective action.

Understanding Community Dynamics

Community dynamics have a direct bearing on risk and its consequences. They influence the capacity of communities to respond to risk—divided communities, for example, experience difficulty in mobilizing consensual opinion and collective action. Community dynamics also influence citizen perception of company commitment to community well-being. People in tightly knit communities engage with organizations as part of a broader context touching families and friends, and a general public that can readily access information about what goes on in the workplace. Companies rise and fall as a function of the extent to which they are perceived as contributing in demonstrable ways to community betterment. To make informed decisions about how they can best contribute, business leaders need wide-ranging information about community dynamics. What issues garner attention? What allegiances and ideologies divide and integrate the community? How do community agencies address and resolve problems? How do people react in times of crisis? What resources does the community have available for recovery? What roles have local government and community organizations played in recovery? With what level of success?

Beyond Knowing

In communities facing catastrophe, physiological and safety needs prevail and compassion is a critical leadership skill. Leaders who can relate to people on an emotive basis are uniquely positioned to help in times of crisis. Their strength is contextual understanding—an ability to understand people and an evolving environment and adapt to it.[23] They have a curiosity about people—how attitudes and values take shape, what motivates behavior, and how people respond to change. They know that context is both real and perceived and encompasses elements such as geography, organizations, cultures, attitudes, beliefs, politics, ideologies, and personal ethics.[24] They also know that context is complex with many intangible aspects. Contextual leaders fit decisions and actions to current circumstances through observation and inquisition. They ask questions and venture outside of an existing context to acquire intelligence about people and the world in which they live. Answers to questions are aggressively pursued and quickly turned into action using multiple sources of information.

Contextual leadership is not new to business. It has been employed by leaders for years and rose to prominence in the 1990s through the work of business theorists, most notably Mayo and Nohria and Rosabeth Moss Kanter.[25] In "How Great Companies Think Differently," Kanter described the process by which leaders of preeminent companies think their way to success by creating frameworks that use societal values and human values as decision-making criteria.[26] For example, Cemex, a multinational Mexican building materials company, has developed products on the basis of unmet societal needs. Among Cemex's innovations have been antibacterial concrete, which is important for hospitals and farms; water-resistant concrete, useful in flood-prone areas; and road surface material derived from old tires, desirable in countries that are building roads rapidly.[27] The contextual focus of Cemex and companies like it is at the societal level. Similar, but smaller in scale is a contextual focus at the community level. When disaster strikes, the rubber hits the road at the level of community. This is where contextual leadership has the greatest potential to make a difference.

Contextual leadership plays out in communities facing risk through people and community impacted by crisis.[28] Researchers have identified five phases of crisis: (1) signal detection, (2) preparation and prevention, (3) damage containment, (4) recovery, and (5) learning.[29] Contextual leaders use knowledge and intuition in each phase to guide planning and response. In the signal detection phase, they look for cues that indicate the possibility of a crisis. Prior learning about types of crisis provides a framework for action to alleviate or avert harmful effects. In the second phase, preparation and prevention, leaders work to mitigate the threat of crisis and develop tactics for response should the crisis occur. The third phase entails curbing the worst effects of crisis and minimizing harm to people and community. During the recovery phase, leaders guide resources to where they are most needed. For contextual leaders, the final phase—learning—is perhaps the most important of all phases. Lessons extracted from crisis are committed to memory and join prior learning to shape decision-making in situations involving risk.

There is a clear role for business leaders in bringing communities together during crisis. Their response is not simply one of throwing money at a problem and doing the right thing at the right time on the ground. It is about the ability to craft a narrative that clarifies the dimensions of risk and about building trust to attain "permissive consensus"—the opportunity to motivate people and mobilize them to collective action. Permissive consensus does not happen without effort. It requires different ways of thinking about business purpose, about how to do business and who to do it with, and how to engage with communities.

Thinking Differently about Business

The need to think differently about business in a world at risk is not a matter of question, it is an imperative. It cannot be divorced, however, from the need to think differently about organizations and their relationships with stakeholders. Mobilizing resources in support of communities, leveraging resources across organizational boundaries to optimize benefit, forging alliances with competitors, redeploying employees for service in communities, balancing the profit motive and social responsibility, and promoting and valuing new skills in leaders all require new ways of thinking about the organization. Just as the current language describing the purpose of business is not up to the consequences of risk neither is the current language of organizational practice.

Over the past several years, companies in significant number have incorporated social responsibility into their purpose statements. Highlighted by the 2019 Business Roundtable statement on the Purpose of a Corporation, to engage in social responsibility means, that in the ordinary course of business, companies are conscious of their impact on all aspects of society, including economic, social, and environmental.[30] Companies have worked diligently to balance long-standing goals of profit and growth with goals of sustainability and societal well-being and have sought to repurpose assets to support communities in times of need. They have deemphasized competition in favor of collaboration and have enlarged the operating world of employees to integrate work and life. They have valued and promoted new skills in leaders and tried to redefine success as an amalgam of goals internal and external to the company. The mantra for companies that have taken social responsibility to a new level is *social consciousness*—awareness of being part of an interrelated community.

Social consciousness in an environment of unprecedented risk takes on a new meaning. During the pandemic, companies pivoted and worked with competitors, customers, and community to provide critically needed products and services. Among them were Unilever, Procter & Gamble, Ford Motor Company, Johnson & Johnson, IKEA, Under Armor, Nike, and a whole host of small companies.[31] In the risk environment ahead, organizations will be tested by changes of unparalleled magnitude and duration. Under the best of circumstances, change is a complex dynamic with a paradoxical nature. Organizations that move too slowly will be passed by competitors and those that move too fast may exceed the capacity of people to adapt. Organizations adjust to this paradox by pursuing change on a graduated scale ranging from *intermediary* goals—those likely to be achieved to *stretch* goals—those to strive for.

Leaders know all too well the importance of pursuing change on a graduated basis with safeguards and off ramps to ensure success. The risk environment ahead, however, may require a different approach. Facing unprecedented risk, companies may have no choice but to pursue stretch goals as the clock runs out on aversion of catastrophic events like climate change. Stretch goals in five domains of business practice bearing on risk are part of a continuum.

Antecedent	Intermediary	Stretch
Shareholder profit	Corporate citizenship	Societal well-being
Company assets	Social responsibility	Shared value creation
Competition	Collaboration	Synergy
Work	Work–life balance	Civic engagement
Models of leadership	Leadership motive	Context for leadership

The tendency toward the safe haven of intermediary goals is borne out of caution learned through experience. This would be perfectly reasonable in the change tapestry of a risk neutral environment, but it is not sufficient for the magnitude of change required to mitigate catastrophic risk. To ensure a sustainable future, business will need to pursue stretch goals in partnership with people, organizations, and community.

Beyond Corporate Citizenship to Societal Well-Being

One cannot speak meaningfully about profit in the absence of a beneficiary. Traditionally, shareholders have been the beneficiary of profit although the notion of "beneficiary" has changed in recent years to include stakeholders outside of corporate walls. As stakeholders have demanded more from business in sustainability practices and corporate citizenship, companies have adjusted purpose statements, plans and budgets, and corporate reports to reflect these aims. This is all well and good in a risk neutral environment, but will it be enough in an environment of extreme risk where benefit must broaden to include society?

Societal well-being is built on active participation in a thriving community, culture, and environment.[32] In a post-COVID world, it doesn't take much to conjure up images of extreme risk. Its social and economic impacts are clear and visible as has been amply demonstrated: declining physical and mental health, declining economic activity, and breakdown in families and social norms. Add to this, the multiplier effect of human stress—a level of distress that constrains rational decision-making—and one is left with the realization that societal well-being is an idealized state. In periods of stability, life decisions are self-contained and personal—a matter of personal concern.[33] In periods of extreme risk, life decisions are no longer self-contained—they become a community concern. If conditions become so severe as to jeopardize public safety, decision-making leaves the hands of individuals and elevates to community.[34] In other words, when facing extreme conditions, individual behavior gives way to collective behavior for the benefit of society.

There is a substantial role for business to play in societal well-being—a role vastly beyond corporate citizenship. This role is realized when business and community jointly explore major societal challenges and work together to integrate societal improvement into economic value creation. Well-being is assured when policies and practices that enhance profit simultaneously advance social and economic conditions in the communities in which a company sells and operates. In the domain of risk, the stratagem would be corporate policies and practices that protect company assets and simultaneously contribute to the capability of communities to mobilize in response to risk. There is always the possibility that pursuit of profit will weigh more heavily than contribution to community, but this is more likely in a risk neutral environment when safety and lives are not at stake. When the elements that contribute to well-being fall out of balance, the risk equation changes and businesses enter a whole new realm of operation.

Beyond Social Responsibility to Shared Value Creation

The potential for conveying value from company assets to community well-being is realized when corporate largesse and social responsibility give way to shared value creation. This evolution emerges not as a result of short-term effort but from a process where company leaders come to recognize the benefit of shared value creation. Shared value exceeds the aims of corporate social responsibility—a business model driven by a sense of philanthropic responsibility and a desire to act in a responsible manner that helps businesses remain connected to communities. CSR lacks specifics for implementation—a void leading to questions about its authenticity and the possibility that it may be driven more by corporate need than community benefit.

Shared value is driven by a different mindset than CSR. While philanthropy and CSR focus on "giving back" or minimizing any negative effect business may have on society, shared value is a management strategy in which companies find business opportunity in social problems.[35] Conceived by Michael Porter and Mark Kramer, companies that pursue shared value use business thinking to solve problems that have traditionally been considered social issues.[36] Issues such as hunger, environment, water, and health are addressed through a capitalist model. Examples abound. Bank of America has brought largesse to environmental issues through a "green bonds" program that has raised $442 million connecting investors with businesses working to foster the renewables revolution.[37] Weight Watchers is working with people and communities to foster healthy living through a change in mission from weight reduction to becoming a holistic partner in health and wellness.[38] All of its products and programs have been modified to promote healthy living—a step that has improved people's lives while strategically growing the company. Ford Motor Company and 3M partnered during the pandemic to improve health care by increasing production of 3M's powered air-purifying respirators using off-the-shelf components from Ford F150 truck's cooled seating as well as 3M's existing HEPA filters.[39] These respirators offer a significant advantage in use because they are battery powered and capable of filtering airborne virus particles for up to eight hours on a single, swappable, standard-power battery pack worn at the waist.

Companies can put shared value into practical use by thinking outside of traditional products and markets, redefining productivity, and sourcing products locally. Reel Gardening based in South Africa reconceived the gardening market by recognizing a social need to empower others to take over their own food security through accessible gardening.[40] For every product it sells, Reel Gardening donates seed tape to schools and communities in South Africa. It further equips schools and communities with the gardening knowledge and education they need to grow their own food successfully. Dunia Designs, an eco-friendly design company, has redefined productivity by up-cycling plastic bottles, plastic bag waste, and other recycled materials to create furniture.[41] Dunia employs numerous individuals from communities to collect plastic waste—a practice that not only provides employment opportunities but also lowers its operating cost. Dunia receives the majority of its raw materials at zero cost. Nando's Chicken, a South African restaurant chain recognized for its vibrant restaurant atmosphere, sources products locally by personally curating each of its restaurants worldwide with the art of its African community.[42] With over 9,000 pieces of contemporary South African art, Nando's has been able to create opportunities for local artists to advance their careers and personal development while simultaneously growing its brand.

Beyond Collaboration to Synergy

During the pandemic, many companies learned the value of becoming less competition-driven and more synergy-driven. There is, of course, a danger in representing corporate purpose as a dichotomy between competition and synergy. Competition will always drive business behavior. But when hard times prevail, as they did during the pandemic, advantage can be realized through collaboration. Company behavior will shift to fit circumstance.

The goal is not simply to collaborate over the short term to protect company assets and ensure continuity. The objective is to forge durable alliances which create a combined outcome greater than the sum of individual company outcomes. Short-term situational alliances to weather tough times are not the basis of synergy. For example, the move of one company to partner with another to expand capability during the pandemic is not a synergistic strategy if the partnership is dissolved following the restoration of economic activity. More to the point is the move of four news organizations in 2020—Scripps, Tegna, Fox-owned stations, and the Howard Center for Investigative Journalism—to forge an alliance for remote news delivery projects between stations, universities, and station groups.[43] Consolidating news gathering operations and redistributing the resulting content enabled these organizations to expand their market reach. It also led to efficiencies in communication and technological fluency that carried forward because of collective advantages that could not be realized on an individual station basis.

Understanding where advantage can be achieved through synergy involves information about customer preferences, awareness of company capabilities, and deep insight into the capabilities of competitors. Customer preferences change constantly as do company capabilities. For example, the convenience of online purchasing became a clear customer preference in the COVID economy. In this economy, Amazon's overwhelming advantage in e-commerce spelled trouble for retailers trying to stay above water, yet a number of retailers lined up to partner with Amazon. In 2020, Sears Holdings announced that it was joining forces with Amazon to sell tires. In 2019, Sears paired with Amazon to sell its Kenmore brand, putting it on par with brands such as Chico's, Best Buy, Calvin Klein, Kohl's, and Nike seeking to ride Amazon's e-tail proficiency to higher sales.[44] These retailers read the tea leaves of changing customer preferences, carefully examined their own capabilities, sized up Amazon's e-tail advantage, and decided to align themselves with Amazon rather than fight. Chico's and Nike opened storefronts on Amazon, and Calvin Klein partnered with Amazon to open pop-up stores.[45] For its part, Amazon recognized that even though consumer shopping preferences had turned online, brick and mortar stores still had advantages. By teaming up with retailers, it could gain insight into competitive advantage linked to last-mile delivery of products and services.

Beyond Work–Life Balance to Civic Engagement

Companies learned during the pandemic that work and personal life could be integrated albeit with mixed results. Employers moved to remote work out of a concern for employee safety and operational continuity. Workers performed surprisingly well in the early going while juggling child care and distractions from home. Months into the transition, however, cracks began to emerge. Projects took longer, training proved to be more difficult, and hiring and integrating new employees more complicated.[46] Workers expressed feelings of isolation and loss of connectivity—sentiments that impacted productivity. On balance, executives found advantages in worker safety and cost savings counterbalanced by concerns about productivity, performance appraisal and communication. Tipping the balance sheet, however, was the opportunity remote work offered for transformation on multiple levels. Companies gained access to resilient and adaptive ways to deliver economic value; leaders embraced the opportunity for an organizational mind-shift to platform mentality; and managers and employees began to think differently about the future of work.[47]

Work–life integration is now part of everyday reality for the majority of American workers. What began as a need to maintain continuity will transition to a goal of enhancing productivity by enabling workers to design their own jobs, manage their own time, and perform more effectively while allocating time to competing roles. Work and family, however, are not the only draw on worker time. Workers are part of a community and there is an obligation to contribute to betterment especially in hard times. Communities do not have the resources to navigate crisis alone as the pandemic amply demonstrated. Business reached out to communities and worked in front-line response during the pandemic, but the front line lacked an orchestrated strategic focus. Missing was an established network of organizations with unique capabilities that could be deployed to meet pressing needs. A critical component of this network was business employees.

Business leaders tend to restrict their thinking about roles employees can play with communities to volunteerism—helping with food banks, delivering supplies, making calls to isolated individuals. Employees are capable of much more and the "more" has to do with easing crisis conditions for people in distress. Employees can play a role as *sensors*—bringing crisis conditions in communities to the attention of managers. They're close to the community and closest to the issues at hand. They also have first-hand knowledge of community needs and company capabilities and can act as two-way *communicators* between company and community. Employees can serve as *mediators* of citizen response to crisis: working with distressed individuals to deliver accurate information about the magnitude of crisis, determining what the community is doing in response, and describing actions being taken to protect citizens. A host of possibilities exist that businesses can explore for deploying employees with communities. These possibilities need to be carefully considered and factored into jobs as part of the future of work.

Beyond Leadership Models and Motive to Context

The dance among different theories and models of leadership began decades ago when organizational theorists uncovered multiple factors driving leader behavior. Among the factors contributing to behavior was motivation. Leaders are driven by extrinsic rewards, intrinsic motives, or a balanced combination of the two.[48] This distinction is important because leader motivation in the fast-changing world of business is more likely a combination of motives than any one type. The old saw of leaders primarily in pursuit of extrinsic rewards—profit, growth, or recognition—doesn't play well in a post-COVID business world where humanitarian objectives have become increasingly important. Even when leaders intuitively pursue extrinsic rewards, internal satisfaction gained through the experience may open new vistas of leadership. It is not uncommon, for example, for leaders in pursuit of rewards to plateau and reset goals when a goal has been achieved. On the surface, this may seem like an exercise in futility because leaders may eventually tire of resetting goals. Quite to the contrary, however, the experience may fuel pursuit of goals outside of organizational boundaries. Goals that contribute to the common good such as forging alliances with competitors to achieve altruistic objectives, redeploying workers to help communities in distress, and broadening the concept of work to include community betterment.

Defining leader behavior in terms of models is overly simplistic in an environment in which context has much to do with what leaders can and cannot do. Models recede in importance when risk rises to a level that threatens well-being. What counts in tough times is an ability to make sense of a complex and uncertain environment and to find a clear direction. Leaders rise and fall on the basis of their ability to adjust personal style to context and situation. This involves a broad understanding of context, the nature and consequences of risk, and the needs and capabilities of people. Leader behavior explained through models or context is, like most dichotomies, ultimately sterile. In a world at risk, context is the architect of behavior that will be effective or ineffective. The objective is not to say that one approach to leadership is better than another nor to maintain that leadership style should change to fit changing conditions. The goal is to find the higher ground of leader awareness of risk and what it will take to unlock human potential in response to risk.

Looking Ahead

Most of us had not come face-to-face with catastrophic risk until 2020 and COVID-19 arrived. Lifestyles were uprooted and dramatic changes were made in how we live, work, and relate. One of five American adults moved because of the pandemic or knew someone who did; millions of workers lost their jobs or indicated a need to make a career shift; office buildings gave way to remote work; mental health declined with sharply rising rates of depression and anxiety; and parents struggled to homeschool their children.[49] Study after study has shown that traumatic events and crises can prompt people to re-examine their values and make life-changing decisions. Looking ahead, what will exposure to catastrophic risk mean for business? Will companies re-examine their values and broaden their purpose? Will leaders embrace and employ new skills? Will employee roles broaden and be more closely tied to life and community?

There are countervailing themes in response to these questions, one reactive and myopic and the other proactive and strategic. A 2020 World Economic Forum survey of business leaders on the likelihood of major risks business would face in the aftermath of the pandemic revealed a predominant concern with economic fallout of the pandemic: prolonged recession, failure of industries to recover, high levels of structural unemployment, weakening fiscal position of major economies, and disruption of global supply chains.[50] Of lesser concern were social and environmental issues: erosion of global decarbonization efforts, worsening mental health, political dissent and government mistrust, failure of education to adapt to prolonged crisis, and investment in global crisis response.[51] Immediate economic concerns took precedence over social and environmental issues—evidence perhaps of leader reluctance to invest in protection against risk that is looming but not an immediate threat to business continuity.

A converse perspective is more strategic in focus. Business leaders are beginning to shift their perspective to risk that could disrupt the fundamental assumptions of business strategy.[52] Climate change, emerging technologies, and global competition are continually evolving and without limit. These risks cannot be handled in typical organizational silos and can destroy sources of value creation if not prioritized and managed effectively. Yet they also have the potential to deliver advantage. Risk is proactive in this perspective—a performance enabler with the potential to drive value.

As more becomes known about catastrophic risk, businesses will increasingly be able to determine upside value and elevate performance to achieve rewards. Managing risk will become a challenge of managing paradox. Leaders will need to be simultaneously aware of occurring elements of risk—immediate and long term, perceptible and imperceptible, and operational and strategic. Analytics will help with this task as well as emerging technologies. Ultimately, however, it is judgment and foresight that will spell the difference between success and failure in a world edging toward catastrophic risk.

More Than Profit

Can business put the greater good ahead of self-interest? Can companies broaden their purpose to include engagement in social issues and attention to society's ills? Can leaders think beyond financial performance to the impact their companies have on wider society? On one level, these are business questions. On another level, they raise fundamental questions about the capacity of business to pursue and achieve humanitarian goals. This is the raison d'etre of this book: "purpose" has become so fundamental that companies without social purpose will achieve limited success in the long term. People and communities are looking for leadership in responding to broad societal challenges. To prosper over time, every company will need to make a significant contribution to society as well as to deliver financial performance. What business does to help people and communities matters. The business of business is not business. In a world at risk, it is contribution to the common good.

Notes

1 Admin, "What Does Well-Being Actually Mean?" *Wellbeing People*, July 20, 2018. Retrieved: December 4, 2020.
2 Reinberg, S., "Rates of Depression Are Triple of Pre-COVID Levels." *WebMD*, September 2, 2020. Retrieved: November 30, 2020.
3 Wilkie, D., "Workers' Mental Health Suffers During the Pandemic: How Managers Can Help." *SHRM*, October 22, 2020. Retrieved: November 20, 2020.
4 Shern, D., Blanche, A., and Steverman, S., "Impact of Toxic Stress on Individuals and the Community: A Review of the Literature." *Mental Health America*, September 16, 2014.
5 Kastelle, T., "Few People Understand the Difference Between Risk and Genuine Uncertainty." *Business Insider*, March 27, 2013. Retrieved: December 5, 2020.
6 Horowitz, E., "Why Are People Bad at Evaluating Risks." *Psychology Today*, March 1, 2013. Retrieved: December 6, 2020.
7 Ibid.
8 Ibid.

9 Ibid.

10 Teigen, K., Juanchich, M., and Riege, A., "Improbably Outcomes: Infrequent or Extraordinary?" *Cognition*, 127(1) (2013): 119–139.

11 Derbyshire, D. and Duell, M., "Nuclear Hysteria Infects the U.S." *Survivalist*, March 16, 2011. Retrieved: December 5, 2020.

12 Blumberg, A., "Trump on Climate Change Report: 'I Don't Believe It'." *Huff Post*, November 26, 2018. Retrieved: December 2, 2020.

13 Ropeik, D., "The Psychology of Risk Perception: Are We Doomed Because We Get Risk Wrong?" *Psychology Today*, August 23, 2010. Retrieved: December 2, 2020.

14 Pervin, L., Cervone, D., and John, O., *Personality: Theory and Research*. Hoboken, NJ: John Wiley & Sons, 2004.

15 Clarke, R. and Eddy, R., *Warnings: Finding Cassandras to Stop Catastrophes*. New York: HarperCollins, 2017.

16 Pam, M., "COGNITIVE DISSONANCE (Dissonance Theory)." *Psychology Dictionary.org*, November 28, 2018. https://psychologydictionary.org/connitive-dissonance-theory. Retrieved: October 7, 2019.

17 Kunreuther, H., Slovic, P., and Olson, K., "Fast and Slow Thinking in the Face of Catastrophic Risk." August 19, 2014. SSRN: https://ssrn.com/abstract=2488653

18 Ibid.

19 Simon, H., "Rational Choice and the Structure of the Environment." *Psychological Review*, 63(2) (1956): 129–138.

20 https://en.wikipedia.org/w/index.php?title=Normalization_(sociology)&oldid=892692859. Retrieved: September 8, 2019.

21 Ropeik, D., "How Do We Perceive Risk." *PBS.Org*, December 21, 2012. Retrieved: December 3, 2020.

22 Gibbs, L., *Risk Assessments: A Community Perspective*. Falls Church, VA: Center for Health, Environment and Justice.

23 Kutz, M., "Contextual Intelligence: An Emerging Competency for Global Leaders." *School of Global Leadership & Entrepreneurship*, August 2008.

24 Ibid.

25 Kanter, R., "How Great Companies Think Differently." *Harvard Business Review*, 89(11) (November 2011).

26 Ibid.

27 Ibid.

28 Wooten, L. and James, E., "Linking Crisis Management and Leadership Competencies: The Role of Human Resource Development." *Advances in Developing Human Resources*, 20(10) (2008).

29 Ibid.

30 Business Roundtable, "Business Roundtable Redefines the Purpose of a Corporation to Promote 'an Economy That Serves All Americans'." August 19, 2019.

31 Guillen, M., "How Businesses Have Successfully Pivoted During the Pandemic." *Harvard Business Review*, July/August 2020.

32 Davis, "What Is Well-Being? Definition, Types and Well-Being Skills."

33 Baggio, M., "Here's Why Society Is Reacting With Panic to Coronavirus." *World Economic Forum*, March 10, 2020. Retrieved: December 24, 2020.

34 Ibid.

35 Mrema, R., "How to Create a Shared Value Business Model." *Creative*. Latitude Fifty Five, November 14, 2018. Retrieved: December 28, 2020.

36 Porter, M. and Kramer, M., "Creating Shared Value." *Harvard Business Review*, January/February 2011.

37 IE University, "5 Businesses That Are Creating Value for Society." *Driving Innovation*, May 6, 2019. Retrieved: December 28, 2020.

38 Ibid.

39 Tambun, T., "Applying the 'Creating Shared Value' (CSV) Concept During a Pandemic or Natural Disaster." *Linked In*, April 25, 2020. Retrieved: December 29, 2020.

40 Mrema, R., "How to Create a Shared Value Business Model." *Creative*, November 14, 2018.
41 Ibid.
42 Ibid.
43 Albiniak, P., "TVN Focus on Journalism/Collaboration Lessons for a Post-Pandemic World." *TVNewsCheck*, December 22, 2020. Retrieved: December 28, 2020.
44 Duprey, R., "What's Up With All These Retailers Partnering With Amazon.Com?" *The Motley Fool*, May 28, 2018. Retrieved: December 30. 2020.
45 Ibid.
46 Cutter, C., "Companies Start to Think Remote Work Isn't So Great After All." *Wall Street Journal*, July 24, 2020. Retrieved: December 28, 2020.
47 Stewart, K. and Menon, A., "How to Navigate the Transition to Remote Work During the COVID-19 Pandemic." *World Economic Forum*, March 19, 2020. Retrieved: December 29, 2020.
48 Butkus, D., "Extrinsic vs. Intrinsic Motivation at Work." *Creative Leadership*, April 11, 2020. Retrieved: December 30, 2020.
49 Khan, A., "The Pandemic Is Prompting People to Make Big Life Decisions." *Time*, December 29, 2020. Retrieved: January 2, 2021.
50 Ghosh, I., "What's at Risk: An 18-Month View of a Post-COVID World." *Visual Capitalist*, June 24, 2020. Retrieved: January 3, 2021.
51 Ibid.
52 Albinson, N., Blau, A., and Chu, Y., "Disruption Dominates the Executive Agenda." *Deloitte*. Retrieved: January 3, 2021.

Index

Note: Page numbers in italics indicate a figure and page numbers in bold indicate a table on the corresponding page.

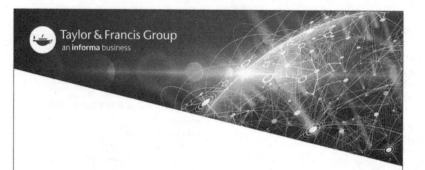